SLEEP—YOUR SILENT PARTNER

IN MENTAL HEALTH

By MARGARET STEGER

Hypnoidal Psychotherapy. 1951

SLEEP -

YOUR SILENT PARTNER

IN MENTAL HEALTH

A NEW METHOD OF DYNAMIC
SELF-DEVELOPMENT

by

MARGARET STEGER, Ph.D.

THOMAS NELSON & SONS

Edinburgh NEW YORK *Toronto*

TO E. H. AND L. S.

Sleep hath its own world,
And a wild dream of wild reality,
And dreams in their development have breath
And tears, and torture,
And the touch of joy.

LORD BYRON

What was formerly a method of medical treatment now becomes a method of self-education. . . . Our civilization is still young and young civilizations need all the arts of the animal tamer to make the defiant barbarian and savage in us more or less tractable. But at a higher cultural level we must forego compulsion and turn to self-development. For this reason we must have a way, a method which . . . has so far been lacking.

CARL GUSTAV JUNG

CONTENTS

INTRODUCTION TO
A NEW METHOD

Would you like to discover an oil-well in your own backyard? Probably you will answer: "Why bother to wish for something which is merely a pipe dream!" And yet, making good use of the hypnoidal stage (falling-asleep and waking-up stage) can well be as important to you as finding an oil-well; and this is no pipe dream.

It should be pointed out immediately that the expression *hypnoidal* has no connection with hypnosis. At no time does the term *hypnoidal* describe or refer to anything but the initial drowsiness which we all experience as we fall asleep, or the natural drowsiness which may linger on for a while, as we awaken from sleep. You will find explanations and proof of these statements in this book.

Ever since the publication of my book *Hypnoidal Psychotherapy,* I have been asked over and over again whether my technique could be made available for psychological self-help. I had to answer, of course, that hypnoidal psychotherapy was designed for therapeutic purposes only and that sick people should never "doctor" themselves either physically or mentally. But the idea of using the hypnoidal stage for psychological self-help presented an interesting challenge. As a consequence, I have adapted the technique of hypnoidal psychotherapy to the requirements of self-help. This new method, which I call Hypnoidal Self-Development, has proved to be dynamically effective.

Over more than twenty-five years, my observations have confirmed that, properly used, the hypnoidal stage becomes a powerful ally in preventing and remedying emotional discomfort and personality shortcomings. It facilitates access to the depths of the human mind and permits the meaning of thoughts and spoken words to be absorbed by the unconscious. To make this absorption possible, however, the constructive meaning of thoughts and spoken words has to fall on well prepared ground.

This has been recognized and clearly stated by the noted French mathematician Henri Poincaré, who said: ". . . unconscious work is not possible or in any sense fruitful, unless it is preceded . . . by a period of conscious work" . . . In the method of hypnoidal self-development, this "period of conscious work" is referred to as *preparatory work*.

The method of hypnoidal self-development is a new approach to psychological self-help, new and different as to method and also as to the manner in which the method is conveyed to the reader. Hypnoidal self-development combines the interaction between:

a) the necessary preparatory work with

b) a specific form of utilizing the hypnoidal stage and

c) the administration of specifically designed suggestions, namely: *hypnoidal suggestions*.

Hypnoidal self-development represents, for the first time, a systematically organized technique by which our faculties, talents and desirable personality-traits may be developed to their fullest extent.

In the method of hypnoidal self-development, hypnoidal suggestions are self-administered by reciting them in a specific manner which will be explained in detail in Part Two of this book. They can also be self-administered by playing back recorded hypnoidal suggestions while the person using them is in the hypnoidal stage.

The recording of suggestions as such is not a new idea, of course; neither is the playing back of suggestions while a person is falling asleep. It is well-known that recorded suggestions exist which promise to build up a "fascinating personality," and so on. But fairy-tale suggestions which allegedly fulfill any wish or desire with scarcely any personal effort involved, are alien to reality and more harmful than helpful.

There are essential differences, however, between these suggestions and hypnoidal suggestions and the principle of building the hypnoidal stage into the method of hypnoidal self-development is new and different also. The contents of this book will make these differences quite obvious.

By the method of hypnoidal self-development, we can stimulate an increase of our mental and emotional capacities. This will permit us to correct unfortunate character-traits, attitudes and habits and also to replace them with more favorable ones. In other words, proper use of the method of hypnoidal self-development enables us to practice constructive self-direction based on co-ordination between emotional response and constructive thinking. This mental-emotional self-direction is essential to mental health.

It is lack of co-ordination between feeling and constructive thinking which so often interferes with adequate self-direction and keeps people from putting their good intentions into action. In fact, a great many people know exactly what they should do, or not do, concerning their life-circumstances, habits and attitudes towards themselves and others and yet they keep on acting against their better judgment. Why is this so?

The following comparison will give you an illustrative answer. Just as the eyes of an astigmatic person do not focus correctly in the same direction and, as a consequence, give a distorted picture of whatever they perceive, in like manner a great many people have difficulty in focusing both their constructive thinking and their emotional response thereto, in the same direction. Astigmatic eyesight, if not corrected, will result in eye-strain and other more or less serious trouble, whereas improperly functioning co-ordination of emotional response to constructive thinking will interfere with satisfactory self-direction and lead to mental-emotional conflict of various forms and degrees.

Increasing awareness of the most unfortunate effects of inner conflict on our physical and mental health brings the importance of mental hygiene into the center of professional and public concern. But mere awareness is insufficient without appropriate tools for the improvement and maintenance of mental health; the method of hypnoidal self-development, however, provides these tools.

But, perhaps, there is no need for you to correct personality-shortcomings. Instead, you may wish to awaken latent faculties and talents, or to improve abilities you have already developed. You may feel an urge to write, or to paint; or you may want to increase your efficiency in your profession, in your business, or, maybe, you want to better your financial circumstances—whichever is the case, the method of hypnoidal self-development can be of decisive help to you.

While this method makes no pollyanna claims and does not cater to wishful thinking and futile day-dreaming, it can and does give added meaning and greater incentive to your worthwhile aspirations. This is not merely an assertion. It will be explained within these pages precisely *why* the *method* works and *how* it can be used beneficially to maintain and further mental health. The better the reader understands what he is about to do, the more likely he is to get the best results.

For this reason, and having in mind that a book on psychological self-help should be within the mental grasp of as many readers as possible, I have abstained, whenever it could be avoided, from using technical jargon. But I have also avoided underestimating the public's intelligence by employing "baby-talk, designed for adults," in the conceited assumption that people don't understand, or don't need to understand, anything above grade-school level. It has been my gratifying experience that, once intellectual curiosity has been kindled, there is usually a good capacity and willingness to grasp ideas and to go on from there to independent thinking.

For this reason, I have inserted quotations whenever they provide authoritative confirmation of important views and opinions, phrased with singular eloquence and succinctness. An apt quote will serve a good purpose in the sense of the *preparatory work,* whenever it stimulates the reader's interest and prompts him to explore the infinitely varied and fascinating territories of the human mind. To be mentally alert and to read, need not make us bookworms, if we realize the following fact: "The art of reading and the technique of research are the primary instruments of learning, of being taught things and of finding them out. That is why they must be the primary objectives of a sound educational system . . ." as Mortimer J. Adler has said.

Any method of psychological self-help automatically excludes "live" contact between client and psychotherapist. In "live" contact, the client and the psychotherapist can establish rapport, a relationship which, in psychotherapy, influences the outcome of therapy either positively or negatively. Beginning with the very first interview, the client has the advantage of finding out whether or not the psychotherapist's attitude pleases or displeases him. On the other hand, when starting to read a book on self-help, the client-reader is left in the dark about the author's personality. It was therefore deemed in the interest of the reader to provide a brief glimpse of some of my general views on matters of psychological self-help.

It goes without saying that the therapist should not moralize regarding individual attitudes of people, or try to impose his personal approval, or disapproval, or his convictions, on those who seek aid. Nevertheless, certain ideas had to be pointed out, because they contribute fundamentally to the upkeep of mental health and belong within the scope of the *preparatory work*. In a book, these ideas are bound to be laid down with seeming rigidity, whereas in "live" contact, the therapist is able to adapt the form of their presentation to the individual needs of each client.

But regardless of whether the therapist's contact with the client is direct, as in his office, or indirect, as by means of a book, the therapist's function always resembles that of a tourist guide who points out to the stranger which places are advisable and rewarding to visit and which had better be avoided. He should also be able to give valid reasons for his selections and rejections when asked to do so. Beyond that, it will be up to the stranger to choose where he wants to go. But there is a difference: in psychological guidance, the "stranger" may often have to develop his ability to choose, before he is able to make his own choice.

In the course of many years of practice, questions, singularly pertinent to the subject of self-help and the use of the hypnoidal stage, were put to me in writing, or during interviews. I am incorporating a few of these questions together with my answers at points where they may contribute to the clarification of certain aspects.

Part One and Part Two of this book serve as a directive for the *preparatory work* and to facilitate the reader's mental orientation. In addition, Part Two supplies an understanding of the tools with which to make the best possible use of the hypnoidal stage as well as detailed directions for the practical administration of hypnoidal suggestions.

The combination of Part One with Part Two forms an entity and ensures successful results with the method of hypnoidal self-development.

PART ONE

ROAD MAP TO

MENTAL HEALTH

1. RIGHT AND WRONG
FORMS OF SELF-HELP

Two men were driving a seldom-used mountain road; suddenly their car developed engine trouble. Unable to effect repairs, they had to continue on foot. When finally they reached their destination after a strenuous uphill walk, one of the men was not unduly tired, whereas the other felt completely exhausted. The first was a good tennis player and his body was in excellent training. The second man, however, had always shunned physical exertion; as a result, his muscles were flabby and he simply couldn't stand up to any strain.

The same kind of thing happens when people come under emotional strain. Those who have been taught and conditioned, or have conditioned themselves, to face life sensibly and courageously, will endure strain and cope with their troubles much more successfully than the ones who have remained flabby emotionally.

Unfortunately, we do not all start out with the same capacity to withstand strain and stress. We are lucky indeed, if wholesome mental-emotional attitudes are instilled into us during childhood-training; but many of us have to build up mental strength and develop wholesome mental attitudes on our own. The human personality expresses a great variety of attitudes toward an infinite variety of subjects. Some of these attitudes will be positive and beneficial, others, negative, distorted and, perhaps, destructive. A person whose every attitude is positive is as rare as one with nothing but negative attitudes and usually we find an assortment of positive and negative attitudes in one and the same person. We have certain attitudes toward our families, ourselves and our friends. We have certain attitudes toward particular persons and toward people in general; toward life and its meaning, toward work and recreation. Many of us feel very definitely about art, religion, morals, ethics, and even the simplest everyday incidents affect those reactions on which we build our attitudes. But in almost every case, changes of attitudes, either for the better or for the worse, are likely or possible.

To correct negative attitudes and to foster positive ones is to develop and strengthen mental health or, in other words, is applied psychological self-help.

Designing a workable method for psychological self-help and writing a book about it in a way equals the feat of having to walk a tightrope across a deep abyss. Although here the abyss is only an imaginary one, to cross it was tricky none the less, because two diametrically opposed viewpoints had to be taken into consideration. On the one side, there was the profession's viewpoint, with few exceptions in stern opposition to the very idea of psychological self-help. On the other side was the necessity to avoid encouraging the general public's eagerness to accept pushbutton techniques which promise to provide all the "wonders and treasures" that life can offer. But pushbutton techniques are most unlikely to lead us out of a maze of confusion and conflict.

Among those who discover this fact by bitter experience, a fortunate few may later find truly helpful guidance through competent professional help. The others split into two groups. One group goes ahead and continues to sample psychological panaceas, while those of the other group simply drop the whole matter once and for all and go on being dissatisfied, mixed-up and miserable, usually making their environment miserable too. For this reason and in apprehension of outright quackery, the profession's misgivings with regard to psychological self-help are understandable enough. To be just, however, let us also evaluate some reasons for the public's frequent credulity. Although the question cannot be answered conclusively here, one of the factors has to be mentioned, as it contributes greatly to create confusion in the minds of laymen.

All too often, remedies or therapies, denounced to the public as quackery yesterday, are given recognition by legitimate professions today and vice versa. Some remedies as well as therapies have been praised and endowed with almost miraculous powers at one time, only to be pronounced harmful and warned against at some other time. This state of affairs is most conducive to general confusion and the psychiatrist Abraham Myerson comments on it by observing: ". . . what doctors say today, they unsay tomorrow . . . there are fashions, ever changing, in medical belief . . ." Myerson continues by relating an amusingly illustrative anecdote about a man who suffered from continuous belching. It seems he consulted a prominent specialist who advised him not to drink any water during meals. The patient followed this advice for several months, but found no relief. So he returned to the doctor, who now told him to drink plenty of water during meals. When the patient expressed surprise at this contradictory prescription, the doctor "looked him over with a gracious and pitying glance. 'Ah,' said he, 'science makes great strides these days!' " (*Speaking of Man*, 1950).

The average layman can scarcely be blamed for finding it difficult to separate the wheat from the chaff when, seeking help for his own confusion, he is confronted by confusion among professionals. While controversies among the experts are on the whole an encouraging sign that a strenuous and unceasing battle is being waged against mental disorders and emotional disturbances, they indicate also that we are still in the experimental stages. This fact cannot be helped, of course, but the public is constantly reminded of it in a manner which often beclouds the issue and increases people's insecurity. Hence, those who are enmeshed in mental and emotional quandaries and turmoil, are often at a loss to decide where to turn for aid.

Quite a number of people reject legitimate help and fall for quackery because of their inability, or often mere unwillingness, to listen to anything they don't wish to hear. But countless others, who are in urgent or even desperate need of help, are confused by obvious contradictions among professionals and are therefore likely to grasp hopefully at whatever straw promises them a temporary illusion of support and relief. And herein we find some of the reasons why quackery is having a heyday.

People who are not severely maladjusted emotionally or confused mentally, should be given the opportunity to overcome their psychological imperfections "under their own power," so to speak. To those who succeed, even if only partially, that success in itself will instill increased self-confidence and thereby contribute enormously to their psychological well-being. Many reputed members of the psychiatric and psychological profession have recognized this and also the important benefits which psychological self-help can exert on an individual's mental and emotional welfare; but only a few of them have given it practical support. Among the most noted ones, Karen Horney contributed to the idea of self-help in emotional quandaries with her book *Self-Analysis* and Sigmund Freud himself wrote a foreword to a book with the title *Psychoanalyze Yourself,* although he said in one of his letters to Wilhelm Fliess: "I can only analyze myself . . . as if I were a stranger . . . As I have come across some puzzles in my own case, it is bound to hold up the self-analysis."

Indeed, psychoanalysis is a most subtle instrument and not always handled too successfully even by some reputed to be experts. It is, of course, a less suitable tool for self-use by a layman who, in addition, is in a psychologically disturbed state. And yet, as Carl Gustav Jung points out: "We need not be neurotic to feel the need of healing." These words contain a powerful motive to justify a search for some form of psychological self-help.

Actually, one of the main obstacles to the profession's acceptance of psychological self-help is based on a faulty premise. There is a tendency among psychiatrists and psychologists to assume that self-help implies psychotherapy. It goes without saying that psychotherapy should never be self-applied nor should self-help attempt to replace psychotherapy. But it shouldn't be overlooked by those who belittle the value of self-help that any successful form of psychotherapy depends on re-educating the patient in order to enable him to direct his personal and social life more harmoniously. As he works towards this goal, the psychotherapist will have to get the patient ultimately to help himself. Why then should anyone who feels the need, or inclination, to try and make the best of himself and of his life, not endeavor to do so *before* possible trouble has had time and opportunity to develop into sickness!

Self-help is not synonymous with "cure," but more often than not, adequate self-help may diminish any future need for a cure in the clinical sense. The basic idea of self-help lies in the purposeful development and application of our mental and emotional assets. This makes competent self-help an excellent safety-device to prevent psychological malfunction and sickness and one of the most active and important factors in mental hygiene.

2. PREPARATORY WORK

Perhaps the expression *preparatory work* sounds a bit formidable to you and you may ask: "What is it supposed to mean? I only hope that no *work* is expected of me!"

Well, you will very soon find out what the *preparatory work* consists of and discover that the effort required of you is minor compared to the results you can achieve. Part Two of this book will make you familiar with the tremendous role which the unconscious mind plays in solving all kinds of scientific, artistic and other problems. You will also learn why a period of intensive study and sometimes of concentration must precede the moment of triumphant solution.

"It is certain that the combinations which present themselves to the mind in a kind of sudden illumination after a prolonged period of unconscious work are generally useful and fruitful combinations which appear to be the result of a preliminary sifting . . . How can we explain the fact that, of the thousands of products of our unconscious activity, some are invited to cross the threshold, while others remain outside? Is it mere chance that gives them this privilege? Evidently not . . . Perhaps we must look for an explanation in that period of preliminary conscious work which always precedes all fruitful unconscious work." These words of Henri Poincaré clearly show the importance of making the unconscious mind work for us; they also point out that in order to achieve this goal a "period of preliminary work"—the *preparatory work*—is indispensable. The following illustration will give you an idea of how the conscious preparatory work may stimulate activities of the unconscious.

Howard M., a very successful man in the advertising field, was asked to work out a novel and effective presentation for a new product. All through the week, his head buzzed with ideas day and night, but nothing he came up with seemed right. Finally, his wife insisted that he take her out for the evening. Although Howard was anxious not to interrupt his work, he gave in, but felt certain he would go on thinking of his difficulties instead of enjoying himself. Nevertheless, a companionable dinner followed by an excellent play kept him from mulling over his assignment. As a result, he slept soundly that night and awoke refreshed the next morning. Immediately, his thoughts returned to his work and suddenly he knew exactly what to do. Rapidly, almost as though following dictation, he jotted down the plan of a brilliant advertising campaign. The preceding intense concentration on his work had *equaled the preparatory work* and supplied the necessary data to his unconscious mind. The evening of distraction, followed by sound sleep, then made it possible for his unconscious to propel a solution of the problem into his conscious mind.

A different and special type of preparatory work is required, however, if the difficulty you are intent on solving is a personal one and involves your emotions. In this case, your thoughts will be concentrated painfully on what is troubling you and it would therefore be a great mistake if the wrong kind of preparatory work were to intensify your mental-emotional preoccupation. This has to be avoided, of course, because it would only result in an increased intensity of brooding and worrying and, as a consequence, your thinking would take place on an entirely emotional level. For instance, if you feel strongly resentful towards a certain person, or in a certain situation, and if you concentrate your emotional thinking on your problem, then you apply the *wrong* kind of preparatory work—in fact, it is not preparatory work at all! Instead, you are feeding your emotionally negative attitude of resentfulness to your unconscious mind. The *right* preparatory work consists, at least in part, of correcting our negative emotional thinking by acquiring a gradual mastery of more objective thinking. This is a process of learning and conditioning which results in self-education.

A good example for this type of learning is the conditioning-process which takes place as we learn some new skill. Do you remember how you felt when you learned to drive an automobile? At first it seemed to be quite a complicated job. You had to pay close attention to every motion you made, to handling the steering wheel, using the brakes and gas pedal, to giving signals, and so on. But, as you became increasingly proficient, you found yourself doing the right thing more or less automatically without having to concentrate consciously on your motions. While we are learning, awareness and alertness, often coupled with apprehension, are strongly in the foreground of our mind. Our uneasiness and over-awareness of what we are doing decreases proportionately with our increasing skill and experience. We feel more secure and so long as this security is based on actually increased skill and knowledge, it is a normal process; finally our learning becomes transformed into a series of well-conditioned physical and mental reflexes. In a way, all successful learning is based on the same principle; it depends on how well we integrate that which we have learned into our mental-emotional make-up so that thereafter it can manifest itself reflexlike in our reactions and actions.

While you are reading this book, provided your attention is focused on the subject-matter, you will acquire a fresh slant on many questions and also sharpen your evaluative faculties. Thus you will be doing your preparatory work "learning as you go." You will reach a wider understanding of your own attitudes and personality and, with improving insight, you will become better equipped to understand others.

But in order to improve your insight, it is most important that you begin answering the questions of the "Guide to Self-Examination," starting on p. 229, *now,* while you are reading this book. However, under no circumstances self-administer hypnoidal suggestions during the hypnoidal stage, until and unless you have finished reading the whole book and have answered all the questions in the "Guide to Self-Examination."

At first glance, the "Guide" with its many questions may appear to you as one of the usual personality-tests; but this is not the case. Mindful of the static character of a great many personality-tests based on the scoring of "Yes—No," "True—False," "Often—Never" answers, I have endeavored to leave your answers unrestricted. Consequently, you are not forced into a set of cut-and-dried personality types which can never reflect quite adequately the wide range of mental and emotional potentialities. After all, life is not static; life is dynamic and changes continually in form and expression.

Should you consult a psychotherapist, he too would ask you questions, some of them quite similar to, others different from those you will find in the "Guide." But any and all of the therapist's questions would be intended to make you focus your mind temporarily on your mental and/or emotional reactions and actions. The questions in the "Guide" have been selected for the same reason. They will stimulate you to seek for the motives why you do, or don't do, certain things and why, and under what circumstances, you react, or don't react, in a certain manner. This helps you to improve your insight and herein lies one of the main reasons why you have to finish answering the questions of the "Guide," *before* you self-administer hypnoidal suggestions during the hypnoidal stage.

Although the improvement of your insight is indispensable, it is often not sufficient to make you function better psychologically, because, in addition, you must be able to transform your improved insight into action. You have to develop the sincere insight to accomplish this transformation during the course of your preparatory work. Often, this may not be quite easy for you, but making use of the hypnoidal stage as described in Part Two of this book, will *decrease* your difficulties and *increase* your ability for constructive mental-emotional self-direction.

During the preparatory work, the importance of sincere self-examination is matched by the importance of developing an adequate and applicable philosophy of life. Quite a few psychologists, however, are of the opinion that philosophy does not belong in the psychologist's consulting-room. This is correct so far as confused philosophizing is concerned. But a sound philosophy of life undoubtedly belongs in the domain of the psychologist. After all, philosophy means love of wisdom and wisdom should not be measured by possession of a parchment scroll or the length of a white beard.

In a chapter on psychotherapy and a philosophy of life, Carl Gustav Jung recognized the value of a philosophy of life by saying: ". . . it guides the life of the therapist and shapes the spirit of his therapy." But when using the method of hypnoidal self-development, it is not the therapist, it is *you* who are going to shape your own life and it is *your* philosophy of life which will influence your viewpoints and attitudes. Your philosophy of life forms the basis of your attitudes and is expressed in everything you think and feel. Like a catalyst, it affects the whole manner in which you conduct your life.

Should your philosophy of life be entirely materialistic, however, you will find yourself at a great disadvantage. Here again, Jung gives the best explanation of why this is so. In his opinion: "You get nowhere if you assume that the vital basis of a man is nothing but a very personal and therefore very private *affaire scandaleuse*. This is utterly hopeless . . . but pierce the veil of that sickly illusion and you step out of the narrow, stuffy personal corner . . . into the healthy and natural matrix of the human mind, into the very soul of humanity. That is the true foundation on which we can build a new and more workable attitude." (*The Practice of Psychotherapy*, 1954). These words clearly demonstrate that gaining and retaining mental health depends to a great extent on the quality of one's philosophy of life.

You should also take stock of your ideas regarding what you wish to accomplish. Think over carefully in what way and to what degree you would like to improve yourself and your life-circumstances, and then plan how to go about it. And keep in mind that it is not enough to *know* what you want, at least it is not enough in most cases. You have to find out also *what*, thus far, has prevented you from being or getting what you want. To use a trite illustration: if you want to make a million dollars, you should do your best to discover whether or not you have the qualifications which might enable you to make that much money. If you are able to appraise your personal potentialities and limitations objectively, then, maybe, you will find that you are justified in trying to make a million dollars—or a little less! But if you only dream about it, then you had better give up wishful thinking and choose a goal better suited to your capabilities. After all, there are other things in life just as desirable as making a million dollars! In fact, there are many other fine things: for instance, making the very best of our qualities and possibilities.

But whatever you want to accomplish, you will have to develop your ability to direct yourself constructively, because: "Personality can never develop unless the individual chooses his own way consciously and with conscious moral decision." (C. G. Jung.)

Within these pages, you will find some viewpoints which may not seem to have a direct bearing on mental health in the narrower sense, and yet they are closely connected with *living* a mentally healthy life. They belong therefore to the domain of preparatory work because, together with your self-examination, they will give you directional ideas which may help you ultimately to "choose your own way"!

3. ◆ THE CASE OF THE
NEUROTIC OYSTER

As an intelligent man or woman, you may think you know fairly well what is meant by a neurosis. But should anybody have referred to you as a neurotic, or should you suspect somebody else of being neurotic, you might want to know a little more about it.

Although definitions are to be found in encyclopaedias, in psychological dictionaries and, of course, in books on psychology and psychopathology, these definitions may deviate from each other to a considerable extent.

While it is true that the medical profession has reached a relatively high degree of success in diagnosing and treating physical diseases, the same measure of progress has not been achieved in dealing with mental and emotional disorders. Unfortunately, this fact only contributes to the confusion of a great many people seeking to work out their emotional problems and it is not surprising that the average person's ideas about mental health remain rather nebulous. Consequently, when a physician finds that a patient's health is adversely affected by some emotional conflict and advises him to undergo psychotherapy, the patient often rejects his physician's advice by saying: "I couldn't face my family and my friends if they knew I were consulting a psychotherapist. After all, doctor, I am not crazy!"

But the patient cannot be blamed entirely for his attitude. Apart from the fact that psychotherapy and psychoanalysis usually are time-consuming and expensive undertakings which not everybody can afford, emotional malfunctioning is regarded on the average with far less understanding and sympathy than physical malfunctioning. The same person who commiserates warmly with a relative or friend, suffering from some virus infection or a broken leg, may consider a neurosis almost as a degradation from so-called normal to inferior behavior. Anyone who admits candidly that he visits a psychotherapist may quite likely, although most unjustifiedly, risk disadvantages in his profession as well as in his private life. On the slightest excuse, doubts may be raised about his efficiency and his reliability, and any quite natural mistakes he happens to make may frivolously be attributed to his "mental condition"!

But does a neurosis actually have to signify mental deficiencies or inferior human qualities? To this question, the psychiatrist Jung answers: "We do our patients grievous wrong if we try to force them into the category of the unfree. Among neurotics, there are not a few who do not require any reminders of their social duties and obligations . . . Neurosis is by no means only negative; it is also positive. Only a soulless rationalism could and does overlook this fact, supported by the narrowness of a purely materialistic philosophy of life. . . ." (*Psychological Reflections,* 1953.)

Sometimes, it may be extremely difficult for a physician to differentiate between neurotic and non-neurotic malfunctions, and under certain circumstances even the most skilled psychiatrist or psychotherapist may find it difficult to diagnose a case unequivocally as a "neurosis." Speaking from a psychiatric viewpoint, Abraham Myerson expresses great caution regarding the neuroses when he points out: "Although psychologizing is a very alluring exercise, the simplest neurosis is not understood in any complete way . . ." And Jung says: "I have yet to come across a respectable specimen of a neurosis of which one could give anything like an adequate description in a short lecture, to say nothing of all the therapeutic intricacies that are far from clear even to the shrewdest professional. . . ."

Therefore, if we are to avoid the fallacy of "having dealt the devil a serious blow by calling him neurosis," it is important to consider at least a few facets of this "devil" neurosis.

During our life-span, we all are confronted by countless motives for mental and emotional struggle and conflict—in love, in hate, in sexual relations, in our various and often greatly exaggerated aversions and predilections, in actual aberrations and in those which are, to a degree, socially determined—the list could be endless. At times, the emotional battles we wage for all kinds of reasons may appear to be losing battles, because mental fogginess and confusion prevent us from recognizing the true origin of the actual or imagined difficulties which bedevil us. The resulting frustration and despondency may cause the kind of incessant inner conflict which nurtures a potential neurosis.

This warfare within ourselves, however, need not turn into a neurosis any more than falling into icy water need result in pneumonia. In both cases, of course, an unfavorable predisposition and/or adverse circumstances may have lowered our powers of resistance, hereby making us more likely to succumb to actual disease. But anybody who finally succeeds in re-establishing his emotional equilibrium by making a supreme effort to extricate himself from a maze of conflict, frustration and fear, may prove to be in basically better mental health than some other person who appears to be well-balanced. The latter may never have been subjected to circumstances and experiences causing emotional upheaval, or he was fortunate enough to react differently to them. However, it would be unjust and false to believe that this difference of emotional reaction means a difference between emotional sickness and health! This difference is a question of individual sensitivity; but sensitivity is not sickness, although it may lead to sickness if it turns into disproportionate and constant hypersensitivity. It is this complex sensitivity which, on the other hand, is a prerequisite to creativeness and may become a powerful stimulus to productivity in the fields of science and art.

Unfortunately, hypersensitivity also contributes to a mental and emotional climate which may favor the development of neuroses. We have only to recall the well-known case of the oyster in which disease results in pearls. It is quite possible that the poor oyster, while producing the pearl, has to suffer miserably and is found obnoxious by her non-pearl-producing colleagues! Yet neither the oyster's "subjective" discomfort nor her "obnoxiousness" can detract from the objective beauty and value of the pearl. I have to admit, though, that I don't know how to help a neurotic oyster in its misery, but I do know that frequently a neurotic condition in human beings can be straightened out or measurably improved.

It goes without saying that great achievements in art and science, or in any other field, are not necessarily anchored in what is clinically called a neurosis. Ironically, hypersensitivity as such is often, although erroneously, regarded as a sign of exceptional artistic or intellectual gifts. Consequently, some people consider it an interesting distinction to be highstrung and temperamental, even when these pseudo-assets are no more than a disguise for a maladjusted personality or, sometimes, simply indicate an adult spoiled brat! People of this kind want to be "different" at any price and may display their neurotic manifestations as "intellectual exclusiveness," claiming thereby a spurious superiority over their fellowmen. As a rule, these people do not shy away from psychoanalysis and psychotherapy; instead they may pamper themselves into a neurosis and, if they can afford it, are eager to be psychoanalyzed as a necessary adjunct to the sophistication they like to parade.

A neurosis, however, need not be earmarked by irritability or by other conspicuous signs of emotional distress and imbalance. Some people appear perfectly poised and in full control of themselves and of their life-circumstances although, at the same time, their emotional undercurrents are highly neurotic. It is not easy at all to evaluate the psychodynamic forces operating in this type of person; very often he is the primary cause for the allegedly neurotic behavior of some other member, or members, of his family.

Another rather strange type of neurotic behavior should be mentioned here. It is represented by the men and women who, as soon as they are confronted with some kind of emergency, surprise everybody by apparently shedding the neurosis with which they had been plaguing themselves and their environment. Temporarily, during a crisis, they may show more composure, decisiveness and matter-of-fact energy than those who are the pillars on whom they usually lean.

As you can see, the concept of the neuroses, like many other scientific concepts, is not clearcut and may, in part or as a whole, be declared invalid tomorrow by what science might be on the point of discovering today. But whatever this may be, Jung's definition of the neuroses will remain valid. He says: "Neurosis is the suffering of the human soul in its whole, world-wide complexity, and this is so enormous that any theory of neurosis may well be described straight away as a worthless *aperçu* unless it is a gigantic image of the soul . . ." (*Psychological Reflections,* 1953.) These words reveal a profound respect for the healthy, as well as the non-healthy manifestations of human beings and, regardless of whether or not we believe in the existence of the human "soul," this basic respect is indispensable if we are to function well as human beings.

All this indicates that we are not quite able to explain what a neurosis *is,* although we are only too often confronted with what a neurosis *does.* A neurosis can interfere drastically with an individual's day-by-day well-feeling and well-functioning and can deprive him of his natural faculty to appreciate and enjoy the greater and lesser gifts life has to offer. In extremely severe neurotic cases, crippling frustrations and anxieties can darken a person's whole life; besides, the effects of a neurosis do not remain restricted to the person afflicted with it. A severely neurotic individual may affect his environment like a contagious disease and even one who is not severely neurotic may be difficult to get along with. For these reasons, wouldn't many people gladly use some pills which would prevent a neurosis? Unfortunately, no such pills are at our disposal . . . yet; but the method of hypnoidal self-development can often prevent a neurosis.

As has been mentioned before, many of us are apt to display neurotic and hysterical symptoms *without actually being neurotic.* These symptoms may amount to nothing more than neurotically tinged behavior and they could be called *neurotic surface-symptoms.* There are many varieties of these surface-symptoms and the circumstances under which they may appear also vary greatly. Temporarily, we may suffer from moodiness, crying spells, increased irritability, listlessness, certain forms of anxiety, fatigue, gastric disturbances, headaches, and so on. If there is no physical cause for them, they may easily belong in the category of neurotic surface-symptoms. At their roots may be unfavorable environmental influences, disharmonious or even unhappy relations with parents, children, marriage partners, superiors or subordinates, colleagues, associates, or fellow-workers. Then there are the pressures of an uncongenial occupation or unfavorable economic circumstances and a host of other breeders of conflict-matter which may provoke seemingly "neurotic" behavior.

But tangible difficulties are not the only ones to produce neurotic and hysterical surface-symptoms. There are also people who display these symptoms as a result of their own negative character-traits, such as excessive selfishness, possessiveness, resentfulness, or continual self-pity, to name but a few. Very often, these negative mental attitudes are coupled with an unwillingness, or an imagined inability to recognize and correct them. Jung refers to this type of person: "People whose own temperaments offer problems are often neurotic, but it would be a serious misunderstanding to confuse the existence of problems with neurosis." Unless people of this type can develop objective insight and come to recognize their faulty attitudes, no psychotherapy or self-help, with or without the use of the hypnoidal stage, will have much chance for success.

It is important to keep in mind that at present we are only concerned with neurotic surface-symptoms and are not discussing the actual neuroses. The surface-symptoms could be compared to a most unpleasant and plaguing cough brought on by a severe cold. The cough as such is not, or not yet, a sign of tuberculosis. If sensible measures are taken, the cold will clear up, although the cough may hang on for quite a while before disappearing completely. And just as we can re-establish physical health by giving proper attention to bodily malfunction and discomfort, we can, in a different way, of course, and by different means take proper measures against the discomfort of psychological malfunctions by which we hurt ourselves and others as well.

"But," you may ask, "how can I take proper measures against psychological malfunctions?" Well, the method of hypnoidal self-development as described in this book provides you with the necessary explanations and directions to be used as protective means against psychological malfunctions. However, when we realize how difficult it can be to distinguish between an actual neurosis and neurotic surface-symptoms, we may ask ourselves whether the method of hypnoidal self-development can be practiced safely and without restrictions. The best way to answer this query will be to insert here several questions and answers which clarify the point.

QUESTION: Can any and every person make use of the method of hypnoidal self-development without disadvantage to himself?

ANSWER: Yes, provided that the instructions outlined in this book are observed.

QUESTION: Are there any counter-indications for the use of this method?

ANSWER: The method of hypnoidal self-development should not be used by people suffering from delusions and hallucinations, especially not by those who hear hallucinatory commanding, accusing, or threatening voices. Furthermore, it should not be used in severe obsessional neuroses with the compulsion of repetitive thoughts of a terrifying, or disgusting nature; all such people are beyond self-help and need psychiatric treatment. With these exceptions, the method of hypnoidal self-development, when applied according to instructions, can only be beneficial.

QUESTION: Can talents and special faculties be revealed and developed by this method?

ANSWER: Yes, they can. It is amazing how often neglected or ignored faculties and talents will germinate and develop to a remarkable extent following the use of hypnoidal self-development. This method can bring to the surface many hidden gifts which otherwise would remain dormant.

But hypnoidal self-development does not merely play the role of a "divining rod"; it is likewise effective in helping a person to develop valuable facets of his personality, thereby furthering his progress towards mental and emotional maturity.

Needless to say, personal problems cannot be expected to vanish from one day to another, nor can everyone achieve exactly the same results and hope to be transformed as by some "magic formula" into a brilliant artist, a mental wizard, or an infallible success in his profession. Much will depend on the amount of good will and perseverance invested, as well as on the individual degree of understanding and responsiveness. However, all *inherent* positive mental and emotional capacities and talents will become activated. This will open up increased chances for a full life, for greater accomplishments and deeper contentment. At the same time, the chances for mental-emotional malfunctioning will decrease together with the chances for acquiring neurotic ills.

QUESTION: What would happen if a person with an actual neurosis, but without the counter-indications mentioned in the second answer, were to try the method of hypnoidal self-development?

ANSWER: It cannot be stressed enough that the complexity of a neurosis should be dealt with by therapy and not by any type of self-help technique. However, in many cases, it is not possible to decide offhand whether or not a person is neurotically ill. I realized this difficulty for those who may use hypnoidal self-development and who don't know whether they are merely in a temporary state of emotional confusion and conflict, or whether they are on the verge of a neurosis, or actually neurotic.

I had also to consider those individuals who wish to use hypnoidal self-development to bring to light certain talents and faculties they might have. Some of these people, possibly unaware of it themselves, could be suffering from one or another mild form of neurosis. It was imperative, therefore, to devise the technique for hypnoidal self-development in such a manner that, above all, it could not be harmful to those who might be afflicted with a neurosis. Actually, a neurotic person may benefit from this method, because hypnoidal self-development will probably serve him better than either doing nothing at all or risking inadequate psychotherapy, which happens more frequently than we care to believe. To paraphrase Bertrand Russell on bad philosophy: "I shall suggest that psychotherapy, if it is bad psychotherapy, may be dangerous and therefore deserves that degree of negative respect which we accord to lightning and tigers." I do not mean to imply, of course, that persons who suffer from a neurosis should use the method of hypnoidal self-development rather than consult a psychotherapist. My intention is only to stress these two points: first of all, there is no disadvantage involved for those who may use my method in possible unawareness of being neurotically ill, and, secondly, it is necessary to choose carefully when selecting psychotherapeutic aid in emotional disturbances, because, as Jung says, "it is not possible to bring the patient to a more advanced stage than one has reached oneself."

Regarding psychological self-help, many people believe that such methods consist of nothing more than common-sense advice. Although common-sense advice can be of great value, we have to realize that very often common sense is not sufficient to bring about improvement. Dr. Lawrence S. Kubie gives us the reasons very succinctly: "If a patient can use common-sense advice effectively, no more is needed and our patient cannot have been very ill. If common-sense advice rolls off the proverbial duck's back, then that duck is ill . . ."

But common-sense advice may "roll off the duck's back" for other reasons than illness! Confused thinking, certain negative character-traits, lack of adequate emotional control and self-direction, and any number of other factors can render it very difficult for a person to make good progress under his own power.

For a great many of these people, improvement and progress are possible in spite of the difficulties with which they are faced, provided that their efforts for mental-emotional self-direction are made easier by the method of hypnoidal self-development.

4. ◆ OVER-AWARENESS OF MENTAL
HEALTH IS SELF-DEFEATING

The prevalent fondness for borrowing from psychiatric and psychological terminology keeps the awareness of mental sickness and emotional disorder constantly awake in our minds. Nowadays, clinical terms are used to describe every harmless mental quirk or individual peculiarity that doesn't conform to generalized patterns of standard behavior. If one likes privacy and enjoys being alone now and then, one is called an introvert. If one is a cautious soul and slow to reach a decision, one is told that one acts that way because one "feels insecure." The current fashion of being "bewitched by psychiatric jargon" has invaded our lives. And so we may rashly call a person who has no more than adequate self-confidence and who refuses to hide his light under a bushel, a "paranoiac," whereas another one may be accused of being "hysterical," just because he is going through a crisis and consequently displays a temporary and understandable moodiness.

The habit of calling a person "neurotic" and "hysterical" at the drop of an argument has become all too frequent and is almost frivolous. I recall a woman patient who came to my office one day complaining bitterly: "I can't go on living with Bob * [her husband] any longer! Whenever we have an argument, he stops me by saying 'Don't be hysterical!' and I resent that. After all, he is a neurotic himself, isn't he?" The attractive young woman, puffing one ciga-

* All names in case histories are fictitious.

rette after another, looked at me expectantly, followed by pained
surprise, when I did not confirm her "diagnostic" opinion of her
husband. Her marriage had begun as a love-match approximately
four years ago. After the birth of their twins, a boy and a girl, their
happiness was complete. But trouble started when Bob obtained
an important executive position. Now business trips kept him away
from home for long periods. Shirley, his wife, began feeling lonely,
neglected and sorry for herself. Her imagination, misled by jealousy,
started to work overtime and she suspected her husband of being
unfaithful. Shirley's suspicions were quite unfounded, but that didn't
prevent her from welcoming Bob with spiteful reproaches and a
flood of accusations each time he returned home. Afterwards, she
would become remorseful at the scenes she had created and thus
her moods vacillated between jealous fury and self-torturing guilt-
feelings. Continuously subjected to her emotional outbursts, Bob
became more and more dissatisfied with his married life. Although
he still loved Shirley, his increasing exasperation over her tantrums
now prompted him to find fault with her even on occasions when
there was no adequate reason to do so. To Shirley, on the other
hand, Bob's frequent censure seemed added proof that he no longer
loved her.

In this atmosphere of almost constant tension, Bob's own behavior began to develop several peculiarities; he became over-
sensitive to noise and, when he was at home, the children were
never permitted to play near him. Then Bob began complaining
of dizzy spells, and on weekend outings with his family, he refused
to drive into the mountains, because he had become fearful of high
places. These symptoms might well be regarded as neurotic, while
Shirley's emotional violence, overshadowing her good reasoning,
could easily be classified as hysterical. Aided by the hypnoidal
technique, Bob and Shirley finally overcame their difficulties. They
learned to think and reason clearly, even in matters with an emotional impact.

I have dealt at length with this habit of clinical name-calling,
because it is harmful for many reasons. For instance, if an individual has definite character shortcomings, the idea that he is considered a neurotic may be grist to his mill. Although people usually
object to being seriously thought of as neurotics, yet at a semi-

conscious level of their minds, they often sense the pseudo-advantages to be derived from a neurosis. As a result, they may rationalize like this: "After all, being a neurotic, I cannot possibly be expected to behave as would a non-neurotic, healthy individual under the same circumstances." Acting on this premise, these people often shrug off the obligation to face and remedy their maladjustments; instead they feel protected and exonerated by the implication of illness contained in the label "neurosis." On the other hand, should somebody really be suffering from a severe neurosis, the ill-advised words "Oh, you are just neurotic!" may easily kindle this person's morbid anxiety and frustration and make him feel trapped in his neurotic loneliness.

Perhaps you will exclaim: "I would never speak of anyone as neurotic unless it were absolutely true!" But how can you be so sure that your "diagnosis" is correct? Rarely do we think of our own emotional malfunctions as neurotic. Usually, we consider our touchiness, our frequent temper flare-ups and many other emotional malfunctions as quite natural and justified. Yet when another person displays the same traits and habits, we are inclined to interpret them as "neurotic." Very often we do so, because we just don't understand, or approve of them, and what we don't understand or approve of, we often tend to condemn as "bad" or "sick."

The tragic element involved in actual mental disease and also in some forms of neurosis should, of course, never be underestimated. However, at times, one is apt to wonder if an over-awareness of neurotic disorders and a constant harping on psychological interpretations does not result in turning a desirable and necessary ounce of prevention into an undesirable and unnecessary pound of prevention.

When used to safeguard *physical* health, it is undeniable that the proverbial ounce of prevention can avert a great deal of trouble. Regarding emotional disorders, a well-measured ounce of prevention is even more important because of the profound part psychological factors play in our social and individual lives. In fact, the disturbing influence of confused thinking and uncontrolled emotions often extends its detrimental effects over a far wider radius than any merely physical disease. Apprehensive over-awareness of possible ill-effects, however, is contrary to precaution and prevention.

It is this over-awareness which often turns into an almost morbid attempt to read some form of baleful psychological significance into every small thing that goes on in ourselves and in others as well.

Now we have discussed a few factors which are adverse to mental health; but what do we actually understand by mental health? The answer to this question seems to be fairly simple. But, apparently, even renowned psychiatrists find it difficult to give a precise reply and prefer to answer indirectly as did Abraham Myerson. "In my day," he said, "I have lectured a great deal both as professional teacher in medical schools and as a so-called lecturer to lay-audiences . . . in the somewhat comic role of 'speaker at a Women's Club,' I was suddenly assailed by a demoralizing fantasy. It was that the faces turned toward the platform were those of monkeys listening gravely and uncritically as I, another monkey, spouted forth—what? How did it come about that I had become an 'authority' in fields of such importance and such vagueness as mental health . . ."

Another answer, this one quite direct and directive, is contained in a brochure published by the National Association for Mental Health in 1951. It catalogues the characteristics of people with good mental health. A few of these characteristics are:

"They are not bowled over by their emotions—by their fears, anger, love, jealousy, guilt or worries.

"They can take life's disappointments in their stride.

"They have a tolerant, easy-going attitude toward themselves as well as others; they can laugh at themselves.

"They neither underestimate, nor overestimate their abilities.

"They can accept their own shortcomings.

"They feel able to deal with most situations that come their way.

"They have self-respect.

"They are able to give love and to consider the interests of others.

"They have personal relationships that are satisfying and lasting.

"They expect to like and to trust others, and take it for granted that others will like and trust them.

"They can feel that they are part of a group."

And the brochure went on to explain: "There is no line that neatly divides the mental healthy from the unhealthy. There are many different degrees of mental health. No one characteristic by itself can be taken as evidence of mental illness."

So far so good; but if it is true that no single characteristic can be taken as evidence of mental illness—and it *is* true—then a single characteristic cannot be taken as evidence of mental health either. But, in that case, why set up a long list of mental health characteristics in the first place! No doubt, most of the listed attributes are worth striving for; yet it may be questionable, for instance, whether a "tolerant, easy-going attitude towards oneself" might not hinder rather than further the attainment of desirable objectives.

Besides, not too many people are born with all these excellent character-traits. Most of us have to struggle and, at times, struggle hard to develop just a few of them. Strangely enough, the brochure does not say *how* we should proceed to develop the mental health attributes we may lack. And yet, it is an essential part of mental hygiene in action to point out ways and means of improving mental health, whereas the mere listing of favorable mental health characteristics resembles the wishful dream of an accountant trying to bring the ledger of life into perfect balance.

However, several of the characteristics named can be endorsed wholeheartedly, provided they are interpreted correctly. It is indeed a priceless mental attitude to be able to "laugh at oneself," so long as it is not bitter laughter, and it is also a priceless attribute to have self-respect, provided that self-respect is not confused with false pride.

The secret of these, and of so many other distinctions, must be sought in the wisdom which we can hope to acquire by savoring every moment of our lives instead of just passing through a form of mere existence. C. G. Jung understands the essence of this wisdom. He says: ". . . contradiction moves me; for how can one see light without shadow, or feel peace without noise, or achieve wisdom without foolishness? . . . To become foolish is certainly not an art; but to draw wisdom from foolishness is the whole of art. Foolishness is the mother of the wise, never cleverness." (*Psychological Reflections.*) Ralph Waldo Emerson, who can hardly be accused of flippant thinking, evidently did not expect people to fit into standardized grooves of mental health, for in his view you should "congratulate yourself if you have done something strange and extravagant and have broken the monotony of a decorous age." And Theodor Reik, the disciple of Sigmund Freud, says: "It is doubtful whether we could go on thinking and acting like reasonable people if we did not from time to time think and act as if we were almost crazy."

This should not mislead us into believing that these men advocate foolishness. Of course, they don't. But in their profound understanding of the workings of the human mind they realize that we do not develop mental and emotional maturity unless we have, at least at some time in our lives, been "bowled over" by love, by the grandeur of nature, by some form of art, by religious fervor, by a longing for adventure, or, in a different sense, of course, by grief, fear, or guilt.

Like the act of creation, wisdom, in a strange way, is related to elation. In the act of creation, elation is acute—in the manifestation of wisdom, it is retrospective. In its many forms, elation may range from the intoxication of drunkenness rolling in the gutter to the enchantment of inspiration reaching towards the stars. If elation is to result in wisdom, it will leave residues of experiences bearing the fragrance of vintage wine—the beauty of the setting sun which has known the day—and even though the stars themselves are not quite within our reach, wisdom will at least know in what direction to search.

5. ◆ MIXED-UP EMOTIONS

Do you worry and brood a good deal? Do you often feel apprehensive or as if you were running around in circles with the restless futility of a squirrel in a cage?

Do you believe that you are unloved or unable to love? Or, maybe, you feel bored frequently?

If you have to answer "yes" to some of these questions, chances are that you feel harassed at times, or perhaps undefinably guilty. Possibly, you put the blame for whatever befalls you on actual or imagined inadequacies; you may even hold the "injustices of fate" responsible for your "sorry lot"! And then again you may be inclined, quite often and without justifiable reasons, to suspect that those for whom you care reject you or don't appreciate you; or you feel suspicious that people are taking advantage of you. If so, you should realize that you are fostering negative mental attitudes which sooner or later will impel you to all kinds of destructive emotional reactions, such as frustration, resentment and hostility. Reflexlike, you may then be driven to counterbalance the actual or imagined unfair treatment which disturbs you so much, by developing a hypersensitivity with regard to your steadily increasing emotional demands. Inevitably, however, this very preoccupation with your inflated demands for love and consideration will blunt your own capacity to sense other people's needs.

Possibly though, you are only slightly though chronically discontented, out of sorts, yet unable to put your finger on any precise reason for your blue moods. And so it happens that you blame your family, your friends, your work, or a combination of many reasons for "what is eating you"—and it might well be that you have a point there! But whatever the case, all these negative mental attitudes, fears and fancies comprise mere samples of a vast variety of emotional patterns which, potentially, constitute an active or a latent part of our psychological make-up.

Should these negative attitudes bother you all too often and with excessive intensity, then they can, and frequently do, result in grave neurotic disturbances. To avoid this, we must learn to understand our emotional reactions and train ourselves to deal with them satisfactorily. Only if we are well equipped to make successful efforts to correct our negative emotional attitudes, or to change the circumstances which call them forth, do we manage and direct our mental and emotional conduct constructively.

The first step towards accomplishing this is to realize that many forms of emotional unease often stem from a negative outlook on life and from inadequate and negative mental attitudes which we either have failed to recognize, or have been unwilling to admit to ourselves.

Another possibility often enters the picture. Theoretically we may recognize the beneficial role of positive mental attitudes and even admit to ourselves that some of our own attitudes are far from being positive. Nevertheless we may consider ourselves unable to do anything about them, or be too indolent to try. As a consequence, when the errors in our behavior are pointed out to us, we usually acknowledge them either by saying somewhat sheepishly: "Yes, I know!" or we answer with an undertone of finality: "That's just how I am!" The first statement is likely to be made by people who actually do "know better" and realize their failings, yet are not able to apply the necessary self-discipline and self-direction. The second answer is more frequently heard from those who don't even intend to improve their faulty attitudes, because they fail to see, or admit, any reason to do so.

But there are others who come to recognize their inadequacies and wish to correct them. Some do so unaided, others with professional help. Some accomplish what they set out to do fairly easily, whereas for others it may be a very hard job. The latter group will find that the method of hypnoidal self-development can bring them greater success with less effort.

Let there be no mistake; constructive mental attitudes and a positive outlook on life as described and understood in this book, are *not* identical with the kind of "positive" thinking which supposedly has the power to fulfill all the dreams and ambitions of those who practice it. The most effective form of positive thinking could not be that powerful any more than the most potent medicine could keep a finite body alive forever. Man cannot get whatever he desires just by convincing himself that anything is within his reach; for one thing, there are usually too many factors involved which he is incapable of controlling.

Although the Pollyanna type of positive thinking is quite evidently inadvisable, it is, beyond any doubt, necessary to practice a sensible form of positive thinking. It is equally evident, that negative thinking and a chronically gloomy outlook on our personal life as well as on life in general, will reduce or nullify our chances of reaching desirable goals, whereas a sensible form of positive thinking certainly increases our chances for achievement.

Just the opposite effect is evoked by negative emotions such as chronic and exaggerated fear, anger, resentfulness, hostility, suspicions, self-pity and many other negative mental attitudes, be they freely manifested or apparently controlled. These negative emotions have a decidedly harmful effect not only on our mental, but also on our physical health, for they interfere directly and indirectly with the functioning of some of our bodily organs and with normal glandular secretion. This vicious circle, created between psychological and glandular malfunctioning, is viewed with increasing concern by physicians and psychologists as they give more and more credit to sound positive mental attitudes for their beneficial interaction with healthy glandular functioning. For a better understanding of the potential harmful effects of undue stress on our mental and physical health, mention should be made of the important research conducted by Dr. Hans Selye and his associates at the University at Montreal. Their findings demonstrate how essential it is to develop sound mental and emotional attitudes by which we can cope with external stress as well as avoid harmful emotional reactions which will cause stress.

As causes for stress, we might also consider attitudes which become inculcated in us as part of an educational system during childhood and later during our formative years. For instance, the overemphasis of competitiveness has an unfavorable effect on the healthful functioning of many individuals and also on the formation of sound character-traits. In this connection, some interesting ideas in regard to youth education were introduced by Count Duerckheim in West Germany. In his opinion, young people are hampered in their development of a healthful personality, if they are forced into trying to outdo each other constantly. Duerckheim believes that incessant competition and comparison with others is less advisable than the endeavor to make the very best of oneself regardless of competition. This concept seems to be a most commendable one for adults also, because overemphasis on competition often amounts to incessant comparison of other people's accomplishments and status with our own. If we are inclined to underevaluate our own faculties, characteristics and life-situation and to overevaluate those of others, it is obvious that envy, resentment and frustration will ensue which, in turn, will cause continual and dangerous stress.

Of course, competition is inevitable in many fields, but it should not be allowed to become the instigator of undesirable character-traits, or cause health-undermining strain. In fact, competition might gain better results, if we were trained, or would train ourselves, to give our very best in every situation. This would prepare us to become not only good winners, but also good losers.

But let us reconsider those motivations which bring forth undesirable emotional reactions. It is imperative to realize that emotions of any type, expressed or unexpressed, if permitted to run wild and to rule us unchecked, are comparable to a culture-medium for bacilli, except that in our case emotional disorders will thrive, instead of bacilli.

Perhaps, you are now wondering: "How does one prevent, or break, the vicious circle between emotional and glandular functioning and how does one develop favorable mental and emotional attitudes?" It would be relatively simple for you to find the right answer if, instead of a human brain, you were to possess an electronic one, provided your electronic brain were given accurate information. But, unlike the electric computer, the human brain does not calculate answers *automatically*. The human brain responds to and interprets each individual sensory perception and intellectual or emotional experience. Then, by complex selective processes of thoughts and emotions, we accept or discard the "information" received in this manner.

You will have to apply this selective mental process to all the information laid before you within these pages and determine which ingredients and precepts of mental health you consider most applicable to your own needs.

6. ◆ CONTROL—DON'T SUPPRESS—
YOUR EMOTIONS

There exist many psychological panaceas from which people are supposed to benefit. Among them, to make a random choice, you are told by some psychiatrists and psychologists, "Blow your top if that's the way you feel!"—"Beware of bottling up your emotions!"—"Self-expression is all-important!"—"Give your emotions free rein!"

Then again you are advised to "Discipline yourself!" "Control yourself!" and you are told, and very rightly so, that frequent emotional outbreaks and temper tantrums are dangerous to mental and physical health. For instance, Dr. Alvarez points out: ". . . temper tantrums . . . I have never had any use for such advice, and I don't think any doctor or psychiatrist would give it, if he had ever had much experience working alongside of a man who blew up over small annoyances and ranted and screamed."

Undisciplined behavior can manifest itself in many forms and degrees. It may appear in the guise of the "sullen silent treatment" which somebody may inflict on those around him, or it may erupt in violent fits of rage. But one thing is certain. Frequent undisciplined behavior has an unfavorable to detrimental effect not only on the person who displays it, but on his or her environment as well. Under whatever circumstances unruly emotions make their appearance and whatever form they assume, inevitably their consequences are deplorable, especially in the home, where the whole family is apt to become victimized.

Should we then exert rigid mental and emotional control to the extent of never daring to permit ourselves any emotional outlet? Yet therein lies danger too, for there are correct and incorrect ways to control and direct our emotions. It is not sufficient, therefore, simply to *know* that we have to control ourselves, it is far more important to know *how* to control ourselves. Incorrect emotional control, most of the time, amounts to wrongly applied will-power by *suppressing* our negative emotions. If you are angry and force yourself not to be angry by thinking, for instance: "I must not be angry—I have to control myself!" or, when a depressive mood begins to overcome you and you attempt to ward it off by saying to yourself: "I shouldn't give in to 'feeling blue,' instead I should try to smile and be gay!" you use *incorrect control* by wrongly applied will-power. The suppression of negative emotions engenders a permanent state of emotional and physical tension and thereby aggravates other forms of stress to which we may be subjected. It is similar to sweeping a room and then hiding the collected dirt beneath the carpet; the room may appear to be clean, but the dirt is not only present, but accumulates.

But whether we suppress our emotions or let them run wild, in either case we shall be living on an all-out hyper-emotional level with more or less harmful consequences to our physical and mental health. The only difference between the two states is, that in the first one, emotional vehemence is subdued, whereas in the second one, emotional vehemence is explosive. In both cases, however, we are apt to vacillate from feelings of anxiety to feelings of aggressiveness and resentment towards others. These emotional undercurrents are forerunners of emotional disorders.

When unhealthy emotions are suppressed, they become even more distorted and cause all sorts of disturbing psychological and physical symptoms. Although the physical symptoms often have no vestige of organic justification, they are nevertheless very real to those who are plagued by them and little comfort is derived from being told by a physician: "There is nothing wrong with you physically—your discomfort is only in your mind!" Should this happen to you, you might well be inclined to retort: "But if it is all in my mind, what can I do to prevent my mind from playing these harrowing tricks on me?" Whereupon you would probably receive the answer: "Take it easy! You need to become more mature emotionally and feel more secure, then everything will straighten out!" And if your doctor has delved into modern psychology, perhaps he will add: "Your symptoms are psychosomatic; stop being emotional and don't worry too much!"

All this is quite correct as far as it goes, except that psychosomatic symptoms are not a recent discovery. They were known in the days of Socrates over two thousand years before the term *psychosomatic* came to be made a symbol of medical-psychological progress. Besides, the hypothetical doctor's advice leaves an important question unanswered: what is the unfortunate fellow or the unhappy woman to do about becoming more mature—more secure —less emotional—and about not worrying too much!

A profusion of advice, good and bad, has been given on how to worry profitably, on how not to worry at all, as well as on how to avoid innumerable other possible pitfalls. Sometimes people may find good sense in what they are told to do, or not to do, and they may easily agree to what they are told. Nevertheless, for many of them, and maybe for you too, it is often difficult and frequently it seems impossible, to put acceptable advice, or even one's own decisions, into practice. And so long as you have to continue to grit your teeth in order to succeed—and even if you do appear to succeed—the problem will remain basically unsolved. The need for sound emotional control and self-direction varies with each individual, of course. The ultimate goal, however, should always be to develop into the kind of person to whom the need for self-directional control has become less frequent as a result of well-conditioned, healthy emotional reflexes. This can be accomplished by developing mental attitudes which enable us to direct and control our emotions beneficially. But first, we must recognize and re-evaluate our emotions and also learn what triggers them, before we can bring them into proper focus. For some people, this realization will be sufficient to make them function better psychologically, whereas others will need some additional device which will help them to control themselves satisfactorily.

There is a popular saying that one should count up to ten before giving an angry answer. The basic idea here is to *neutralize* one's mind before responding to an unpleasant situation. The simple device of counting ten would not suffice, however, to ward off depressive moods or to combat unfortunate mental attitudes; but here too, the idea of neutralizing one's mind remains valid, only one has to go about it in a different manner.

The ability to neutralize one's mind consists of directing one's thoughts deliberately toward subjects which have *no emotional impact at all and to concentrate on them.* This presupposes adequate mental-emotional self-direction and the ability to concentrate.

Among powerful devices by which to neutralize your mind against the intrusion of undesirable or painful moods or thoughts are the following. Invent, for instance, more or less complicated patterns of counting; or try to form as many words as possible of, let us say, six given letters; or, if you are studying a foreign language, test your vocabulary by translating words and sentences from your own language into the foreign one. Or, try to solve a crossword-puzzle or a "brain-teaser," such as you may find in a newspaper or magazine. And, by the way, it is not necessary that you really *solve* that puzzle or "brain-teaser"; the concentrated attempt to do so serves the purpose. Any mental occupation without a personal emotional undertone to which you can direct your mind and that you can concentrate on, sometimes for five minutes, at other times perhaps considerably longer, will intercept the circuit of your unpleasant thoughts or painful moods.

If you keep up the practice of mental-emotional self-direction and concentration and if you are persistent in neutralizing your mind whenever needed, you will be surprised how much easier it will be for you to control your moods successfully.

It is well to remember, however, that the popular notion of emotions causing distressing psychological and physiological symptoms is only a half-truth. Emotions, even strong emotions, need not amount to trouble; it is confused emotions and rampant emotionalism which can turn us into nervous wrecks. Unfortunately, the distinction between emotions and emotionalism is often tricky. And yet, in this distinction lies the crux of the concept of mental health, just as the crux of practical mental hygiene *consists of being in command of constructive mental-emotional self-direction.* This latter ability constitutes one of the most important factors in the attainment and preservation of mental health.

Nevertheless, it may be quite normal for some people to feel emotions strongly and to express and display them freely. Others, also normally, feel less keenly in the first place, or, due to their disposition, are more inclined to conceal their emotions. But even emotional malfunctions such as temporary anger, resentment, passing moods of depression, whether secretly felt or visibly manifested, should not always be considered as a menace to mental health unless these negative emotions are too frequent, or grossly disproportionate to their motivating causes. If this is the case, we have to learn how to handle these emotions so that, as a result, they will eventually diminish in intensity and frequency.

No, there is nothing wrong with emotions and it can never be the task of psychotherapy, or mental hygiene, or of psychological self-help, to curb perfectly sound emotions and natural emotional reactions. Therefore, we can fully agree with Robert Lindner when he says: "I have been shocked to learn that they [analysts and patients] have felt themselves to have achieved their analytical goal when patients become placid, accepting, undisturbed by the condition of the world, uncaring for the fate of their fellow-men and able without guilt or strain to pursue wholly selfish goals."

The ability to live a full life, satisfying to oneself and to others as well—and who can think of better mental hygiene?—presupposes a sentient human being and not an automaton. It is obvious that one cannot be a sentient human being and an automaton at the same time. As Ralph Waldo Emerson once said: "God offers to every mind its choice between truth and repose; take which you please—you can never have both." And in connection with Emerson's words, Karl M. Menninger gave expression to the following thoughts: "To me it is a strange and dismal thing that in a world of such need, such opportunity and such variety as ours, the search for an illusory peace of mind should be zealously pursued and defended . . . The continuous encounter with continually changing conditions is the very substance of living . . . striving for personal peace means . . . losing one's life in trying to save it. On the other hand, peace or something near it is often achieved by those who do not seek it, who, seeking truth, forget themselves." But, forgetting oneself, although a noble goal, might seem too big a task for the majority of people. A more down-to-earth directive in the words

of T. S. Eliot advises us to avoid excessive and undue preoccupation with ourselves. This is not quite as difficult as to *forget oneself*
entirely. Besides, it will lead us to take ourselves seriously, without,
at the same time, fostering feelings of self-importance, because:

> "Half of the harm that is done in this world
>   is due to people who want to feel important.
>   They don't mean to do harm—but the harm does not interest them.
>   Or they do not see it, or they justify it
>   because they are absorbed in the endless struggle to think well
>   of themselves."

> (*The Cocktail Party*).

There is a great difference between the "endless struggle" to think
well of oneself and striving to make the best of one's potentialities.
It is the difference between reluctance to take a good look at one's
flaws and faults and the sincere endeavor to gain objective evaluation and understanding of oneself and others. This may be rather
difficult at times, because most of us tend to dislike deflating our
ego. However, if we make an honest effort without getting to feel
smug at having become paragons of virtue, we may acquire an
independence of spirit which makes outward success relatively unimportant. And, strange as it may sound, this *relative* impervious-
ness to outward circumstances might eventually increase our chances
for material success.

7 ◆ AS THE TWIG IS BENT...

The foundation for future wholesome attitudes should be laid as early in life as possible. The topic of child-guidance, however, goes beyond the scope of this book. It is a highly specialized field which cannot be treated here with the thoroughness it would require. Therefore, only a few basic factors will be mentioned insofar as they reflect on the *adult* personality. They will prompt the reader to examine his own conduct in their light.

Although the importance of avoiding possible mistakes in bringing up children is obvious, it should nevertheless be kept in mind that these mistakes are not invariably the cause of subsequent personality-shortcomings. No adult is justified in shrugging off responsibility for his shortcomings by blaming everything on the mode of his upbringing. Aldous Huxley, for instance, points out: "Many psychologists are turning away from the view that all neuroses are due to some crucial experience in infancy. The conditioning process which takes place during childhood does not completely determine the behavior in man. To some extent, at any rate, he can be conditioned by the circumstances of his adolescent and adult life; to some extent his will is free, and, if he so chooses and knows the right way to set about it, he can re-condition himself." (*Ends and Means*, 1937.)

The prevailing tendency to generalize and blame most of the adult's failings on his childhood-experiences and his parents, is, in many instances, although not always, unjustified and unsound. Very often it involves the psychological "scapegoat tendency" of seeking to blame things on somebody else. The adult who is led to feel that his parents were entirely responsible for his emotional discomfort and malfunctioning may, at times quite instinctively, acquire this "scapegoat tendency" and apply it later on in his family, business and social life. The "It's all my parents' fault" attitude provides a welcome excuse to shake off responsibility for one's own reactions and actions.

Nevertheless, a reasonable regard for the infant's and the growing child's individual requirements, combined with a gentle but firm and consistent correction of negative traits, cannot start too soon. Infants have a natural tendency to regulate their physical needs by their impulses of pleasure and displeasure. At times, the infant cries just because it wants to be carried around; probably it yearns instinctively for the animal warmth of another creature, or for the pleasant and calming rhythmical sensation of being rocked to and fro. Therefore, a flagrant disregard of the infant's individual needs may add up to a severe violation of the infant's emotional equilibrium. In some infants, the violation can easily amount to provoking and stressing any predisposition they may have for rebellion to such an extent that they may grow up to become extremely aggressive and hostile. With other infants, violation of their individual requirements may lower their normal endurance level for physical and/or mental discomfort; they may become conditioned to subsequent attitudes of depression and defeatism.

It should not be ignored, however, that over-indulgence in demonstrative affection and blind compliance with all of the infant's and child's impulses and whims, may likewise have unwholesome after-effects. This may produce a subsequent attitude of "I-must-always-have-what-I-want-regardless-of-anything-and-anybody!"

If a child tends to develop this type of personality and if his demanding and dictatorial instincts are catered to, instead of discouraged, he may, as he grows up, be inclined to feel sorry for himself at the slightest setback. As fate is rarely considerate enough to grant our every wish, such an individual is bound to become increasingly apprehensive, frustrated and resentful. These negative mental attitudes constitute some of the most powerful prerequisites for mental and emotional malfunctioning. *That is why it is essential not only to respect individual inherent needs in the infant and in the growing child, but also to ensure that these needs are wholesome.* For example, great care has to be taken to prevent a child's growing into the kind of adult who shuns the normal tasks and obligations of adulthood or, at best, regards them as far more onerous than they actually are. These individuals are bound to become dissatisfied, for they are perpetually trying to run away from their obligations. Often, their constant restless need for excitement and thrills compels them to be "on the go" all the time. But even excitement and thrills soon become blunted and the ensuing boredom must be assuaged at any price by new excitement and headier thrills. But after a while, these too will pall until, gradually, the tension and torture of boredom increases to the point of becoming unbearable and turning into *pernicious boredom.*

Pernicious boredom is a real disease and can assail rich and poor, old and young alike. A child who is always asking the grown-ups around him: "What shall I do now?" may well be predisposed to become one of the unfortunate victims of pernicious boredom, especially if his lack of initiative and his craving for amusement and attention are overindulged instead of reasonably curbed. A predisposition of this kind can usually be corrected in a child, although the "What-shall-I-do-now" attitude can also be inculcated in him, if he is never allowed to occupy himself in accordance with his own wishes.

People, in whom the predisposition to develop pernicious boredom was not checked at a tender age, may ruin their whole existence by letting boredom interfere with their work and also with their private lives. They get easily bored with other people, with their life-circumstances and, above all, with themselves.

Too little attention has been paid so far to the dangerous impact that pernicious boredom can exert on human behavior. There is, however, a type of boredom quite different from the pernicious kind. It is *normal boredom* which may be caused by certain life-circumstances. All of us may experience it temporarily, but do not let it become unmanageable. On the other hand, pernicious boredom acts like a somber-tinted dye, staining and permeating the very lives of those over whom it pours its components of fear, tension, feelings of inadequacy and a constant obsessive desire to "get away from it all!"

Again and again it can be seen by any objective observer, that the more an individual is given to a definitely materialistic outlook on life and disregards or repudiates spiritual values, the less capable he will be of discovering his own inner resources. Their lack makes him more and more dependent on material gratification and, as a consequence, an easy prey to pernicious boredom, one of the most dangerous forms of mental stress.

These are only a few of the "nursery-rhymes" which may affect our later life. There is still another subject, the mere mention of which gives rise to widely divergent viewpoints on the part of *laymen* and experts alike. Nevertheless, it deserves serious consideration because of its far-reaching effects on our adult life. The subject is sex-education.

8. CONSEQUENCES OF UNWISE
SEX-EDUCATION OF CHILDREN

It was reported in *Time* magazine that on his 80th birthday Carl Gustav Jung was asked by an interviewer: "What . . . first made you take up psychology as your life work?" Jung's answer: "When I was a child . . . once an aunt of mine took me to a museum to see all those stuffed animals. The bell rang and we had to hurry for the exit, crossing through a gallery of antique sculptures . . . My aunt said 'You horrible boy, shut your eyes, don't look at these things!' . . . I thought 'Now why did she say such a thing?' And then I discovered that these wonderful figures were naked. And that was why my aunt could not stand it."

Even today, some parents tell their children gruesome stories about the physical and spiritual risks they incur whenever they show a quite normal interest in sex. Sons are told that they should avoid girls because "they are evil," and daughters are persuaded to believe that "all boys are cruel, callous and out to harm them." Very often, the overall idea is instilled into these boys and girls that members of the opposite sex are untrustworthy and that sex is utterly sordid. It is evident that this type of parent is badly in need of enlightenment regarding some essential facts of mental health.

But enlightenment would also be of benefit to those parents who go overboard in their wish to be "progressive." I know of a young father, quite well-meaning, who gave his four-year-old daughter a detailed description in technical terms of the female anatomy. As a result, when the little girl was in the swimming-pool one day and happened to feel an itching between her legs, she called out to her mother: "Mummy, my vagina itches!" Friends, gathered around the pool, roared with laughter at the little girl's advanced vocabulary and a discussion ensued on whether sex-education helps children in their approach to life later on or whether the old-fashioned methods were preferable. There were as many different opinions as there were persons present.

Sex-education is, of course, in no way objectionable so long as it remains within reasonable bounds. But it *is* objectionable, if it goes so far as to ignore or deny the vital fact that human beings do not and cannot thrive and develop to their fullest extent on a mere biological and materialistic approach to life.

It is misinterpretation of what is "modern" and what is "old-fashioned" that causes people to become confused about the meaning of these terms with the result that new problems are created. The fact is often overlooked that not everything which is modern or new is actually progressive, neither is everything now called progressive invariably new. Clinging to old ideas, customs, traditions and ideals may be regressive in many instances, but we find also that old ideas stimulate new ones and thus lead to real progress. Sound traditions may lend their faithful followers a steadfastness and natural dignity which will contribute greatly to make them human in the best sense of the word. History shows that it is the eternal cycle from primitive simplicity to complex civilization followed by a return to simplicity, which ensures ultimate progress in the evolution of mankind from cave to cathedral, from cauldron to multiple computer.

Each time the cycle is completed, the quality of primitive simplicity is somewhat changed and often enhanced, offering a more fertile seed-bed from which progress may spring once again. Thus the saying "Nothing is new under the sun," is only half accurate, because everything is new and old at the same time.

Sex is certainly not an innovation—it always has been, as it will remain, a highly important factor in human lives. But its importance has been almost morbidly exaggerated by those who assert that sex absolutely dominates our mental, emotional and physical living from the cradle to the grave. This concept has assuredly been a chief incentive to the present widespread opinion that children should be given sex-education in their homes or at school. What a contrast to the days, still remembered by older people, when a leg was delicately referred to as a limb! The prudery of that era was most unwholesome, as are extremes of any kind; on the other hand, the present trend of talking sex to death is equally extreme. It is therefore just as unwholesome, sometimes even to the extent of becoming an obsession and dangerous to mental health.

While it may be quite normal for one child to be curious about sex and ask questions about it, it may be equally natural for another child not to be curious and not to ask questions. Curiosity is usually normal for children; it may range from the fascination of observing an earthworm disappear into the ground to watching mother bake a cake, or father tinker with his car. Curiosity may extend from taking apart every toy in order to find out what's inside and how it works, to the curiosity of the "peeping Tom." But even the latter type of curiosity in a child need not cause concern so long as there is good reason to assume that it is only a transitory phase and well compensated for by other more favorable characteristics.

If a sound "sex-talk" may be advisable, or even necessary for one child, it may be unnecessary or even inadvisable for another one and not just because this child "knows it all anyway!" Sex-talks, indiscriminately imposed on children by "authority," may prove more injurious to some types of children than just hearing their playmates talk about sex in their own way.

Whatever we explain to a child, be it sex functions or anything else, we must try to approach as close as possible to the child's mental-age level. In doing this, let us beware, however, of "talking down" to him and of believing that to reach a child on his own level means to use baby-talk. On the other hand, we should also refrain from imposing our own manner of thinking and feeling on a child, expecting him to understand and adjust to our adult level. Unfortunately, modern psychological concepts often seem to ignore *psychology* by stressing the biological approach. For instance, it will be of small benefit to children, if they are shown graphs and pictures of how the male sperm travels to fertilize the female's egg. Bringing the biological aspects of sex into the limelight while disregarding

the emotional and spiritual values essential to *adult* human relationship between man and woman, is likely to create the impression in
a child's mind that human sex relationship is merely a functional
matter. This impression may well tend to blunt the natural idealism
most adolescents feel towards the opposite sex and stifle a potential
emotional sensitivity which could have enriched his or her adult life.

If sex-education is to consist mainly of emphasizing biological
facts, the deplorable results will manifest themselves in adults as an
increasingly impaired ability to distinguish between love and sex.

9. EFFECTS OF LOVE AND SEX
ON FAMILY ATMOSPHERE

Like some animals, children sense the mental and emotional climate of the environment to which they are exposed. They are badly affected by an atmosphere of discontent, of anger, of fear; in short, the quality of the mental and emotional atmosphere of the home definitely has an effect for ill or good on children.

Educating a child means nurturing his potential ability to develop his mental and humane qualities and instilling in him the incentive to use them. But the best and wisest guidance by teachers, or through books and other sources, will be severely handicapped by an adverse or unhappy atmosphere in the child's home. A child's receptive mind will absorb impressions of chronic insecurity and fear much more easily, if they are conveyed to him through the parents' behavior towards each other. Long ominous silences between parents, or endless bickering and recrimination, can harm a child even more severely than a so-called broken home.

There is no question that the separation of parents is usually most harmful to children, mainly because it means depriving them of a normal family life. But it may be even worse for children if the parents remain together in an atmosphere of bitterness, resentment, and often of hate. For this reason it is imperative to realize that the lack of a wholesome and serene family atmosphere may become more damaging to the healthy development of a child than other mistakes made in his upbringing. But a sound family atmosphere is not created just by avoiding a divorce! It is created by preventing, or correcting, those characteristics of parents, or parents-to-be, which may result in causes for divorce.

The nature of these characteristics is, unfortunately, a highly controversial subject. For instance, some time ago at a psychiatric meeting, a psychiatrist expressed the opinion that "men must wear the pants," because women are not equipped by nature to be the head of the family. But the outcome of a marriage depends on a great many imponderables and cannot be solved merely by applying the "head of the family" theory. It is a fact that some women feel the need of a "lord and master" for a husband. If they are lucky enough to marry this type of man, their marriage will probably work out well. Other women, however, will neither be happy themselves, nor make their husbands happy, should they marry the "masterful" type of man. Regarding who should be the master in the home, let us turn to the very different opinion of another psychiatrist. Carl Gustav Jung states: "Where love rules, there is no will to power; and where power predominates, there love is lacking."

Other elements besides love constitute a good marriage. It is not simple to give a description of these elements, but we find an almost perfect one in *A Dreamer's Journey* by Morris R. Cohen. He said that if he had an opportunity to write an epitaph on his father's and mother's grave, it would read:

> Here lie the remains of two brave souls
> whose courage was never daunted by hardships
> and whose fidelity to the ideals of honesty, piety and devotion
> to all those dependent on them never faltered.
> They were married throughout sixty-seven years and remained
> absolutely faithful even when separated for years.
> She never uttered anything foolish and he never did or said
> anything base.

Unfortunately, many young people get married in haste and with only the most rudimentary ideas of what marriage implies. After childhood and teen-age years with too little sound discipline and too much freedom, a freedom which is often misunderstood and sometimes abused, these young people have come to believe that the main purpose in life is "to have fun!" As a consequence, the responsibilities of married life gave an unpleasant jolt to their illusions and instead of facing the changed circumstances and trying to adapt to them, many young wives, and almost as many husbands, indulge in self-pity. They imagine that they have been "gypped by life" and keep the divorce-courts busy.

Of course, many young and older people are well aware of the responsibilities marriage and parenthood entail and accept them willingly and gladly. But it would seem that they are no longer a majority, to judge by the alarming increase of mentally and emotionally disturbed individuals about to marry, or married already. The offspring of these unfortunate marriages are bound to suffer. Growing up, as they so often do, in a tension- and hate-laden atmosphere, they may all too easily fall into a condition of morbid anxiety which appears later on under many disguises, one disguise, for instance, being the form of destructive hostility.

Every human being harbors potential feelings of fear and anxiety from the very beginning of his existence. They are necessary for man's survival, because without these warning-signals man would lack the possibility to guard against dangers of all kinds. Anxiety is also ethically essential for discriminating between right and wrong; if well proportioned to its cause, anxiety is normal. However, the harmful quality of an adverse home-atmosphere may cause a child's normal propensity for anxiety to deteriorate into highly exaggerated and therefore morbid anxiety.

The indispensable ingredients of a good marriage are the capacity to love—to love unselfishly—and a willingness to give companionship and mutual respect. A marriage, based on these prerequisites, will succeed. But where the emphasis is laid on one-sided domination, or placed exclusively on physical attraction and sex-relationship, the likelihood of a happy and enduring marital relationship and of a harmonious family-atmosphere is sadly limited.

The Oregon obstetrician, Dr. Goodrich G. Schauffler, voices a severely critical opinion on: "The precocious sex-activities of . . . young people . . . greatly increased awareness of sex . . . stimulated and maintained by the sex hysteria which is a calculated instrument of modern journalism and so-called entertainment. There are loose practices . . . bad examples and lack of supervision in parental and home influences . . . The result is an emotional shambles."

It is difficult to pick a quarrel with Dr. Schauffler's opinion except when he overshoots the mark by saying: ". . . young people nowadays are exposed to teachings such as those of Freud and Jung . . ." Certainly, Jung does not belong in the category of sex-obsessed psychiatrists! This can be proved by letting Jung speak for himself: ". . . sexuality breaks into all possible fields which do not belong to it, and uses such an indirect mode of expression that we can expect suddenly to detect it practically everywhere. Thus even the idea of the intimate understanding of a human soul, which is actually something very beautiful and pure, becomes besmirched and perversely distorted by the intrusion of an indirect sexual meaning . . . The erotic instinct is something questionable . . . it blossoms only when spirit and instinct are in true harmony . . . Most men are blind erotically. They commit the unpardonable mistake of confusing Eros with sexuality . . ." (*Psychological Reflections*).

It is beyond any argument that satisfactory sexual relations and normal sex desires will greatly contribute to the harmony of a marriage. Therefore, it is most fortunate when both marriage-partners are well mated in regard to their sexual needs, or are able to mutually adjust to each other's requirements. If no adjustment takes place, then we hear accusations like "My husband is too demanding," or "My husband is impotent," and quite a few husbands will say: "My wife is frigid," or "My wife expects too much affection and lovemaking." Some may have good reason to complain, but often these types of accusation are based on the fact that the sex-needs of the couples do not coincide and either no attempt at adjustment and mutual consideration was made, or if any attempts were made, they were ineffectual.

The degree of sex-need varies with the individual and ranges from abnormal sex-coldness through various degrees of normal sex-need and sex-desire to abnormal sex-greed. An excessive preoccupation with sex denotes more than normal sex-desire and like any other form of greed, it is pathological. The very nature of greed is insatiability; its obsessive and frantic search for ever new stimulation is a futile chase, which may end in pernicious boredom.

The over-emphasis on sex—and nothing but sex—has been the cause of a legion of books on sex-mechanics. Some of these books may contribute to the betterment of sex-techniques, but they add little towards creating the kind of human relationship that actually constitutes a good marriage; at times, these books don't even improve sex-relations. A patient of mine whose husband, following the advice of his analyst, had studied a book on sex-techniques, said to me one day: "My husband told me I should read this book too and now, after I have read it, our sex-relationship is worse than ever before, because I can always tell exactly which page he has just been reading!"

Sometimes animals are more subtle than human beings. I remember seeing on television a delightful short subject film of big game hunting with cameras. Hippopotami were shown swimming and playing in the water; they rubbed their heads together and opened their colossal mouths; they did what among human beings would be called kissing. In their own hippopotamus manner, and without having swallowed a single book on sex-techniques, these "wild beasts" showed more gentle and heartwarming affection for each other than many human beings seem capable of. Their love-making in its natural spontaneity might serve better to enlighten humans than volumes of professional directions on sex-mechanics.

10. EMOTIONAL TEAMWORK AND EMOTIONAL GENEROSITY

Sex-problems are not the only causes of confusion, emotional upheavals and suffering. Uncountable elements making up the human personality and innumerable situations that occur in human life continually supply material for the offices of psychiatrists and psychologists. This makes it all the more regrettable that greatly conflicting and often misleading advice is frequently given regarding the most vital subjects, such as handling one's emotions, the processes of growing up and aging, rearing children, and marriage and sex. Some psychologists, for instance, advise married people never to give up sleeping in a double bed and, with a tinge of threatening authority, they warn that only by sharing a double bed can marital togetherness be achieved.

Unquestionably, many people fit this behavior-pattern; nevertheless, a married couple's decision on how to sleep should, as a rule, not be dictated by a third person, be it parent, friend, or psychologist. There are many reasons which can make occupying twin beds, or even separate rooms, commendable, provided that the home situation renders this feasible. Naturally, if husband and wife agree that sharing a double bed contributes to their happiness, then, by all means, they should do so, with or without a psychologist's blessing. Should, however, the husband or wife or both prefer twin beds, why should they be frightened into believing they will lose their feeling of unity unless they conform to the notions of an "expert"!

Physical togetherness is a very important factor in a marriage—
everybody knows this. But the good quality of a marriage relation
is far more likely to endure, if unnecessary mental-emotional friction can be avoided in day-by-day living. Mutual attractiveness may
quite possibly be better preserved, if togetherness is not overly
stressed to a point where it can deteriorate in custom-jaded indifference or even aversion. With a poet's sensitivity, Rupert Brooke
described that situation in the lines:

> Taking
> Their poor dreams within their arms and lying
> Each in his lonely night, each with a ghost.

These lines reflect an awesome picture of real lack of togetherness.
They indicate a profound sense of aloneness which is manifested
so often in marriages based exclusively on sex relations.

In spite of all that is being said and written about sex and sex
drives, and with all the research going on in biology and psychology,
not too much is known as yet about the real nature of the sex drive
and its origin. Can we assume that we know more about love?

It is almost impossible to give a concise answer to the question:
"What is love?" Attempts are made to explain love as a chemical
and/or electrical field of attraction, but this seems rather like trying
to determine the beauty and fragrance of a flower by peering at it
through a microscope. Libraries are full of books on the subject
of love and while interpretations vary extensively and definitions
are difficult to formulate, we can nevertheless recognize the "real
thing" by its manifestations. When two people understand each
other, even in their failings, when no sacrifice appears too great,
when the need for each other remains after the fires of passion have
cooled with age, then these people have found true love. They have
experienced the blending of physical and spiritual togetherness into
a sublime entity and, to paraphrase Dostoyevsky, they have known
moments in which time suddenly stood still and gave place to
eternity.

Some people might say: "It's very nice to read about this type of
love in poetry and romantic fiction, only it doesn't exist in reality!"
To argue with these people would probably be useless as would

be the attempt to point out the greatness and the beauty of a Bach oratorio to someone whose musical understanding doesn't go beyond the enjoyment of a catchy tune. This comparison is not intended to make a snobbish distinction; catchy tunes can be entertaining and affect our moods, but sooner or later they are forgotten, whereas a Bach oratorio or any other great music will abide with us.

Adjustments of all kinds are necessary in a marriage and love will not make them superfluous, but love will make them easier. Adjustment in itself, however, is not the solution to every problem, either in marriage or otherwise. Sometimes an adjustment might be undesirable; it may even be inadvisable. It is important, therefore, to keep in mind just how severely one or the other person is adversely affected by an adjustment which is apparently required. Any decision on how to carry out adjustments should always take into consideration, which partner will be making the *smaller* sacrifice and be able to yield more easily to the other partner's reasonable wishes. This is important in every situation, and in a marriage adapting oneself to the new duties and responsibilities becomes paramount.

But to be married also means to make living together a joyous experience. At the very least, it should amount to a sincere attempt to make life mutually pleasant. To accomplish this, emotional teamwork will have to be developed and this signifies more than just to reason coldly that it is preferable "to get along together"! Emotional teamwork is based on warmth of feeling, tact and generosity —emotional generosity—which automatically makes one think of the other person and try to feel with him. Emotional generosity encompasses a willingness and readiness *to give* without any expectation, even any semi-conscious expectation, of receiving something in return.

Emotional generosity doesn't have to make a sucker out of one, either financially or otherwise. It requires, however, character-traits which would make one choose voluntarily rather to give than to take, provided a choice were possible. To possess, or to develop these character-traits, is important to mental health, because they preclude feelings of resentment. Emotional generosity is a necessary forerunner to emotional teamwork.

Strangely enough, emotional teamwork is much more frequent

where the "big things of life" are concerned and is apt to function least well in the routine of everyday-living. And yet, as we human beings live and work together, it is the sum total of "little things" which makes the vital difference between constant friction and contented harmony.

Emotional teamwork is actually a game which you play with a partner, be it your husband, your wife, parents, children, or your co-workers—everybody is a potential partner. But to make this game successful, your partner has to share in the game and second your attempt to cooperate with him, otherwise the chances of succeeding in the game are greatly limited. But be sure you don't merely imagine that your partner is *not* being cooperative in the teamwork. In this case, ask yourself whether perhaps you expect too great a contribution from him while, at the same time, you yourself may be contributing too little.

11. ETHICAL VALUES AND MENTAL HEALTH

We all possess a greater or lesser capacity for emotional teamwork and if this gift is dormant in us, it needs to be awakened and then trained systematically. The earlier in life emotional teamwork is taught and encouraged, the better the results. Otherwise, lack of emotional teamwork contributes extensively to many forms of mental-emotional malfunctioning and creates disharmony in human relations.

Excessive reading of bloodthirsty, so-called "Comic" books and similar mental nourishment will not supply children and teen-agers with desirable examples of emotional teamwork. Neither will the unending procession of crime and brutality, parading across movie and television screens, convey to our minds and hearts particularly valid ideas of emotional maturity and of ethical values.

Yet, when the harmfulness of the all too numerous tales of murder and mayhem is pointed out to us, we usually answer: "Oh, one gets used to that kind of thing and hardly pays attention to it any more!" Should this be true, then, apparently, we have lost our ability to grasp the significance of all the brutality, crudeness and vulgarity to which we are exposed incessantly. If this is true, haven't we become in our reactions similar to workers in slaughter-yards, who can spend forty hours in every week killing cattle or hogs! Inured to their type of work, it is unlikely that these men give a thought to the fact that they are inflicting a cruel death on creatures capable of suffering fear and pain.

People who stifle their better judgment by assuring themselves and others that we are not unduly impressed by the beatings, burglaries, killing and other "entertainment" of this type, should think of these desensitized men in the slaughter-yards! It is really difficult to determine which attitude is more lamentable from the standpoint of mental health: to remain unimpressed by brutalities and crimes, or to come to the point of enjoying, or even imitating and participating in them. It is not necessary to serve up a steady diet of goody-goody stories and of entertainment which carries a "message" in order to preserve and stimulate the fundamental good qualities in human beings. But, at least, we ought to make sure that these qualities don't become weakened and destroyed by a one-sided diet of distorted ethical values and commercialized sex-stimulation. The ideal of "good" can never quite be materialized, nor can the "bad" be completely abolished; but we can raise the level of probability for achieving the "better" instead of catering to the "worse."

Again you may ask, a little disdainfully perhaps: "Are these reflections an invitation to philosophize about good and evil?" No, they are not! But mental health is inconceivable without recognition and awareness of ethical values. It is not intended here to go beyond a mere glimpse of the criteria of "good and evil," of "right and wrong," and only in regard to their impact on mental health. To serve this purpose, an illustration of some facets of evil by a couple of real-life examples will suffice. A woman had a cherished pet, a cat. One day, teen-agers caught the cat and amused themselves by pouring gasoline over the animal and holding a burning match to it. The unfortunate creature burned to death while the teen-agers looked on and yelled with glee. When the woman found out what had happened to her pet, she was deeply chagrined. But far from being vindictive, she refused to lodge a complaint with the police, saying through her sobs: "I guess the youngsters only wanted to have some fun!"

Another story which I read in the newspaper some time ago—and, by the way, it was only one among many similar incidents one reads about almost every day—reported that a boy of about twelve years was standing quietly at a street corner on the sidewalk, when a nineteen-year-old youth, driving a car, deliberately steered his vehicle onto the sidewalk, knocking the younger boy to the ground and injuring him severely. When the older boy was asked why he had made this wanton attack, he answered without any sign of remorse: "I wanted to scare the kid and have some fun!"

There is certainly nothing wrong with the desire to have fun, even if the fun sometimes becomes rather wild. But it depends on what kind of thing one considers and *feels* to be "fun!"

Fun derived from torture of helpless creatures is neither *good fun* nor is it *wild fun;* it is just plain evil. In fact, it makes one wonder whether it is actually so difficult to distinguish good from evil and whether there is any distinctive difference between cruelty to animals and cruelty to human beings, as is sometimes asserted. You may object to this statement and point out that children may develop into normally kind and decent people in spite of having shown traits of cruelty during childhood. You are right there; however, it must be determined first whether a child's cruelty is just a passing stage caused by complex circumstances, or whether it is an inherent pathological disposition. A potentially wholesome-minded child will come to realize what he has done, and feel honest regret. In contrast, the pathologically inclined child will fail to show or feel any compunction and continue to derive vicious pleasure from being cruel and destructive.

I have used two examples concerned with teen-agers to illustrate the idea of "evil"; I have done so because age plays an important role and one and the same deed will have a different connotation if committed by a child under ten years, or by a teen-ager, or by an adult. Children, of course, should be given the benefit of the doubt whenever possible, yet we also have to be mindful that, as Jung says, "The wine of youth does not always clear with advancing years, oftentimes it grows turbid."

Ethical values, however, should not be confused with moral codes. Moral precepts are devised and imposed by groups of individuals and tied up with specific cultures and civilizations; they are, therefore, subject to change and may become obsolete or too dictatorial and rigid. In contrast to moral precepts, ethical values such as those expressed in the Ten Commandments or in the Sermon on the Mount are timeless. In our civilization, the inability to recognize ethical values, or to respond to them, definitely indicates a specific sickness of the soul, a condition more dangerous than any physical disease.

Well, you might object here and say: "I don't want any *mystical* references to the soul . . . I want *practical* advice on psychological self-help!" If so, you should realize that the kind of help you demand is by no means *psychological!* The word *psychological* is derived from the Greek word *psyche,* which means *soul.* As a consequence, the word *psychological* refers to conditions and manifestations called forth by the soul and thus implies the reality of the soul.

"Reality of the soul? What is *real,* if you please?" you may be provoked to ask now. And you may continue: "Real is a tree, a table, a bruise on my knee which I got when I hit a *real* chair entering my room in the dark. Real is food, real is—anyway, it goes too far to call the soul real!"

Does it actually go too far? That depends on what one understands by the words "real" and "reality." Walt Whitman didn't hesitate to say "The soul is also real," and Aldous Huxley gives the following interpretation: ". . . reality is actual experience, contains intuitions of value and significance, contains love, beauty, mystical ecstasy, intimations of Godhead. Science did not, and still does not possess instruments with which to deal with these aspects of reality."

Herein seems to lie one of the main reasons why it is so difficult for science and religion to find a common meeting-ground, essential as this would be for the welfare of mankind. If, at this point, you are inclined to say: "So now you are trying to impose religion on me—and what about the teachings of Freud and many other representatives of modern psychology?" Let us assign the answer to this question to one of the most outstanding and lucid minds in the province of psychology. Jung says: "Religions, in my opinion, with all which they are and assert, are so near the human soul that psychology least of all can afford to overlook them . . . Is there, as a matter of fact, any better truth about ultimate things than the one that helps us to live? . . . If . . . in doing so I use the concept of God or an equally metaphysical concept of energy, I am bound to because these are the things which have been in the human soul from the beginning." (*Psychological Reflections.*)

Psychology will have to recognize that it is adverse to mental health to consider religious experience as a neurotic manifestation, a viewpoint shared by many, although not by all psychologists. Unfortunately, to many of us, God merely means a kind of super-father, expected to erase grievances and to fulfill our requests. This attitude is reflected in the following anecdote. A little boy was saying his prayers on the evening of his birthday. He included in them everybody who had given him something. Finally he turned to his mother and asked: "Have I forgotten to pray for anyone else who gave me a present?"

Yet how frequently do adults share this approach to prayer! Eckhart said: "Some people want to see God with their eyes as they see a cow—and to love him as they love their cow, for the milk and cheese and profit it brings them . . . They do not rightly love God when they love Him for their own advantage." Although praying for material things is a somewhat selfish form of prayer, it is nevertheless a good act of faith and trust from which we can derive great comfort. But we should pray for both our spiritual and material needs; and we should also turn to God to worship and to give thanks, opening our heart to Him, as the lotus opens its petals to the sun.

Communion with God is a very real spiritual experience; it is known to many who follow the teachings, rites and dogmas of a creed. It may be perceived also *extra ecclesiam* by those for whom, perhaps only once in a lifetime and only for an instant, the dense veils of human limitations rend asunder. This experience is touched on by Maxwell Anderson in the following lines:

> ". . . . yet is my mind my own,
>   yet is my heart a cry toward something dim
>   in distance, which is higher than I am
>   and makes me emperor of the endless dark
>   even in seeking!"
>   (*Winterset*).

This gropingly sublime search for God can be regarded as a religious experience, though not in the theological sense; but it too encompasses psychic strength and a readiness for reverence and humbleness.

It is by no means the task of psychology, or of mental hygiene, to "prove" God, to argue about religion, or to attempt to talk people into believing in God. Spiritual-religious guidance has to be left to those on whom vocation confers that task. Nevertheless, we must come to realize that we would suffer from fewer neurotic afflictions and be sounder psychologically, if we were, and would remain, able to transcend our own ego by seeking "something dim in distance, which is higher" than we are.

12. GROWING INTO EMOTIONAL MATURITY

Whenever I am confronted with over-used and ambiguous catch-words such as "Emotional Security" or "Emotional Maturity," I feel like a small child with his rapid-fire questioning "What is this?" and "Why is that?" for I too am tempted to ask "What *is* emotional security?"—"What *is* emotional maturity?"

Half of the time psychological catchwords of this kind are over-simplifications which prove quite inadequate when it comes to measuring psychological complexities and describing emotional conflicts. Over-simplifications are a constant source of misinforma-tion, a fact on which Aldous Huxley comments as follows: "Over-simplifications! . . . the penalty for making them consists in our inability to realize our ideals, to escape from the social and psycho-logical slough in which we wallow." (*Ends and Means.*)

Let us see what happens if we attempt an answer to "What is emotional security?" Does emotional security signify a feeling of soothing certainty that everybody approves of us? If so, will we not be lulled too easily into assuming that we cannot be, or do, wrong? Or is there an emotional security which deceptively may give us a feeling comparable to that of a drunken driver behind the wheel of an automobile who is sure that he can safely drive ninety miles an hour!

An illustration of how the idea of emotional security, of self-confidence, can be misunderstood, is demonstrated by the following case. A woman who consulted me complained that her daughter was extremely self-conscious about being ugly and the mother implored me to direct every effort towards making the girl believe she was beautiful and admired by everyone. When I met the young girl a few days later, I saw that she was unusually homely and painfully aware of the fact. This made her awkward, diffident and reluctant to meet people. She was always apprehensive of being laughed at, or criticized, or, worst of all, of being told by her mother how to make herself attractive. The mother's request to make her daughter believe anything so completely at variance with reality as that she was beautiful—provided that I could have done so!—was out of the question and revealed how much the mother's attitude was aggravating her daughter's situation.

It was difficult to convince the mother that the only way to help her daughter was to minimize, without exaggeration, of course, the all-importance of her looks and, above everything else, to awaken in the girl an awareness of any other qualities or proficiencies she might possess. In the course of hypnoidal psychotherapy, we discovered that she had great talent for dress designing; this talent was stimulated during therapy and she became increasingly interested in her work. Although she had to overcome all kinds of difficulties in her studies and also later on when seeking a market for her designs, she developed a happier and more relaxed frame of mind which in turn reflected even on her external appearance. Gradually, she acquired a more confident attitude and finally she became quite successful professionally as well as popular in her private life.

Emotional security or emotional maturity cannot materialize in an otherwise mental and spiritual vacuum. They are facets of each personality as a whole. Whatever our deficiencies may be, we merely intensify their unfortunate effect on ourselves, if we concentrate on them excessively, yet without an active attempt to correct or to compensate for them.

On the other hand, if we ignore our deficiencies, we intensify their unfavorable effect on others and this in turn usually increases their disturbing effect on ourselves. A deficiency of appearance, let us say, which we may be powerless to alter, can become much less conspicuous, if we succeed in compensating for it by developing a more engaging personality. By compensating thus for deficiencies in our appearance, we will make them not only less apparent to others, but more bearable to ourselves. In psychoanalytical terminology, this process is called sublimation; but whatever name is used to describe it, the fact remains that voluntarily or involuntarily, consciously or unconsciously, we compensate for one thing with another most of the time. And so we try to compensate for deficiencies in ourselves, for actual or imagined insufficiencies in our life-circumstances, for longings which cannot be fulfilled; the important thing about this psychological mechanism is to compensate *constructively* and not *destructively*.

We compensate constructively by seeking and creating values of some kind for ourselves and for others; by work, by tasks we set ourselves to accomplish, by increasing our perceptivity of whatever joy and satisfaction we can find in life—in short, by sustained endeavors to develop positive human qualities.

But even these efforts for constructive compensation may turn into a potentially destructive over-compensation, if our endeavors become tainted with excessive and blind ambition, or with possessiveness and the drive to dominate at any price. Destructive compensation for unfortunate life-circumstances is frequently expressed in negative escapism such as alcoholism, spending money far beyond one's means, debauchery, gambling and, quite in contrast to all this, by complete withdrawal into a dream world of "How wonderful life *could* be, if . . . !" Unless a real and constructive attempt is made to materialize these and similar day-dreams, at least to a certain extent, they only amount to futile indulgence in wishful fantasies which may become just as obsessive and almost as dangerous as any other form of addiction.

If we improve, condition and apply our ability to compensate constructively for any shortcomings in ourselves or for adverse life-situations, we increase our emotional security. But emotional security as well as insecurity may have entirely different meanings to different people. Besides, it is not possible for us to foresee exactly what life has in store for us.

Consequently, we can speak of *justified emotional security* only, if we realize that it equals our readiness to meet, and to cope with, the many occasions for inner and outer *insecurity* as they arise. This, at the same time, will help to bring us nearer to *emotional maturity*.

Unfortunately, most people speak of emotional maturity now-adays as if it were a measurable quantity. We seem to forget that since time immemorial, wise men have struggled with doubt regarding maturity and immaturity in the individual. With the humility of the wise, they have realized that the most we humans can attain is some measure of knowledge as to the nature of wisdom and how to strive for it. If we learn from every experience, good or bad, this learning will become an active and well-integrated part of our whole being, whereby we may attain a certain degree of wisdom and emotional maturity. However, we are not born wise, although we may have a predisposition to become wise—and mature. Yet absolute emotional maturity is only a descriptive term, because: ". . . in the adult there is a hidden child—an eternal child, something that calls for unceasing care, attention and fostering. That is the part of human personality that wishes to develop and to complete itself." (C. G. Jung in *Psychological Reflections.*)

Children, nevertheless, at times display an intuitive kind of wisdom and with it an intuitive kind of emotional maturity, which seems to get lost later on in the tussle and bustle of "adult" living. We find this illustrated in a true anecdote of a little girl who said to her mother on their return home after a vacation: "I am glad we brought all these shells back from the beach. It doesn't make you so lonesome for the good times when you bring part of the vacation back with you."

Many an adult might well emulate this child's mental attitude. But if we are not endowed with a natural gift of bringing back into our everyday-life "part of the vacation," then we must learn how to develop and integrate this potential faculty into our personality make-up.

Whether one's mind is healthy by disposition, or whether it harbors merely a kernel of health and strength which will have to be nurtured before it can develop and become active, the goal to be pursued remains the same: to learn how to discover and practice the art of living benignly with regard to ourselves and to others.

In every kind of artistic creation, the artist will have to blend his individuality with craftsmanship and thereby transform his work into genuine art. In like manner, each of us has to shape his own individuality, blend it with the manifold facets of life and thereby transform mere existence into the art of living.

There are, of course, no one-way directions on how to practice the art of living, although its nucleus is highlighted incomparably by Henry Thoreau: "It is something to be able to paint a particular picture, or to carve a statue and so to make a few objects beautiful. But it is far more glorious to carve and paint the very atmosphere and medium through which we look . . . to affect the quality of the day . . . that is the highest of arts."

Many of you readers may ask: "How can one go about enhancing 'the quality of the day'? It seems to be more easily said than done!"

Again, different minds will have different ideas and therefore will have to realize diverging goals by different means. However, the difference in goals and in ways of attaining them does not necessarily imply that one way has greater merit over any other, so long as each fulfills its purpose of contributing to the savor of life. And don't imagine that you need to accomplish anything extraordinary! It suffices, if you take time out, perhaps only a few minutes a day, to read maybe, or to listen to, or think of something, which gives you a spiritual lift, or awakens your interest in something worthwhile. It can also be an incident which amuses you, or an occupation which distracts you pleasantly for a short while from everyday duties.

You may feel exalted by the glorious colors of a sunset. Or you may enjoy a short walk in fresh air, gardening, watching animals at play, preparing a fancy dish, tuning in the radio to some music you like, or you may feel good about having reached out a helping hand to somebody. Reading a poem may give you a lift, because ". . . there's nothing so good as a potent brew of well-aged pathos, preferably distilled in verse. At once you feel cleansed and ennobled." (Walter Mehring.)

Or, perhaps, you have the enviable capacity to relax . . . to relax in the manner which Vernon Lee observed in D. H. Lawrence: "he possessed what is, for a highly strung and intelligent man, an even more remarkable accomplishment—he knew how to do nothing— he could just sit and be perfectly happy." And, above all, give yourself, as often as you can, an opportunity to smile—but kindly, understandingly and enjoyably! All this and more is desirable and rewardingly constructive, so long as you are perceptive of the good things life has to offer. You have to keep in mind though, not to let anything you might do, or not do, interfere with the consideration you owe to others. Just imagine what would happen if, for instance, you love to listen to music and have the radio on full blast, whereas your family, or neighbors, don't quite share your delight!

We can "affect the quality of the day" in any number of ways. In other words, we can *practice* mental health as an inner necessity instead of giving generalized anaemic lip-service to theoretical notions about mental health. And if once in a while we may be inclined to do exactly the opposite of what is reasonable, that too may be mentally wholesome, so long as we don't make a habit of acting on every pleasurable impulse.

To give an example of a "wholesome folly," let us imagine that a man whom we shall call George, has been dreaming for years and years of making a certain trip, but the expense, approximately one thousand dollars, is beyond his financial budget. George mulls over all kinds of plans to make the trip possible. He finally sees a way to afford it by cutting down his daily expenditures here and there for several months. In addition, he will have to use all his savings and, besides, he will be uncomfortably short for some time after his return. On the other hand, he will be able to balance his budget eventually and start saving again. Realizing these facts, George decides in favor of the journey. And so he sets forth. However, success or failure of his undertaking will depend on his own mental attitude!

If George, during his voyage were to weigh down his mind by anticipating future discomfort and worry about every cent he spends, it would be most unreasonable. George should have taken all the pros and cons into consideration before making his decision. Neither should George feel "guilty" about the extravagance, provided that nobody else will have to suffer, or be wronged as a result of his pleasurable adventure.

Once George has decided to fulfill his dream and make the journey, he should enjoy it to the hilt; otherwise he would not only use up his hard-earned money, but also fail to derive any satisfaction from doing so. This would make the financial restraints he will have to impose upon himself on his return twice as painful to bear. Do you remember the little girl mentioned before, who wanted to recall the joys of her vacation by bringing back "shells from the beach"? Unlike her, George would bring nothing back except remorse at having yielded to his longing for an extravagant journey.

Situations such as the one illustrated by this example as well as by others cited within these pages, can only demonstrate briefly a few aspects of how to avoid pitfalls and lead a mentally healthy life. However, you may feel that there is no connection between the situation in a given example and the circumstances you may be concerned with personally. But were you to look a little closer, you might find that in many instances you encounter certain attitudes which approximate your own, although the circumstances themselves may be different.

While we travel through life, our attitudes toward ourselves, toward others and toward life, are reflected in the meaningfulness we find in life, in our preparedness to assume responsibilities, and in our ability to feel joy.

The positive attitudes we cultivate in ourselves help us in our striving for emotional maturity, a maturity which renders us fit to cope valiantly and resourcefully with whatever life may have in store for us. But you might say: "There is a catch here! What of the things that are impossible to bear, or to put up with! What about the unending monotony of my work in the office—in the factory— my daily housework! How can my attitudes protect me from the insufferable conceit of my boss—my wife's endless nagging—my husband's complaints!"

Perhaps your specific situation justifies your exasperation and, if this is so, you should figure out what you can do to improve matters, or change your reaction toward them. And if you answer: "This is impossible!" let me remind you that we tend to say "Impossible!" when actually what we have in mind may be "difficult"— very difficult, perhaps—but not *impossible*. Besides, even if your feelings about some person or situation are justified, has it ever occurred to you that your own attitude may be contributing to bring out the worst in this other person, or to aggravate the situation. This possibility cannot be stressed too emphatically, for once you realize that your own attitude is at fault, at least to a certain extent, you *can* change your attitude. If you succeed, you may find that everything else also has changed for the better.

The inconveniences, complications and obstacles we have to face in life will range from the utterly insignificant to the desperately difficult. Our reactions and attitudes toward them may cover just as wide a range. The following eleven behavior-patterns, some favorable, others unfavorable, constitute only a small selection within this wide range, but you may discover that you conform to one or another of them:

1) You try hard to do your best to fight and overcome inner and outward obstacles and conflicts, whatever they may be.
2) If a situation is difficult, you *think it through* and you try to reach a decision as to how far you should and could
   a) influence, or change the situation, or
   b) adapt yourself to it.
3) You accept the situation because you believe there is nothing else to be done, or because you are afraid that any change you might bring about would only make things worse.
4) You resign yourself, but with feelings of self-pity, which may gradually increase until you develop a "martyr-complex."
5) You sulk with life and with a fate that treats you shabbily and unjustly.
6) You resent aggressively the situation you are in and also those you consider responsible for it. You become bitter, quarrelsome, dissatisfied with everything and end up by neglecting your responsibilities towards others and, maybe, towards yourself as well.
7) You seek negative escape from your problems by indulging in too much "fun," or too much alcohol, too much food, or too much sex. Maybe you seek escape in gambling, perhaps you even gamble with your life, or with the lives of others. This can be done so simply nowadays, just by driving carelessly and recklessly. You may also show an increasing lack of consideration for others and become callous and vindictive.
8) You may change the whole situation drastically, because you consider it best for all concerned. You have come to this conclusion, not impulsively, but after having weighed the pros and

cons with regard to yourself and everyone else affected by this situation.

9) You may change the whole situation drastically, affirming that this is best for all concerned, although actually you are not sufficiently objective. Your justification for whatever action you take is merely rationalization. The change serves solely your own good, yet you would make it appear to be a supreme sacrifice of your own wishes and interests and even pretend so towards yourself.

10) You change the whole situation drastically, regardless of how this may affect others, and perhaps even yourself.

11) After having reached a decision based on one of the alternatives described in 1, 2, 3, or 8, you *compensate* your difficulties *constructively* by finding new and worthwhile interests, thus giving added purpose and incentive to your life.

Like a tone scale which consists of only seven whole and five half tones, yet allows us to develop an infinite variety of musical themes, so do emotional reactions present an infinitude of shadings and forms. To navigate in this ocean of emotions, we need a good compass and nothing adds up to a better one than wholesome insight, good evaluative faculties in general and the ability to make up one's mind. This compass helps us to grow into emotional maturity.

13. HOW TO MAKE UP YOUR MIND

Did it ever happen that you couldn't make up your mind about even so trivial a thing as whether to stay at home or to go to the movies? And, after you had finally determined to go, did you find it difficult to decide which picture you wanted to see?

This is a very unimportant decision indeed. However, there are a great many others, just as unimportant, with which you may be confronted more often than you care to admit. Nevertheless, they all affect you in a similar way by reason of several factors, only three of which will be mentioned here. Most frequently, it is one of these three factors, or a combination of them, which is also at the root of indecisive attitudes in matters of the gravest import to ourselves and to others.

The first factor, but first only in regard to the sequence being observed here, is *indifference*. When indifference is coupled with fatigue or boredom or both, we shall find it increasingly hard to make decisions.

The second factor is *reluctance,* justified or unjustified reluctance, to assume responsibility for a decision. It is obvious, that apprehension in various degrees usually motivates reluctance to make a decision.

Although the reluctance to assume responsibility is of no particular consequence in a case such as going or not going to the movies, even here it may have some bearing on our behavior in general.

A wife or husband will frequently say: "I don't want to choose a movie, or a restaurant, because if it doesn't turn out right, I shall be blamed for having made a bad choice."

Reluctance to assume responsibility in these inconsequential cases probably stems only from the wish to avoid hearing a few unpleasant remarks. When it comes to questions of greater import, then a deep-seated lack of self-confidence and the anxiety connected with it, may easily be the far more serious reason for our indecision. We may be desperately afraid that making a wrong decision might result in unfortunate consequences to ourselves or to others; yet, actually, it may be our indecision that causes most of the unfortunate consequences.

In various cases, reluctance to make decisions may be justified, at least to some extent. A person may have either too many responsibilities already, or certain types of responsibility may be obnoxious to him. Then, if he cannot relieve the pressure, he may be brought to the verge of a neurosis or of some physical illness. The outcome of such a situation will depend greatly on the overall personality of the individual who displays the signs of excessive reluctance to make decisions and also on whether he can practice adequate mental-emotional self-direction. If he is well-balanced emotionally in other instances, if he is usually able to make decisions and assume responsibilities, he should not be forced, or force himself, *constantly* to assume duties which are either too much for him, or alien to his inherent character-disposition. Being constantly forced, or forcing himself, might upset his otherwise good emotional balance. In some cases, aversion to assuming responsibilities of a certain type may have been engendered by some previous experience of an unpleasant or, perhaps, even a dangerous nature. On the other hand, reluctance to assume responsibilities may be based on character-shortcomings which would require straightening out.

Finally, there are those who cannot even grasp the meaning of responsibility. If one attempts to clarify their thinking, they simply don't understand. These are the individuals with an almost psychopathic deficiency in their character make-up. It is extremely difficult, and often not possible, to coax them into acquiring enough constructive insight regarding their deficiencies, to make correction take root.

The third factor is *conflict*. If you cannot make up your mind whether or not you ought to go to the movies, you vacillate, also emotionally, between the wish to stay home, maybe rest in your comfortable chair, and your wish to see a picture, or to seek distraction, or not to disappoint your wife or husband. All this, insignificant in itself, if repeated too often, springs from the same source whence far more serious conflicts arise, namely, from a habitual or a temporary difficulty or inability to *think a given situation through reasonably, decide what course to take, and direct yourself into taking that course.*

Indecision need not be a symptom of a neurosis, but it certainly can lead to a neurosis. And, while we are on the subject of conflict, if there is anything almost as unfortunate as perpetual indecision, it is the tendency to make *rash decisions*. If you make a rash decision, you are not making a real choice. While indecision is based on mulling things over too intensely and for too long a time without making a definite choice, a rash decision *omits the weighing of pros and cons* before making a choice and *this too may cause conflict*. A rash decision precipitates action and the conflict arises from the possible consequences of an action prematurely taken.

But it is the chronic state of indecision which traps us in a maze of conflicting thoughts and emotions, and the longer we permit such a condition to continue, the closer we come to a neurotic disorder.

14. BASE DECISIONS ON LOGICAL THINKING AND INTUITION

Decisions in themselves may be good or bad, right or wrong to a varying degree, or they may be neutral and have neither good nor bad effects. Whatever quality applies to a decision may become obvious immediately, or be determined by results far in the future. But whatever the case, the kind and quality of the decisions you come to will depend greatly on:

a) Whether you are able to reason logically and to recognize and avoid the mental traps of ambiguous and confused thinking set either by yourself or by others. In short, it will depend on whether you are able to recognize the type of pseudological reasoning of sophistry, which is directed not towards arriving at the truth, but rather towards proving some preconceived point or winning an argument.

b) Whether you can project yourself into another person's feelings, viewpoint and situation and see both sides of a question.

c) Whether you are able to practice flexibility as well as firmness in your thinking and attitudes, yet *avoid* excessive flexibility or excessive firmness. Excessive flexibility usually results in inconsistency and impairs good judgment; on the other hand, excessive firmness results in mental and emotional narrowness, righteousness and a "Holier than Thou" attitude. This also impairs good judgment.

d) Whether you master and apply the practice of constructive mental and emotional self-direction.

Although sound logical thinking is an indispensable prerequisite for arriving at intelligent and mature conclusions, sometimes it may be preferable and kinder to let our heart speak rather than to listen to the dictates of cold reason. There are certain problems, be they of a personal, or of an objective and impersonal nature, which our reasoning powers are not adequate to solve.

In addition to our ability to think and reason, we are endowed with intuitive faculties by which enlightenment may come to us in a flash. We may even reach the solution to some personal problem in this way and express it by saying "suddenly it dawned on me" or the like. This doesn't indicate that we have come to a rash decision without having thought the matter over. On the contrary, the flash of intuition has almost invariably been preceded by intense concentration on the subject in question. Some of our greatest scientific, inventive, and artistic minds have solved weighty problems in this intuitive manner, problems to which logical and methodical thinking alone had failed to provide a solution.

It is all the more unfortunate that some of those entrusted with the task of teaching us to think logically, look down somewhat condescendingly on others who recognize the value of intuitive faculties. But it is just as unfortunate when the latter ignore the fact that logic is an essential ingredient of our mental processes. Definitely, we have to learn how to master the craft and the skill of sound logical thinking and reasoning, because most of the time this is the correct way to function intellectually.

But, although with reservations, we must also be able to see other points of view such as that of W. MacNeil Dixon when he says in *The Human Situation:* "Those who would have life logical, a pretty geometrical design, a kind of finished garden city, to which no addition can be made, must, indeed, view its confusions and irregularities with uneasy apprehension. To pattern lovers, to neat minds, who prefer things in their proper place, ticketed and pigeonholed, it no doubt presents a shocking spectacle, an inextricable tangle, a wilderness without ways, aflame with conflicting energies, swarming with creatures of a hundred million habits, involuted and convoluted to an indescribable complexity. Let it be so, and let us take a holiday from the requirements of static logic . . . Half-hours with the irrational, the magical, the surprising, have they not a tonic quality . . . the charm of the medieval as contrasted with the modern garden city? Have you observed how much these irresponsible beings, the poets, are in love with such wild things? . . . they would not give a fig for logic. Perhaps nature speaks through them as clearly as through reason."

We are confronted here with colorful, persuasive language, a powerful instrument which can be used in many variations and for many purposes! Without a doubt, this type of language can exert tremendous fascination—and yet it is but a certain type of prejudiced and emotionally tinged thinking, liable to becloud the issue. Dixon uses the seductive sound of words and phrases to discredit logic; nevertheless, involuntarily he weakens his own thesis when he says: "Perhaps nature speaks through them [the 'wild things'] as clearly as through reason" because in these words we find his indirect admission that nature herself speaks through reason!

The tragic error which Dixon and many others in different fields and with different words want to convey to us as "truth" consists in trying to make us believe that there exist only "Either-Or" situations, or only two shades of color, namely, black and white, and that there are only two states of mind, static logic or wonderful irrationality. But logic need not be static and irrationality is not that wonderful! The potentialities of the human mind are vast and while it may function with the force of sharpest precision in thinking and logical reasoning, it may also transcend these tangible forms by intuition, by the capacity to *sense* a solution rather than to figure it out, or to know something without preceding factual cognizance. According to Thomas Aquinas, it is by abandoning "word and discrimination" that one may find oneself on the intuitive "path of realization."

And so we have to realize that the ability to think logically and to reason does not represent the human mind in its entirety— neither does intuition. Only united do logical thinking and intuition blend into human intelligence.

15. INSIGHT AND SELF-EVALUATION

Negative emotional traits such as resentfulness, disproportionate chronic guilt-feelings and others, stem from a malfunctioning of our personality, and in reverse they tend to aggravate this malfunctioning. In the majority of cases, the malfunctioning of personality could be remedied, if we became able to judge ourselves objectively.

If we find ourselves getting emotionally upset too frequently and too intensively, or if we show signs of chronically going haywire, we can be quite certain that there is something wrong. Once we have honestly admitted to ourselves that this is so, the next step should be to try and discover the underlying cause or causes. We will succeed in finding them more often than not, if we try earnestly enough. After we have discovered what is wrong with us, at least to some degree, we have to endeavor just as hard, and probably even harder, to make appropriate changes in our mental and emotional attitudes, or else change the situation which is upsetting our emotional equanimity. Let us take an example at random. Should you, for instance, come to realize that you seek to dominate people, you will next have to investigate whether you tend to dominate

a) people in general, or
b) someone in particular and, besides,
c) in what way and
d) for what reasons you seek to dominate.

Perhaps you try to dominate people consciously or unconsciously, in order to camouflage your own weaknesses. You may try to dominate other people for a variety of reasons and you may use various means. You might take advantage of an actual illness, or pretend a sickness in which, finally, you come to believe yourself. You could dominate by stubbornness, by making a person fear your wrath, your contempt, or some kind of retaliation, and so on.

If you are sufficiently fair-minded and also objective toward yourself, you will want to overcome this undesirable tendency to dominate others. However, there is also a possibility that one or several persons assert that you are trying to dominate them, while actually you are authoritative. Being authoritative is quite different from being domineering. Some special knowledge or skill might give you an authority you would be quite justified to exercise in certain instances, whereas domination is never justifiable. A position of authority, however, combined with the tendency to dominate, constitute a fertile soil for the development of tyranny. This fact alone makes it obvious how important it is to develop constructive insight, self-evaluation and self-direction in order to avoid generating unfortunate personality-traits.

Many people claim they become extremely uneasy and self-conscious at being obliged to watch their attitudes while trying to correct them. Probably, self-consciousness is particularly strong in those who are over-vulnerable to some form of vanity which prevents them from evaluating themselves accurately and causes them to resent anything short of blind approval and flattery.

We also find that people who cannot bear being criticized, have a tendency to criticize others most sharply and willingly. This seems to divert them from unpleasant and sometimes even embarrassing traits and facts they might discover if they were to take a good look at themselves. Going from one extreme to another, the same type of person is often unduly self-critical, especially if deep-seated feelings of inferiority are camouflaged by vanity and this prop is lost in the attempt to practice sincere self-evaluation. But whether hypercritical against ourselves or against others, whenever we criticize unduly, we fail in sincere and constructive evaluation.

Those who complain about increasing self-consciousness during the process of self-evaluation should keep in mind that while we are going through the stages of self-examination and self-evaluation, we are going through a process of learning about ourselves. This makes it necessary, of course, to pay closer attention to our actions and reactions than we would normally do. However, we don't live for the purpose of getting better acquainted with ourselves; to achieve the finding of our own identity can enhance life and make it much more worth living! But it doesn't mean that we have to be *constantly* aware of the greater and lesser worthiness or unworthiness of our character-traits and attitudes.

Various forms of awareness are imposed upon us either by physical pain, or by the painful psychological experience of being obsessively afraid, or, for instance, feeling frustrated, resentful, rejected, misjudged, and so on. But there is also an *intentional and directed form of awareness*. One cannot learn and benefit from learning, whatever the subject-matter, without practicing this intentional and attentive awareness. However, the most observant learning will be insufficient, if what we learn does not become integrated in our minds. If we learn to play an instrument, let us say the piano, we have to practice monotonous finger-exercises over and over, closely watching the position of our hands and fingers, the quality of the tone we produce and many other things. But later on, while we are interpreting the music of the great masters, the finger-exercises as such will be forgotten. What finger-exercises could teach us will have become integrated in our mind and our nervous system and be reflex-like at our command. And so, while we no longer need *think* about the rules of finger-exercises, we play in accordance with these rules.

A great many people also complain that they cannot improve their insight without simultaneously developing excessive tension. This claim is based on faulty observations and false conclusions. The awareness of certain undesirable character-traits in ourselves and of attitudes we may have, coupled with a sincere wish to improve or change them, neither contributes to, nor causes excessive tension.

Tension originates, or increases, only when awareness of one's undesirable character-traits and attitudes *combines* with resentment against having to change them. If the wish for improvement is sincere, resentment and the tension resulting from it are automatically excluded.

16. ♦ THE VENOM OF RESENTFULNESS

Resentfulness and hate are two of the most potent factors in the undermining of our faculty to enjoy whatever would be enjoyable in life. This is generally recognized, but the knowledge remains theoretical. We also know theoretically that the detrimental effect of chronic and disproportionate resentfulness on the human mind is comparable to the physical ill-effects of chronic bacterial infection. Like most comparisons, however, this comparison is not quite accurate because of the difference in our reactions toward physical discomforts as compared to mental-emotional ones. We are usually eager to improve our physical condition and will submit voluntarily to all kinds of uncomfortable and even painful treatments. But as far as improvement of our mental-emotional well-being and well-functioning is concerned, we shrink from having to exert any effort. First of all, we often find it more difficult to realize and accept the urgency of remedying our mental attitudes than to accept the necessity to do something about our physical discomforts. As soon as we feel physical pain, we try to alleviate the pain. But should we suffer from resentment and the consequences thereof, we believe there is little we ourselves can do. Instead we are inclined to blame everything on the person or situation causing our resentment.

Whenever we are afflicted with some emotional disturbance and feel uncomfortable, or become desperate and feel in need of help, we may at the same time be quite uncertain how to go about it.

Finally, when the situation comes to a crisis, perhaps we shall consult a psychotherapist or psychiatrist. Then we may become discouraged and disillusioned on finding out that not all the help needed can be expected to come from the *doctor* and that it is essential for us to participate cooperatively in the therapy. The situation is entirely different when we consult a physician for some physical ailment. Here we consider ourselves as being under the physician's care and rely implicitly on him, because *he is the doctor!* We expect that he will do his utmost to help us and so we assume the attitude of children who trust in a parent's omnipotence when anything goes wrong. This is fortunate and, regardless of whether the doctor has been called on to treat our body or our mind, to trust him is a factor which, as we all know, contributes powerfully towards a "cure." It is, of course, much easier to trust the doctor when he prescribes a gargle for our sore throat and to understand that we have to do our own gargling than to make the necessary effort to overcome an emotional malfunction.

Let me illustrate this statement with a very simple case. Mrs. B., a housewife, neglected her household-work which she regarded as inferior. She felt rather guilty about this neglect, yet did nothing to remedy her attitude. Her husband, quite patient with her at first, finally threatened to leave her unless she changed. From then on, she found all kinds of excuses for her negligence; she couldn't admit to herself that she was wrong and consequently resented being made responsible for the discord in her marriage. This growing resentfulness caused her to develop uncomfortable physical symptoms, stomach ulcers and severe tension-headaches. She blamed these discomforts entirely on having "too much to do!" while, actually, she neglected her domestic chores more and more. Mrs. B. completely failed to realize that those who labor under constant feelings of resentment, foster within themselves a source of all kinds of emotional and physical malfunctions.

Admittedly, it is almost impossible at times *not* to feel resentment towards certain people, situations, or duties. If there is real cause for resentment, we should take care not to let ourselves turn into a "doormat" type of person, who just submits. We should, however, ask ourselves, whether our resentment is not disproportionately strong and, furthermore, what we could do about removing or mitigating its cause or causes. By approaching the situation more objectively, we might reach a better understanding with the person whose behavior we resent. But perhaps it isn't that simple; maybe some other approach would be preferable; usually there are several ways of reaching one and the same destination!

Unfortunately, a great many people do not reach any destination at all. Sometimes, they remain resentful, although they think they have freed themselves from their resentfulness by more or less pushing it into the background of their minds. But nothing has been accomplished if we just say "I am not resentful any more!" Disguising or pushing aside disturbing and negative emotions does not eliminate them; they merely become displaced. The following case illustrates this truth. Mrs. T. considered her husband sexually inadequate; she claimed, however, that she was completely reconciled to this deficiency in her marital situation. But one day Mrs. T. involuntarily revealed that this was not so. She was telling me about a dispute the couple were involved in with an automobile dealer. Mrs. T. expressed furious indignation because her husband was seeking a friendly settlement, whereas she wanted him to be more aggressive. She displayed violent hostility at her husband's attitude, finally saying: "If he were a man, he would handle the matter differently—he is just no man!" These words indicated a clear case of displaced resentment which continued to fester, although on a conscious level Mrs. T. was convinced it had been dealt with satisfactorily.

Different again is the resentment somebody may feel about his job. He may consider it not good enough for him, or he may resent something else about it—people can find countless reasons for resentment—whereas its main effects always remain the same, namely, diminishing mental and physical health and a diminishing quality of work. Resentment between employer and employee, for instance, hardly ever promotes good work or a propitious atmosphere in which to work. However, after eight hours of work, there is usually some chance to counterbalance resentfulness with more pleasant and constructive activities. But in a marriage, resentment differs from the many other forms of resentment. The whole atmosphere in which some couples live may become permeated with the poison of resentment.

Among the most frequent reasons for domestic resentment, the following two should be pointed out. The husband resents the money he is obliged to give his wife for the household. From his point of view, marriage consists of nothing but an endless row of bills to pay. His wife, on the other hand, resents the hard struggle of making both ends meet which leaves her without funds for the things she would like to do. Many a wife also complains that her husband has the advantage of being free to rest and unwind when he gets home after the day's grind, whereas she herself has to cook dinner and, in most instances, also get from one to several children fed, bathed and put to bed. Sometimes, temporary feelings of discontent or even resentment at these chores may be quite understandable. But the husband will only intensify his wife's resentment if he expresses doubt that her day's work is anywhere near as strenuous as his own, or if he exclaims on coming home in the evening: "I am pooped! What did *you* do all day long?"

The same can apply in reverse when a wife expects her husband to help with the chores as soon as he gets home from work. The husband can hardly be blamed for resenting this attitude on the part of his wife—and he usually does! These and similar factors frequently build up marital resentment, but the reason for marital shortcomings and hardships lies in the personalities of the marriage-partners, because a marriage is only as successful as the mental and emotional qualities of each husband and wife.

In every instance of resentment, it is important that you discover at the earliest moment possible *why* and *what* you resent. Then attempt to eliminate, or at least alleviate, the external and emotional causes for your resentment. This may be difficult, at times, because the impact of disproportionate resentfulness, of guilt-feelings, and so on may seriously interfere with your attempts. Nevertheless, the better you are able consciously

a) to recognize your negative emotions as such,
b) to direct your way of thinking into more constructive channels,
c) to come to sound decisions,

the better you will be able subsequently to use the hypnoidal stage in order to succeed in your aspirations.

17 ◆ WHAT TO DO ABOUT
GUILT-FEELINGS

Just as pain is significant physiologically, guilt-feelings are significant psychologically; they are vital alarm-signals.

Guilt-feelings, when justified, are signposts by which to direct our ethical conduct. However, too frequent and excessive guilt-feelings may change from their function as alarm-signals into an increasingly destructive force, if they are disregarded. Unless we react sensibly and in good time to the warning guilt-feelings, their impact may become overwhelming and finally inflict torments quite out of proportion to the original cause.

Each person will be affected by guilt-feelings according to his own individuality; one person, for instance, who has good reason to feel guilty, may light-heartedly think or say: "I am so sorry!" and then consider everything is all right! Some people use their guilt-feelings merely as a device to feel exonerated by taking the attitude: "I feel guilty, what more can I do!" whereupon they continue to do, or to omit doing, what caused their guilt-feelings in the first place. The danger lies in choosing the easiest way out without applying corrective mental self-direction.

The exact opposite of corrective self-direction, however, is suppression. Anybody who suppresses his guilt-feelings by pushing them into the background of his mind and seeking to hide from them behind an endless succession of superficial distractions, will only cause his guilt-feelings to continue to thrive "under cover" in his unconscious. He may pretend that his guilt-feelings don't exist, but they will smolder like the live sparks of a banked fire which glimmer unseen, until some gust of air fans them into flame. Then, suddenly, he may find himself having dizzy spells or severe headaches or beginning to suffer from insomnia, palpitations, or other unpleasant and seemingly unaccountable symptoms. Or, instead of these physical symptoms, or perhaps in addition to them, he may develop psychological symptoms. For instance, he may come to feel guilty about almost everything and identify himself with every unfortunate happening, be it in his family, among his friends or fellow-workers, even where no connection whatsoever can be established between himself and the circumstances that arouse his guilt-feelings.

There is also the type of guilt-feeling that results from apprehensive brooding over possible consequences after a decision in some matter has been acted upon.

Another type of guilt-feeling is based on vacillation between decision and indecision. The following case is a good example of this type. Robert Jones felt he should give his aged mother a more generous monthly allowance. However, this would have meant cutting down on certain small luxuries he loved to indulge in like custom-made shoes and shirts, pleasure trips, and so on. Jones reproached himself about his attitude toward his mother, but he could not resist those luxuries he had longed for all his life and worked hard to obtain. At first, Jones rationalized the situation by arguing that what he did for himself was a necessity, because it gave him a lift and kept up his working-ability. Well, it is difficult to *know* where rationalization ends and truth begins, or vice versa. Undeniably, Jones' mother was quite comfortable with the money she received from him. Nevertheless, Jones had gradually come to feel more and more uneasy and guilty about buying things for himself and, after a while, he began to feel guilty when there was no reason for any self-reproach. Independently of whether or not it was in connection with his mother, whenever Jones had the slightest cause to find fault with himself, he felt unduly depressed and remorseful.

The reason for all this was that Jones didn't come to terms with the facts squarely. Had he possessed the necessary insight and self-direction, he would either have decided that his mother was entitled to a larger share of his income, even at some personal sacrifice, or he would have accepted the fact that his own pleasure meant more to him than increased comfort for his mother. Instead, Jones remained in a state of chronic indecision. As a result, his guilt-feelings gradually became transformed into "free-floating" guilt-feelings.

You may have heard the expression "free-floating anxiety." Well, we can speak of free-floating guilt-feelings with as much justification. In the main, both afflictions show the same characteristics; they don't remain connected with their motivating cause exclusively and may be set off by any direct or indirect stimulus, often completely unconnected with the original cause.

In the case of Jones, hypnoidal psychotherapy helped him to gain full insight into the situation and to coordinate his emotional reaction with his improved insight. Consequently, he became able to reach and to carry out satisfactory decisions.

To avoid the manifold discomforts based on suppressed, and also non-suppressed, guilt-feelings: don't delay to face squarely the cause of what may be plaguing you. Then endeavor to come to terms with it and with yourself! In doing this, you may often be surprised to find that you have less real reason for your sense of guilt than you imagined and, if this is correct, you will have come a long way in reducing your emotional discomfort.

Should the cause for your sense of guilt lie too far back in the past for you to do anything about it, then be firmly resolved not to repeat what originated your guilt-feeling. Instead, prevent yourself in some constructive manner from brooding about what might or might not have happened had you acted differently at that particular time, for this is water under the bridge. But under no circumstances suffer from your sense of guilt passively, or try to suppress it. Facing the issue is only a temporary discomfort and will help you to avert the far greater discomfort and danger of continuing to suffer from the *repercussions* of suppressed guilt-feelings.

In addition, it should be pointed out that guilt-feelings, when suppressed into the unconscious, may cause a compulsory omission, or conversely repetition of certain actions and thoughts. Especially compulsive thoughts with their often self-accusative content can virtually terrify the person who is plagued by them until finally the victim comes to the point of feeling: "I don't want to have these thoughts—why can't I stop them!" But these thoughts cannot be stopped just by the desire to be free of them. On the contrary, the anxiety-laden struggle to prevent their recurrence only increases them and fixates their morbid content in the individual's mind. These thoughts thrive on fear and the more we shrink from them, the more power they gain over us. On the other hand, if we recognize at a relatively early stage that we are indulging in an undesirable thought-pattern, then we can, with great probability, arrest its development into a harmful attitude, in the following manner. We have to:

1) improve our insight by evaluating our own personality and our life-circumstances with unflinching honesty;
2) act in accordance with our improving insight;
3) train our ability to neutralize our mind;
4) train our ability to practice constructive mental-emotional self-direction consciously and conscientiously;
5) condition ourselves in these practices and integrate them into our personality with the aid of the hypnoidal stage and hypnoidal suggestions. You will find the necessary directions for doing this in Part Two.

The farther we progress in our training and conditioning, the better we shall be able to direct our thoughts into constructive channels and to carry out the resolutions our improved insight has led us to make. This is constructive self-direction. By applying it, we shall be able to prevent ourselves from suppressing illogical, excessive guilt-feelings as well as other unfavorable emotions. As a consequence, the upsurge of painful and destructive thoughts will become ever less frequent and less intensive. Nobody, of course, can ordain what thoughts will come spontaneously into his mind, neither can he dictate his first and immediate reaction to the content of a thought or to some experience. This is beyond our conscious control.

But it *does lie within our conscious control* to direct and thereby affect our *counter-reaction* to our *first* reaction; we call this counter-reaction, our *second* reaction. Should you, for instance, hear a shot-like detonation, your first reaction might be to become alarmed. "That was a shot," you might think, "somebody has been shot . . . burglars have broken into a neighbor's house . . . they'll try to escape . . . perhaps into my house!" and so on, conjuring up all sorts of frightening incidents, complete with dire consequences. In this manner you could easily work yourself into a state of abject terror. But if you are capable of self-direction at will, then, on hearing the same shot-like noise, your *first* reflex-reaction may still be one of fear, provided you are a fearful person. Your *second* reaction, however, will be to assume mental control, to evaluate the circumstances clearly and thereby probably come to realize that the detonation was merely caused by a car backfiring or by a tire blow-out.

The practice of self-direction is important for another reason also. It is true that primary reactions to external happenings, or emotional jolts, cannot be deliberately avoided; they are uncontrolled reflex-reactions. There are negative reflex-reactions, and also positive ones, and once the habit of directing *secondary* reactions has been established, it will be found that sooner or later even *primary* reflex-reactions causing fear, anger or confusion, have lost much of their punch.

18. HOW TO PRACTICE MENTAL-EMOTIONAL SELF-DIRECTION

First of all, you should become acquainted with the necessary prerequisites to the practice of mental-emotional self-direction, namely:

a) Selection of a particular goal or goals toward which you wish to direct yourself.

b) Development of adequate means by which to direct yourself towards a chosen goal. Adequate means consist of

   1) your mental and emotional ability and preparedness to cope with possible obstacles and difficulties in the best possible way;

   2) furthermore, adequate means consist of your ability to think logically and to see the different sides of an issue, taking them all into objective consideration before determining in what direction to search for a solution.

c) Once you have come to a conclusion, the next step is to put it into practice. Sometimes this is fairly easy; at other times, it is more complicated and difficult. But in either case you have to face the issue.

d) To acquire these prerequisites for adequate self-direction, we need sound self-discipline. If people understood better what discipline and self-discipline actually signify, they would not cringe at the mere mention of the word. Sound self-discipline is a necessary adjunct to successful living.

Self-discipline need not imply painful self-denial, just as discipline need not consist in punishment. Only when carried to excess will self-discipline deteriorate into extreme self-denial, or discipline into crippling punishment. Quite understandably, both extremes will either cause rebelliousness, or will result in an extinction of individual self-expression.

On the other hand, too little discipline, or none at all, can be considered as a most harmful factor in human behavior and in human relations. If there is one test which is a sure give-away of good and bad character-traits, it is the behavior of automobile drivers. A person, who is considerate by disposition, will be considerate while driving a car; another one, who only thinks of himself and has no self-discipline, will forget that other drivers share the road with him. Adequate instructions and regulations will be powerless to prevent accidents, when drivers have "bad manners of the heart" and have not learned the value of exerting self-discipline and obeying the rules.

But apart from driving an automobile, we should realize that without sensible self-discipline, it is difficult for any one to find his place in life and to get along with his fellow-men, or even with himself. Discipline, especially self-discipline, is a skill, an art. Practice this art and you will have found a key to the widest freedom anybody can attain, for it will preserve you from becoming a slave to your own undesirable or harmful impulses.

The process of conditioning constructive self-discipline is aided greatly by using Psycho-Gymnastic Exercises which I introduced in my book *Hypnoidal Psychotherapy*.

These exercises came to be called *psycho-gymnastic,* because once, when I was explaining them to a patient, he remarked: "That sounds exactly like gymnastic exercises." I replied: "In a way, that's what they are—*psycho-gymnastic* exercises!"

The psycho-gymnastic exercises which I have devised are relatively simple in performance but complex in their effect. Many people, when they start out with psycho-gymnastic exercises, regard them as just an added burden and do not realize at the beginning that these exercises will *ultimately help relieve the actual or imagined burdens* by which they feel weighed down.

Two types of exercises are particularly helpful for the purpose of training and conditioning in constructive self-discipline and mental-emotional self-direction.

In order to make the best use of psycho-gymnastic exercises, you have to understand clearly that both types of exercises should always be carried out with a conscious awareness of the following factors:

1) Psycho-gymnastic exercises should never be regarded as or practiced as just one more onerous or boring obligation.
2) Psycho-gymnastic exercises have to be considered as *specific training-exercises and nothing else.*
3) Psycho-gymnastic exercises are designed to strengthen and condition your general faculty of mental-emotional self-direction.

19. PSYCHO-GYMNASTIC EXERCISES

I. PSYCHO-GYMNASTIC EXERCISES, CATEGORY ONE

a) Select a certain task every day and resolve to *carry it out the following day at a certain time.*

b) The time, let us say 2 P.M., has also to be set on the previous day. Keep as closely as possible to the time you have set, but, *if necessary,* give yourself a leeway of five to ten minutes. Under no circumstances should you exceed ten minutes leeway, because if you do, you would break the interaction of several factors which make psycho-gymnastic exercises effective.

c) The task itself need not take up a great deal of time; it may require *only one or two minutes, or up to approximately half an hour.* You are free to decide how much time you wish to give to the planned undertaking, but it should never exceed half an hour.

d) It is advisable that the length of time you devote to your psycho-gymnastic exercises vary from day to day. For instance, if you have chosen for one day an exercise which lasted about fifteen minutes, plan an exercise which will take no more than a couple of minutes, or so, for the following day.

e) The activity you choose may be a useful one such as writing a letter, cleaning out the drawers of your desk, and so on. Occasionally, you may decide on doing something which doesn't serve any particular purpose. For instance, you may decide:

"To-morrow at 3 P.M., I will take a certain ash-tray, carry it from the living-room to the dining-room and back again to the living-room." As an ordinary action, this, of course, would be nonsensical. But this exercise and many others of a similar type which serve *no other purpose except that of carrying them out,* are of great value as training-exercises.

f) It is irrelevant whether or not you choose an activity for which you have a particular predilection, so long as you don't choose exclusively those activities which you prefer.

g) It is important that the advance-planned exercises be performed in as relaxed a frame of mind as possible.

h) You must let nothing prevent you from carrying out your self-selected and advanced-planned activity. Only a genuine emergency may excuse you. For instance, should the telephone ring just at the time when you start out with your psycho-gymnastic exercise, then, of course, you will have to answer the telephone. But, whenever possible, carry on with your exercise as soon as the interruption is over, provided it doesn't interfere with any other activity you may have to attend to.

II. SOME ADVANTAGES TO BE GAINED FROM PSYCHO-GYMNASTIC EXERCISES, CATEGORY ONE

You practice making a decision, insofar as you have to decide on a certain task.

You practice making a choice by having to select the form in which to carry out that task.

You practice self-discipline, because you have to carry out your decision.

You practice foresight by planning your task so that it will not interfere with anything else you may have to attend to. For example, should you have planned to go into the garden and pick flowers at 11 A.M. on the following day and should you have overlooked that you have an appointment with your dentist at, let us say, 11:30 A.M., you would find yourself unable to do both, or else you would have to carry out your psycho-gymnastic exercise under pressure and, besides, be late at your dentist's.

You also practice foresight, if, for instance, you refrain from planning an outdoor activity in summer during the hottest time of the day, because this might interfere with your health.

In this connection, remember that whenever you plan your psycho-gymnastic exercise, you should always carefully avoid the possibility of choosing an exercise which might be in violation of the rules of good health.

III. PSYCHO-GYMNASTIC EXERCISES, CATEGORY TWO

a) Psycho-gymnastic exercises, Category Two, are *not* to be planned on the previous day.

b) You select your task on the same day, either one or two hours beforehand, or you carry it out on the spur of the moment.

c) Your selection has to consist of something more or less irksome to you or, alternately, of abstaining from something that would give you pleasure.

d) These exercises condition you to practice instantaneous mental-emotional control and self-direction.

IV. GENERAL RULES FOR PSYCHO-GYMNASTIC EXERCISES

1) On days when you have selected a psycho-gymnastic exercise of Category One, don't do any exercise of Category Two and vice versa.

2) Care should be taken, as has been pointed out already, that the exercises don't conflict with the requirements of health: for instance, abstention from regular meals, over-strenuous physical exercise, and so on.

3) Should you, however, like to have a second cup of coffee after lunch, you might decide one day on the spur of the moment: "No, I will not have another cup today!" This would be an acceptable psycho-gymnastic exercise of Category Two. To drink only one cup of coffee instead of two after lunch certainly cannot impair one's health!

4) To decide: "I will have only one cup of coffee after lunch *tomorrow!*" is to plan a psycho-gymnastic exercise of Category

One, especially if you are used to drinking more than one cup of coffee.

5) If a habit such as smoking too much or overeating is a serious problem, one you find almost impossible to give up, then this habit should *not* be made the object of psycho-gymnastic exercises, *not even as a part of them*. These habits have to be taken care of alongside the psycho-gymnastic exercises. For instance, you should not make a psycho-gymnastic exercise out of depriving yourself of a cigarette after lunch, provided it is a problem to you to break the habit of smoking.

6) The same rule has to be observed just as strictly, if you want to acquire a beneficent habit and it is difficult for you to do so.

7) If you were to try and attack any major problem *directly* by means of psycho-gymnastic exercises, it would be like attempting to take an examination without having studied the subject-matter, or like competing for a championship without having conditioned and trained yourself beforehand.

8) The exercises of Category One and Category Two may be omitted on one or two days every week; but they have to be continued until they become routine. This may require approximately three or four months, sometimes more, sometimes less.

9) In the course of time, certain repetitions of exercises will have to take place, but never repeat one and the same task within a period of two weeks.

10) The tasks for the exercises can be of various kinds, of course, and using your imagination to devise them, contributes to good training.

11) Once you have made psycho-gymnastic exercises a routine activity, you can be sure that you are on the best way to become well-conditioned in constructive self-discipline and self-direction. *This is the time to approach and attack directly any problem you may have.*

12) It should be pointed out once more that psycho-gymnastic exercises are not a direct aid in learning to master your problems. However, these exercises will condition you to achieve with increasing ease any constructive goal you have set for yourself.

20. ◆ THE ART OF LOGICAL THINKING

Among the prerequisites for mental-emotional self-direction, you found a reference to logical thinking, and you too might do well to re-appraise your reasoning powers. However, should you say: "Why should I do this? I am quite well able to think and reason logically!" you are probably correct. But all the same, unless you have been trained in the art of logical thinking and practice it consistently, you may often find it difficult to *think through* a problem thoroughly, or tackle a complicated situation successfully.

A well-trained and systematically applied ability to think clearly, logically and objectively, serves as a direction-finder like a compass at sea. It helps to penetrate the mental fog which prevents so many people from navigating safely through life.

The faculty of clear thinking, however, is not always sufficient to make us wary of psychological pitfalls, because, under certain circumstances, people's reasoning faculties may become blinded during the struggle between reason and emotion and, too often, the latter will gain domination. This point is amply illustrated in the "Guide to Self-Examination." These illustrations also show how ambiguous deductions may result from false conclusions.

Unfortunately, not all the textbooks on the subject of logical thinking are reliable tools with which to achieve this important goal. The renowned philosopher Morris R. Cohen comments on this inadequacy by pointing out that "of all textbooks those on logic might be considered the most illogical . . . there is a bewildering Babel of tongues as to what logic is about. The different schools, the traditional, the linguistic, the epistemological, and the mathematical, speak different languages and each regards the others as not really dealing with logic at all."

This doesn't sound encouraging for those who wish to get better acquainted with the art of logical thinking. On the other hand, Cohen gives a very good and convincing idea of what logic can do for you. He says: "To show that logic deals with all the world—with ambiguities as well as clarities, fiction as well as truth, probabilities as well as certainties . . . seemed to me a service in dispelling the mist that envelops a good deal of temporary philosophizing . . . logic . . . an indispensable instrument for the exploration of yet unrealized possibilities might make plain the role of logic as an indispensable element . . . of free thought."

In the "List of Books Recommended for Additional Reading," there are a few books mentioned which give guidance in logical thinking and the sport of applying one's reasoning faculties systematically. But logical thinking does not signify mere skill in logical formulations; we have to realize the many other factors that operate in logical thinking. One of them is semantic thinking; but here again, the semanticists themselves are not on too good terms with the logicians! Apart from any confusing semantic-logical feud, it is evident that our culture and civilization would not be conceivable, if languages, with their intricate structures and forms, had not given us the possibility to express the finest shades of meaning. In everyday-usage, though, language is, comparatively speaking, reduced to the role of shorthand symbols. Most of the time, this is sufficient, because we have become conditioned both to give mere indications of what we want and to an almost intuitive grasping of what is meant. And so, if somebody says, for example: "It is cold in this room," you will not pay much attention to the manifold possibilities which this simple statement contains.

Consequently, unless you are having an argument about temperature in general, or the temperature of one room in particular, you will probably not investigate first how many degrees of Fahrenheit the room-temperature shows, nor raise the point of how low a temperature would justify the statement, "It is cold in this room."

But if you argue about a statement, even a trivial one like this one, it will require sound reasoning to reach a just evaluation of the assertion. Should you be in the same room with the person who claims that the room is cold, you may:

1) disagree with him and mind very much if he closes the window and lights a fire;
2) be indifferent to his statement and indifferent to the temperature in the room; then you will not care if he closes the window and lights a fire;
3) agree with him, because you too feel cold and therefore you welcome his closing the window and lighting a fire.

In the simple statement, "It is cold in this room," still other factors have to be considered. First of all, whether or not this person's claim is objectively or subjectively justified, for justification does not lie exclusively in the measurable temperature of the room. One person, by his physical constitution, may be more justified in his need for more warmth than somebody else with a different constitution. Or a person may be justified in needing more warmth, because he is sick or not sufficiently warmly clad. On the other hand, you, who do not think that it is cold in the room, are adequately dressed or maybe even too warmly dressed. And, of course, there are many other possibilities which could affect the validity of the statement, "It is cold in this room."

The specific reason for elaborating on this very ordinary example is the fact that there are also countless so-called psychological situations which may be based on an even greater variety of degrees and shadings of human perceptions, of mental and emotional reactions, and of individual interpretations. At times these psychological situations and problems may become highly complex, and in order to convey an idea of how even simple problems may get out of hand, let me tell a legend about the inventor of chess.

According to the legend, a Persian king was presented with an exquisite set of chess-men by his Vizier, who had devised the game and taught the king to play it. The king was delighted and, desiring to reward the Vizier magnificently, requested him to name his wish. After some hesitation, the Vizier asked for as many grains of wheat as could be placed on a chess-board in the following manner: one grain on the first square, two on the second, four on the third, eight on the fourth, in short, always twice as many grains as on the preceding square. At first, the king was annoyed at the Vizier's modesty, but then he found out that the modesty was less great than he had believed, because the number of grains finally came to the astronomical figure of 18 446744 073709 551615 or 18 trillions, 446744 billions, 73709 millions and 551615 grains of wheat. Thus the king was unable to grant the Vizier's wish, because his country didn't produce that much wheat. I can't say that I have checked the exactness of these figures! However, they give a fair idea of how deceptive the apparent simplicity of some matters can be. This is especially true of psychological matters, where things may often appear quite simple, while, at the same time, they may be more complicated than we are inclined to believe or perhaps able to comprehend.

The ability to think and reason clearly is of paramount import to mental health, because it makes it easier for us to understand ourselves and others. But we must also be able to coordinate our emotional reactions with our clear reasoning; only then will we function well psychologically.

21♦ THE NEED TO COORDINATE
EMOTIONAL RESPONSES WITH
CONSTRUCTIVE THINKING

One of the simple sounding, yet complex psychological verities is contained in Pythagoras' injunction: "Know Thyself!" This is still sound advice by which to attain and retain mental health; however, Pythagoras could well have added "and make good use of that knowledge!"

Most of us have quite a fair amount of self-knowledge, but do not always apply our theoretical realizations. For example, we may know that we should eat less and yet continue to overeat. Or we may know theoretically that we should be more considerate of some person, but keep on heedlessly, or even deliberately, disregarding this person's reasonable wishes. Theoretical insight alone does not suffice to produce favorable personality changes, unless the acquired theoretical insight is transplanted into appropriate action. Freud himself pointed out that to make a person know intellectually why he feels and acts as he does, is not always sufficient to remedy his emotional malfunction. The following tragi-comic anecdote is an apt comment on the difference between theoretically knowing certain things about oneself and actually applying this knowledge to good purpose. The story goes that a psychoanalyst and his patient were discussing the famous painter Von Gogh who mutilated himself by cutting off one of his ears. The patient asked: "Do you think, doctor, that Van Gogh would have cut off his ear if he had gone through psychoanalysis?" The analyst answered: "Yes, probably . . . but at least he would have *known why he did it!*" A joke like this is funny, of course. But when something like this really happens—and it occasionally does—then it is not so funny.

Improved insight without corresponding action would be similar to the barren studiousness of some people, who accumulate an encyclopaedic store of unconnected facts, but are unable to correlate any of them creatively. Without intellectually realized and emotionally integrated self-knowledge, it will hardly be possible to cope successfully with baffling conflicts, frustrating experiences and unreasonable fears. It is the inability to translate theoretical insight into practice that contributes so much to people's tormenting fears and anxieties. Although these people realize quite often that their fears are not justified, this mere intellectual realization seldom relieves their discomfort. Just as an automobile with a damaged steering-wheel does not obey the guiding hand of the driver, we human beings don't operate properly when our mental-emotional self-direction is impaired by a lack of coordination between our selective mental faculties and our emotional response.

For some people, the step from theory to practice is very difficult, even under quite ordinary circumstances. It becomes more difficult, when bad and harmful habits are involved. It becomes harder still, when it is a case of having to fight some form of addiction (and let us keep in mind that addictions are by no means restricted to alcohol and drugs). People, who are prey to any form of addiction or near-addiction, may resolve over and over again not to give in to their cravings, all the while believing in their own sincerity. Yet they are seldom able to muster enough strength and tenacity of self-direction to carry through what their better insight tells them should be done. When our good reasoning is not in accord with our emotional responses, or in other words, when "The spirit is willing, but the flesh is weak," our mental-emotional self-direction is impaired.

This thwarted capacity to carry out our good intentions, causes inner conflicts and anxiety; it has during our waking condition an effect on us similar to that of so-called anxiety dreams during sleep. For instance, a deep-seated anxiety may manifest itself if we dream of hurrying to pack a suitcase and that all our frantic efforts to do so remain futile. During our waking condition, we generate anxiety and frustration and we magnify the already existing ones, if we brood over what is bothering us without reaching any corrective conclusion and subsequent action. Our inability to convert an intention into action makes us increasingly vulnerable to unavoidable strains. At such times, we maneuver ourselves into a condition of chronic stress which usually results in more or less serious psychological and physiological malfunctions.

Obviously, mental-emotional self-direction can function well only when our emotional responses are, and remain, constructively interlocked with our faculty to think and reason clearly and to evaluate ourselves properly. If this coordination doesn't come naturally, it will have to be acquired in order to ensure psychological well-functioning. This is made possible by the method of hypnoidal self-development. With its combination of conscious preparatory work and the specific use of the hypnoidal stage, this method diminishes negative emotional drives and gradually replaces them with desirable motivations and ways of thinking. As a result, negative emotions will interfere less and less with positive self-direction and cease altogether as you gain new energy and strength of purpose.

PART TWO

SLEEP—

        YOUR SILENT PARTNER

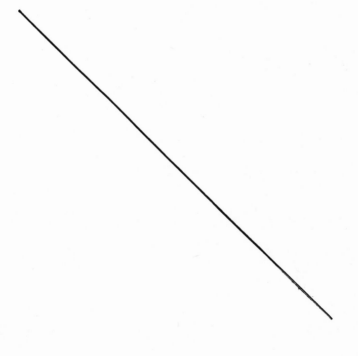

22. WHAT IS SLEEP?

The method of hypnoidal self-development makes the falling-asleep stage (the hypnoidal stage), an incomparable aid to personality-development. It is necessary, however, to make you familiar with the various aspects of natural sleep and also with some peculiarities of dreams, because it will be of added advantage if you understand *why* the use of the hypnoidal stage can help you to fulfill your constructive aspirations.

When we discuss sleep, one question-mark follows another and, in contrast to the exact sciences, we can seldom substantiate our findings. We are forced to leave a very wide field to mere speculation regarding such questions as: "What is sleep?" or "What causes us to sleep?" or "What makes us wake up?" or "What is chronic sleeplessness?" Expert opinions on these matters are as numerous as they are contradictory. Although the question "What is sleep?" has not been fully answered as yet, research has ascertained that during sleep various chemical changes and reactions take place in the blood and in the secretions of the glands; changes also occur in muscle tonus and the rhythms of breathing; the pulse rate slows down and blood pressure is lowered during normal sleep.

If we scrutinize different scientific studies, one school of thought tells us that the cerebral cortex "somehow" causes the process of sleep, whereas, according to the Swiss physiologist and Nobel Prize winner W. R. Hesse, the brain contains a "true sleep center," the sole function of which is to send a person to sleep when he needs it! Another, although not very scientific sounding, explanation is given by a group of scientists; they simply point out that "sleep happens to you when you are not too busy being awake!"

Several controversial opinions have been expressed regarding the effect of fatigue on the cells of the body, or whether sleep results from cerebral congestion or cerebral anaemia. And muscular relaxation is also considered very important to induce sleep; people who were kept awake experimentally could not be permitted to relax physically, because they would doze off when they did so. In order to stay awake, they had to move around constantly or, at least, make use of some of their muscles almost continually. This fact led to the conclusion that complete muscular relaxation is an essential prerequisite for sleep. It has not been ascertained, however, to what extent these people's self-directive mental attitude served as a contributory factor to the deliberate prevention of sleep. Nevertheless, muscular relaxation does contribute extensively to induce sleep. But whatever degree of muscular relaxation may be necessary to favor sleep, the relaxation of the skeletal musculature, though generally increased, is never complete. Taking a few examples from the animal world, birds, for instance, cling, while asleep, to the branches they are perched on; horses sleep standing up, and in human beings, the muscles which close the eyes remain tensed.

Other instances of partial relaxation are the body-positions from which we human beings derive the relaxation necessary for sleep. Like everything else, they vary with the individual. On the point of going to sleep and during sleep, a resemblance to the evolutionary stages has been observed. Some children, and adults also, lie hunched up in the position of an embryo and babies are often inclined to make fists while they sleep and to stick their arms into the air as if they were seeking to hold on to a branch just as their primordial forebears did when they sought protection in trees. Although making a fist is not muscle-relaxing, it doesn't seem to disturb a baby's sound sleep.

23. RELAXATION OF THE MIND
—AND SLEEP

Necessary as muscular relaxation is to falling asleep, the role of relaxation itself is frequently exaggerated and too often is considered as a panacea for every physical, mental and emotional malaise or malfunction. Abraham Myerson pointed this out with some acidity, but also with much truth. "The popular books on psychology," he said, "are almost exclusively fallacious, not only in their optimism, but also in their expressed certainty of knowledge. There are psychiatrists and near-psychiatrists who speak as if they had become the new agents of God, and claim that they can furnish principles fool-proof against illness and despair. One writer says that if you know 'How to relax,' you will be all right mentally, which is like saying that if you gargle with a mouth-wash, you will cure a sore throat, pneumonia and cancer."

Yet, it cannot be denied that a good gargle-mixture may have a soothing effect on a sore throat and make the patient feel better subjectively; although this does not constitute a cure, it might *contribute* to a recovery. It is comparable to the soothing effect of muscular relaxation on a tired body, an effect which may also result in relaxing our minds.

But relaxation of the mind results from muscular relaxation only when and if the soothing effect of physical relaxation is transmitted to the mind. Once the transmittal has taken place, spiritual access to the mind, sometimes even to a more or less severely troubled one, is made easier. In the latter case, however, it takes far stronger measures to produce the required muscular relaxation than routine physical exercises designed to relax the muscles. In other words, only a fundamentally sound mind is strong enough to create the type of relaxation needful to the upkeep of physical *and* mental health.

It is the individual with a basically sound mind who can accept, as well as carry out, the training and conditioning necessary to remain healthy even under adverse and trying circumstances. A sound mind also possesses the faculty to bring about that mental relaxation which opens the door to sleep when sleep is normally due; otherwise a situation is created which Shakespeare described four hundred years ago in one of his Sonnets:

> Weary with toil, I haste me to my bed,
> The dear repose for limbs with travel tir'd.
> But then begins a journey in my head,
> To work my mind, when body's work expir'd.

If in wakefulness you are tense and afraid, confused, or agitated, if you cannot regulate your emotions with good sense and self-discipline, you are sure to remain a victim of your emotional difficulties while you are attempting to fall asleep. For at this stage will begin the "journey in my head to work my mind," and this "journey" will make sleep difficult. But if you can relax your body *and* your mind while you are in the waking condition, you will have a good chance to fall asleep with normal ease and relax body and mind during sleep.

24. OUR PHYSICAL AND MENTAL NEED FOR SLEEP

To everything and to everybody life has set minimum and maximum limits, but these limits differ widely. One instance is the individual need for sleep. I was consulted once by a man who had been extremely worried, because his physician had told him that anyone who complained of "feeling lousy" unless he got nine hours of sleep, was neurotic. I found no indications that would have justified declaring this man a neurotic, although his claim that he needed nine hours of sleep seemed rather exaggerated. Nevertheless, I insisted on his getting those nine hours of sleep. His wife co-operated, and as a result, the allegedly neurotic craving for sleep disappeared after a while and the physician good-naturedly admitted his mistake.

If this were an isolated case, it would not be worth mentioning. However, quite a few medical and psychological pundits assert that *we all* need just so many hours of sleep—no more, no less. And there are "sleep-experts," who hold the debatable opinion that we exaggerate our need for sleep. They affirm that an average of four to five hours of sleep is quite sufficient, saying that we can "bounce back very nicely if we have to!"

This is true—*if we have to,* we can get along, for quite some time, physically and mentally, without the number of sleep-hours we would normally require. Maybe, we can even do without sufficient sleep for a whole lifetime. But that is not the issue. The important point is whether or not we remain healthier, do better work and enjoy life more when we get the amount of sleep we require individually.

In the course of research, several persons were kept awake experimentally for up to one hundred hours. Yet this enforced sleeplessness allegedly did not cause them any lasting harm. On the other hand, we know that for some people a single sleepless night may have quite disturbing consequences. These people will feel abnormally fatigued and extremely irritable, although one subsequent night of sound sleep will usually wipe out these unpleasant aftereffects. Undoubtedly, most of us can adjust physically and mentally to over-fatigue for a certain length of time in such a manner that at least we will appear to be functioning properly. But, unquestionably, we will suffer from the unavoidable after-effects of chronic fatigue caused by prolonged lack of sufficient sleep. In most individuals, the results of too little sleep over long periods will become obvious in a feeling of tension and in having to drag themselves through the waking hours. Finally, this chronic strain and tension will lead to an abnormal increase of mental and emotional irritability. Needless to say, irritability is not exclusively caused by lack of sleep; it can also derive from organic causes or from wrongly oriented mental and emotional attitudes.

However, in an otherwise emotionally well-balanced individual, increasing irritability, one of nature's serious warning signals, might very well be based on lack of sufficient sleep. It always warrants attention and usually makes changes in living-habits advisable.

As a general rule, it is agreed that seven to eight hours of sleep are sufficient for most people. Of course, there are exceptions; to name but two, Humboldt and Leibniz required only three to four hours of sleep in twenty-four hours, and yet they reached old age. While some people, though in good health, require more rest and sleep than the average seven to eight hours, others may need less, and some barely half as much sleep but nevertheless remain perfectly healthy.

What should be regarded as sufficient sleep does not depend on how many or how few hours of sleep a person likes to indulge in. Instead, it depends on the number of sleep-hours necessary to produce the best mental and physical results during waking hours.

Sleep can be a most powerful medicine for body and mind. Nevertheless, an excessive need for sleep may be a symptom of serious physical or mental illness. Usually, the effects of sleep on the mind are benign and blissfully serve to halt the mental revolving door in which our worrisome thoughts may be caught; but some persons seek morbid refuge and protection from reality in an excessive amount of sleep. Exaggerated need for sleep may be the symptom of a deep depression. When the degree of depression is sharply disproportionate to the motivation, or when there is little or no motivation at all, then we are confronted with some form of pathological depression. However, should sufficient reason exist to account for a state of deep depression, then an increased requirement for sleep can help to mitigate the grief or anxiety which caused the depression. For sleep possesses an invaluable power to which Iamblichus referred by saying: "The nighttime of the body is the daytime of the soul."

An exaggerated need for sleep may also be based on laziness and this laziness may stem either from some character-shortcomings, or from neurotic fatigue, or from fatigue called forth by a physical malfunction or disease, such as an abnormally low blood sugar tolerance level or a thyroid deficiency, and so on. Therefore, when a child or an adult seems to be abnormally lazy, a physician should be consulted to check on possible organic causes.

But not every manifestation of laziness need be due to physical malfunctions or imply neurotic symptoms. Some psychological but non-neurotic reason might be contributing to a person's physical discomfort. And, quite apart from all this, in some instances it is actually just plain laziness!

25. ♦ THE FIGHT AGAINST INSOMNIA

The problem of insomnia, of chronic sleeplessness, must be considered briefly here, because it involves the mechanism of falling-asleep. As the falling-asleep stage is of the utmost importance within hypnoidal self-development, obviously anything which interferes with normal sleep and sleep-habits can also affect the proper use of the hypnoidal stage for hypnoidal self-development.

Apart from relaxation, there are certain sleep-patterns and habit-forming influences which often are used as sleep-inducers, but which sometimes may turn into sleep-preventers. One person can sleep only in a completely darkened room, another has to wear ear-stoppers in order to remain undisturbed by any noise, a third will have to arrange his pillows or covers in a certain manner, and so on through innumerable other devices and sleep rituals. A famous general, for instance, is said to have been unable to sleep unless he was wearing an old college T-shirt under his pajamas. A celebrity in the political field is supposed to find sleep only if his harmonica is tucked away under his pillow and a famous actress puts on a flannel nightgown, a bathrobe and a pair of most unglamorous woolen socks whenever she is troubled by sleeplessness. But these examples, and a great many others, should by no means arouse your suspicion that such peculiarities necessarily indicate the strange quirks of a neurotic personality obsessively compelled to do, or refrain from doing, certain things. These peculiarities are simply individual sleep-habits and, although their motivation may be obscure, they needn't be pathological. Even babies and small children have their individual sleep-patterns, a fact which sometimes makes the wish of many an adult that he might sleep "like a baby," appear as an unconsidered remark. A child may demand a drink of milk or water or whatnot, before settling down for sleep and this demand is not always just "naughtiness" and wilful procrastination. It may well be a child's individual sleep-pattern and he may feel instinctively that the milk will help him to go to sleep.

Most children insist on taking to bed a favorite toy or some other trifle of vital significance to them. And we adults, who watch television before we go to bed, or like to read a while before turning off the light, should realize the importance of the bedtime story to some children and, for that matter, the significant role of the cradle song in the earliest stages of childhood.

But in spite of a large industry of mechanical sleep-inducers such as ear-stoppers, muscle massagers, special mattresses and countless other devices, it is said that about fifty-two per cent of the population in the United States complain about sleeplessness.

Insomnia is quite a problem, not only to the person who suffers from this affliction, but also to the physician expected to relieve it. Physicians, of course, do not treat their patients with remedies of the aforementioned kind; usually they prescribe sedatives and sleep-inducing drugs. Although it hasn't been discovered as yet exactly how these drugs function to reduce tension and to induce sleep, we know by experience that modern pharmacology supplies us with remedies which *can* procure relaxation and *do* induce sleep. Of course, nobody should ever avail himself of these and similar drugs such as the so-called "tranquilizers" except when prescribed by a trustworthy physician. Especially in regard to the tranquilizers it is important to know that they do not "cure" and are merely more or less potent supportive aids for psychotherapy. In fact, opinions on these drugs are conflicting, because of their unpredictable physical and mental side-effects on certain persons.

Although it is permissible, and sometimes advisable, to take an occasional sedative, tranquilizer, or a sleep-inducing drug, it is imperative not to become dependent on pharmaceutical crutches.

Efforts should therefore be focused on devising other means with which to provide relief for people who suffer from chronic sleeplessness *not* caused by physical disease and pain or by acute emotional distress.

Treatment of insomnia by suggestions with and without the use of hypnosis has been applied from time immemorial, sometimes, but by no means always, with success. At the Navy Hospital in Memphis, Dr. Ernest Schmidt put a whole ward to sleep by playing a tape recorder with sleep-suggestions. The sleep-inducing effect of these recorded suggestions has often been found to consist in the monotony of the voice reciting the suggestions rather than in the words themselves. Actually, the mere mention of the word "sleep" or "relaxation" may produce quite the opposite result in some insomniacs. Although these people *want* to be relaxed and sleep, their strongly conditioned fear of not being able to sleep is in the foreground of their emotional response and, as a consequence, the word *sleep* may trigger a reaction of restlessness due to anxiety. The fear of not being able to sleep may prevent the insomniac from absorbing the objective meaning of the sleep-suggestion.

This can be easily understood, because suggestive words become effective only in the exact proportion to their capacity to stimulate either positive or negative, favorable or unfavorable emotional responses in the person receiving the suggestions.

Another method of sleep-inducement, sometimes successful, is singing oneself to sleep. By the way, many people will be grateful to the advocates of this "remedy" for emphasizing the necessity not to sing loudly, but to lull oneself to sleep *tonelessly!* The idea of singing yourself to sleep may appeal to you, especially if you agree with the old saying: "Try singing yourself to sleep and you will wake up with a song in your heart!" But you might reconsider on learning that you are supposed to get both lyrics and melody of the song completely right and refrain from letting your mind wander! You are told to penalize yourself for woolgathering by beginning your song all over again from the first line. The idea behind this procedure was to make you concentrate so intensely that the worry or excitement which is keeping you awake, will be crowded out. I cannot see any great advantage to waging so severe a struggle against mind-wandering as such sustained concentration interferes with the initial relaxation conducive to sleep.

The procedure of singing yourself to sleep may become more successful if you modify the strict rules and concentrate less intensely on the avoidance of mind-wandering, but do your singing—tonelessly—in a more mechanical and therefore more relaxed manner. Just try to remember melody and lyrics, then hum them in your mind. Sometimes you will only recall the melody, at other times only the lyrics, but continue with either melody or lyrics or both, until you feel increasingly drowsy and finally fall asleep. When you try to remember the song you have selected, never try hard to remember, because this effort could make you feel tense and restless and therefore wakeful again.

Now, let us abandon the method of the "music-makers" to combat sleeplessness and consider what the Danish psychiatrist Dr. Magnussen has to say in his report to the National Association for Mental Health in New York. Dr. Magnussen recommends that you visualize a restful landscape, with which you are familiar. You are supposed to fill in all the details of the picture and then to concentrate on some small part of it. You should try to hold this section of the visualized picture in your imagination; but if outside thoughts interfere, you have to fill in all the details of the picture and then to concentrate on some small part of it. You should try to hold this section of the visualized picture in your imagination; but if outside thoughts interfere, you have to start all over again, evoking the same picture and concentrating on the same section. Dr. Magnussen states that with this "landscape method," emotionally tinged thoughts interfering with sleep are kept away.

For some people this may have a better effect than simply counting sheep. By the way, I recommend the following modified versions of the well-known sleep-inducing method of counting sheep. Instead of counting straight up to one hundred, or back from one hundred to one, in order to woo sleep, the count goes as follows:

(a) 1, 3, 5, 7, 9, 11, 13, 15, 17, 19, 21, 23, 25, 27, 29, 31, 33 . . . . and so on up to hundred and one, or more, and then back again: 101, 99, 97, 95, 93, 91, 89, 87, 85, 83, 81, 79, 77 . . . . and so on, back to one.

(b) 1, 2, 3, 4, 5——4, 3, 2, 1——2, 3, 4, 5, 6——5, 4, 3, 2, 1——
2, 3, 4, 5, 6, 7——6, 5, 4, 3, 2, 1——2, 3, 4, 5, 6, 7, 8——
7, 6, 5,
4, 3, 2, 1——2, 3, 4, 5, 6, 7, 8, 9——8, 7, 6, 5, 4, 3, 2, 1——
1, 2,
3, 4, 5, 6, 7, 8, 9, 10——9, 8, 7, 6, 5, 4, 3, 2, 1——and so on.

(c) 1, 4, 7, 10, 13, 16, 19——17, 15, 13, 11, 9, 7, 5, 3, 1——
1, 5, 9, 13, 17, 21, 25——22, 19, 16, 13, 10, 7, 4, 1——
1, 6, 11, 16, 21, 26, 31——27, 23, 19, 15, 11, 7, 3——
3, 9, 15, 21, 27, 33, 39——34, 29, 24, 19, 14, 9, 4——
4, 11, 18, 25, 32, 39, 46——40, 34, 28, 22, 16, 10, 4——

and so on. As you see, the method to count in (c) requires
that, at first, you add 3 and you deduct 2; in the second row you
add 4 and deduct 3; in the third row, you add 5 and deduct 4; and
so on. You start out each new row with the last digit of the preceding row. Continue this pattern until you feel drowsy and don't give
up too soon. It may take you from five to twenty minutes to fall
asleep.

If you prefer to count as shown in (a), you may have to count up
to one hundred, or two hundred, or even more; or you may prefer,
once you have reached one hundred or two hundred without getting drowsy, to start out again and count up to one hundred or two
hundred. Almost every person has an instinctive feeling about these
things and chooses that pattern which suits him best.

Should you prefer example (b), you may have to repeat this
pattern until you reach fifty, or even more. If it takes you longer
than approximately half an hour before you get really drowsy, then
you had better design another pattern for counting, one which clicks
better with your falling-asleep mechanism. Sometimes it is advisable to design one's own pattern of counting; besides, it is preferable
to use several patterns interchangeably. These patterns are quite
successful in making people drowsy; they are not as simple as
"counting sheep," which is routine counting and therefore doesn't
succeed so well in preventing other thoughts from crowding in.
On the other hand, it is not so strenuous as the other concentration
methods which often contribute to tension and consequently interfere with the onset of sleep. In this sense, Dr. Magnussen's land-

scape-method of inducing sleep, like other similar methods, can be effective only when the picture, song, or whatever other vehicle is used, does not cause too much tension due to the effort of intense concentration and, in addition, does not call forth conscious or unconscious associations of an unpleasant or exciting nature. After all, it is not strain, mental, physical, or emotional strain, that brings on sleep; it is pleasant relaxation and a temporary remoteness from emotionally loaded thoughts that make falling asleep easier.

There is an exception to this rule, however. Should unhappiness cause a person to cry bitterly, he may cry himself to sleep. Here again we lack an explanation why this is so, whereas other strong emotions or moods, unhappy as well as happy ones, usually prevent us from going to sleep.

Disadvantageous to falling asleep are those methods in which concentrated effort may combine either with excessive stimulation or with boredom, a state which, contrary to common belief, does not always relax, but may give rise to acute tension. Therefore, I consider a preferable device for falling asleep the solving of not too complicated brain-teasers, easy mathematical problems, not too difficult puzzles, and the like. Try to solve them in your mind and, should you become sufficiently interested, your mind will be prevented quite automatically from wandering. This eliminates the strain of "penalties" such as having to start over and over again as soon as another thought interferes with perfect concentration; consequently normal fatigue sets in much easier and leads you into natural sleep.

But whether you fall asleep with normal ease, or find it quite a struggle, your personality is a determining factor. If you are well-balanced emotionally, falling asleep and sleeping, as a rule, will give you little trouble. On the other hand, if you cannot direct your thoughts and emotions, or if you are not in command of yourself during your waking condition, you may fail to derive from sleep that regeneration of your mental and physical strength, which sound sleep normally provides. Consequently, the quality and the quantity of your rest and sleep will likewise benefit from the favorable development of your personality-traits and the strengthening of your faculty of constructive mental-emotional self-direction.

26. VARIOUS STIMULI AFFECT YOUR SLEEP-MECHANISM

No two persons will react in the same way to the stimuli which bombard us incessantly awake or asleep. It is imperative for the reader to realize the powerful influence which stimuli of all kinds exert on our mental and emotional make-up. This is all the more essential, because their influence becomes strongly intensified while we are about to fall asleep. Thus the role of stimuli in the method of hypnoidal self-development is most important and for this reason, we have to become better acquainted with the vast variety of stimuli and some of the effects on us.

Experiments with direct stimulation of the brain by electricity— as a stimulus coming from without—have produced all the features of wakefulness in sleeping animals, whereas restriction or destruction of the brain-stem has put animals into a pathological condition of sleep. These recent investigations into the mechanism of natural sleep have led to the conclusion that the brain-stem, which forms the connection between brain and spinal cord, promotes sleep or sustains wakefulness. But *how* the brain-stem works to control sleep and wakefulness is not yet quite clear.

Another theory is that impulses are sent out by an electric relay in the brain and received, as well as responded to, at the base of the brain. The impulse-current between the higher parts of the brain and the body can thus function undisturbed while we are awake, but during *transition* into sleep the intensity of this current is reduced until the critical minimum has been reached. At this point the current is allegedly too weak to keep the relay closed. Consequently, the circuit between brain and body is interrupted and nerve impulses are prevented from reaching the higher parts of the brain. In other words, the nerve impulses are too weak to project their message into consciousness, unless the stimuli become so intensive that they re-activate the mechanism of this impulse current, thereby closing the relay which was open during sleep.

Regarding the effects of external and internal stimuli in regulating sleep and waking, it is assumed that a lessening of external stimuli induces sleep. However, by some kind of mechanism, our perception of sensory stimuli is sometimes diminished or even shut out altogether, although the stimuli are still present in the same intensity as before they ceased to be apparent to us. This mechanism is an unknown quantity; we don't know *how* it functions, but it is assumed as probable that we possess this sleep-mechanism. It has been observed, besides, that some external sensory stimuli don't interfere with sleep, but actually help to induce sleep; the regular beat of a metronome, for instance, or the sound of falling rain are usually favorable to sleep, whereas the equally monotonous sound of a dripping faucet may interfere mercilessly with sleep.

Why is it that some types of monotonous sound promote sleep while others prevent it? Perhaps the sound of a dripping faucet interferes with sleep because of a component of annoyance directed either against ourselves or someone else, for not having turned off that faucet properly. Consciously, we may not even register the origin of our emotional disturbance; nevertheless, it ferments in us with increasing force and thus prevents us from relaxing and going to sleep. This example of exasperation in the "Case of the Dripping Faucet" may serve to indicate how dramatically some stimuli, whether consciously perceived or unconsciously absorbed, may provoke emotions and therefore interfere with sleep.

Imagine yourself sleeping peacefully and deeply. Then, gradually, you become aware of a clanging sound beating with measured insistence on your auditory senses until, at a certain moment, you are wide enough awake to recognize what is taking place. Now you remember that you are serving as a guinea-pig in an experiment to measure the intensity and duration of external stimuli required to wake you from sleep. Experiments are being carried out for this purpose nowadays; the measurements, however, cannot be quite accurate, because in addition to the measurable *external* stimuli, the sleeper is usually subject to *internal* stimuli which can hardly be evaluated by these measurements. Yet these internal stimuli may be strong enough to awaken the sleeper or contribute toward waking him. For instance, there is the stimulus of the sphincter muscles of the bladder which contract during sleep and build up pressure in the bladder to the point of waking the sleeper. Or, to give another example, a lowering of the blood sugar level, caused by lack of nourishment during sleep, might produce contraction of the stomach walls, creating a sensation of hunger. This is sufficient to waken the sleeper under certain circumstances, although, once awake, he may not feel particularly hungry and therefore does not realize what woke him up. Of course, these are only a few examples of physical impulses functioning as internal stimuli to awaken the sleeper.

Other stimuli, strong enough to break through sleep, stem from completely different sources. There is the well-known experience of a mother who, having fallen into a sleep of exhaustion at the bedside of her sick child, cannot be roused even by the loudest noise. Yet a faint sound coming from her child will awaken her immediately. How can we explain this? Probably by the mother's apprehension and expectation of having to assist the child. Besides, it may be that the emotional rapport between mother and child becomes extraordinarily intensified by an anxiety-laden situation and hence converts every sound coming from the child into an associative stimulus powerful enough to penetrate the mother's sleep.

But apart from a *sentimental* emotional rapport like the aforementioned one, there is also a *professional* rapport, conditioned by professional training. This rapport can be observed in a good nurse who likewise may wake up whenever her patient moves. To give an example of an entirely different kind of internal stimulus: many people can resolve before they fall asleep, to wake up at a certain time and will actually succeed in waking within seconds of the pre-determined hour. The "inner alarm-clock" may be triggered by impulses rising from the nervous system and by signals sent forth by the brain as a *result of pre-sleep thoughts, wishes, or commands.*

But there are times when the brain does not or cannot convey to the body the command to act or to feel in a certain way. This happens when messages sent from the body to the brain, or vice versa, become blocked or transformed within the nervous system. This fact can be substantiated by a very simple experiment. If one tickles the sole of a normal individual's foot, provided the individual is awake, his toes will curl *inward* as if they wanted to grasp something. Yet, if the nervous impulses leading through the spinal cord are blocked at some point, the reaction will be reversed and the toes curl *upwards*. For the neurologist, this may be an important diagnostic sign, because the upward curling of toes when the sole is tickled, may constitute a symptom of disease if it occurs *while the person is awake*. Strangely enough, the same upward curling of the toes when the sole of a foot is tickled *while a person is asleep, or in narcosis,* may be a normal reaction. This experiment shows us the *great changes nervous impulses may undergo, depending on whether we are in a waking, or in a sleeping condition.*

During a nightmare, for instance, the sleeper may be quite aware of the terrifying situation; he may even know what would help him to escape this situation, yet *he is incapable of translating into action what he wants to do*. He feels blocked and this incapacity is sometimes more torturing to the dreamer than the nightmarish terrors threatening him. In fact, the dream sequence may not contain any threatening danger at all and lack the quality of a nightmare. Its content may be an ordinary occurrence like running after a bus and never catching up with it. In these cases, the brain sends out messages as usual to certain parts of the body. But for reasons rarely explicable, these messages, stimulated by sensations and images during the dream, have become blocked at some point in their journey along the nerve pathways and cannot reach their destination. And here we touch on the phenomenon of dreaming, a field in which a tremendous amount of scientific investigation has been and is being undertaken.

27. ◆ THE RIDDLE OF DREAMS

A great deal has already been discovered about dreaming, yet much more remains guesswork. The answers given to the questions, "What makes us dream?" and "Do we always dream while asleep?" are therefore so contradictory that they leave us more perplexed than enlightened.

From a *physiological* point of view, we have learned that people who were used as subjects in experiments, showed a particular pattern of rapid jerky eye-movements occurring several times during the night. Each time the subjects were awakened while their eyes were still twitching, they said they had just been dreaming, but they could not say what they had been dreaming about. The eye-movements were recorded by electrodes attached to the skin above, below, and on each side of the subjects' eyes. At the same time, wires of an electro-encephalograph were attached to the subjects' heads to record their brain-waves. With all these wires affixed to them, the subjects went to sleep—a feat I profoundly admire—and the eye-twitching occurred after a subject had slept from one to one and a half hours. Usually the subjects dreamed for about fifteen minutes, but sometimes for as long as an hour. Then the eye-twitching stopped, but it started again after approximately a couple of hours. The conclusion drawn from these experiments was that the eye-movements did *not* continue without interruption during sleep, but were concurrent with dreaming; therefore dreaming was not incessant during sleep. However, we cannot be sure whether our eyes *always* twitch when we are dreaming, or *whether the twitching only occurs in particular types of dreams, or only in some individuals, or whether everybody's eyes twitch during every dream!* Besides, as sleep and dreams are easily influenced by the sleep situation, we could also ask whether the twitching might not be favored by the experimental "over-wiring" of the sleeper!

So far, no apparatus or device employed to discover *when, why* and *what* we dream, has fulfilled our hopes of obtaining any definite answers. Endeavors to approach the psychical realm of dreams scientifically have been equally unsuccessful. It is with a feeling of relief therefore, that we turn to Doctor Frederik van Eeden, a Dutch neurologist who in 1913 expressed a warning as timely today as it was then. He said: "It is against this scientific arrogance that I utter a warning. No theory has as yet explained *all* about dreams; no! not even the tiniest part. We have not yet crossed the threshold of that world."

Long before the physical "wiring" experiments were made, scientists such as Havelock Ellis had concluded that dreaming was *not* continuous during sleep, whereas Freud and many of those who probed deeply into the psychic manifestations of sleep, believed that we dream incessantly while asleep. But to us it is less important whether or not we dream ceaselessly during sleep than to know what dreams may reveal about ourselves.

Saint Augustine once said: "How thankful am I to Thee, dear Lord, that I am not responsible for my dreams!" To us, this statement seems rather cryptic, as we would have to agree first on what we mean by being or not being responsible for our dreams. We would be *directly* responsible, if we could plan our dreams voluntarily as, for instance, by resolving: "This night I am going to dream about my father," or "I will dream that all my debts are paid and I have all the money I want," or "This night I'll see myself in Africa hunting big game," and then actually have a made-to-order dream. The fact that we hardly ever succeed in dreaming what we deliberately set out to dream, cuts down our *direct* responsibility, although our *indirect* responsibility subsists. For our dreams, most of the time reflect, partially at least, those facets of our personality which we refuse to realize. All kinds of emotions and thoughts also prey on our minds and follow us into sleep. In addition, there are those emotions and thoughts which we repress or try to suppress, yet they abide with us faithfully and become transposed into the symbolic and hard-to-decipher language of dreams.

28. ◆ DREAM-INTERPRETATION

Three hundred years before Sigmund Freud, Montaigne, the French philosopher and essayist said: "I believe it to be true that dreams are the true interpreters of our indications, but there is art required to sort and to understand them." These words give testimony that Montaigne considered dreams as the interpreters of what we *are* and realized that a connection existed between the content of our dreams and our personality.

In spite of the fact that we cannot divorce the content of our dreams from what we fundamentally are, the symbolic language of dreams in its specific relation to the dreamer is very difficult to interpret correctly. Consciously accepted values frequently become either magnified or minimized in our dreams, and quite often something which consciously causes us great concern becomes only a minor disturbance in our dreams and vice versa. The element of time, for instance, may be distorted or completely lost within the dream-content, whereas other factors such as the effect of colors might remain linked to the dreamer's conscious attitude towards colors. Dream-interpretation may deteriorate into a farce or, as Montaigne has said, it can be an art—and art is based on intuition, knowledge, skill and honesty. These ingredients of art also determine the qualification to interpret dreams. When dream-interpretation penetrates to the under-currents of the conscious behavior-patterns and reveals the connections between them and the unconscious, then the interpretation of dreams can be made the key to our personality.

Let me give you a few glimpses now into the complexities of dream-interpretation, because similar complexities may prevail when we set out to interpret our personality. For instance, dream-interpretation reveals most clearly how carefully we should abstain from generalizations. Let us visualize a husband and wife sitting at breakfast one bright morning. "She" says to "Him": "Darling, I had the strangest and silliest dream last night; I have forgotten most of it, but I remember running up and down stairs again and again." With a knowing smile "He" answers: "Oh, that is an easy one! It means you were in an amorous mood, dear." Whereupon "She" displays a rather skeptical smile and says: "You are wrong, dear, it was a most unpleasant dream, I assure you." But the husband knows better; he is an amateur dream-interpreter and has read several books on this subject by Freud and other analysts and psychologists. Consequently, he is convinced that he has the right answer, because, after all, he is only repeating what he remembers from those books.

Yet it is not quite that simple. According to Freud, it is the rhythmical movement of sex-activities which reappears in dream-actions such as climbing stairs, ladders, and so on. The acceleration of movement, of breathing, the leaping forward when running downstairs, are seen by Freud as some of the dreamer's symbolical devices to disguise his desire for sex-activity. No doubt Freud had valid reasons to apply this symbolism to the dream-material which led him to offer that interpretation. But it doesn't follow that *all* dreams of climbing or descending stairs, or similar dreams, should invariably be given a sexual meaning. As has been mentioned previously, consideration should be accorded also to the residue of recent thoughts, emotions and activities taken into our dreams and which are often those of the day just lived through. A housewife, who dreams of climbing stairs, may be obliged to run up and down stairs countless times a day and she can scarcely be blamed for not enjoying it. She may also have experienced some annoyance during the day, perhaps only a minor one and completely unrelated to climbing stairs, yet this specific annoyance was nevertheless strong enough to stimulate her chronic gripe at always having to run up and down the stairs, and so that is what she dreamt about.

Of course, our dreams are not influenced by the residue of the past day only. The changing world we live in also affects our personality and with it our dreams. For example, in the eighteen-nineties a housewife may have dreamt she was climbing stairs, carrying buckets of coal from the cellar to the top floor of the house. Today, a housewife living in the city might dream she is carrying a large bag of groceries up several flights of stairs, because the elevator isn't working. Why did they have these particular dreams? Probably "Mrs. Nineteenth Century" disliked trudging up and down stairs with heavy loads of coal, whereas "Mrs. Twentieth Century" resents the fact that the elevator in her apartment house is out of commission too often, forcing her to use the stairs. And so they re-live their resentment by projecting into their dream "what is eating them."

A dream about climbing stairs might also be a sex dream or could equally be caused by some organic stimulus, by gastric distress, for instance. The accompanying physical discomfort may cause the sleeper's breathing to become very heavy and, dreaming in pictures and images as we do, he may find himself breathlessly climbing stairs.

Dreams, insofar as they can be interpreted with any degree of certainty, depend on multiple factors and therefore should never be explained by tagging them with a handy list of ready-made symbolic meanings. One and the same symbol usually has a great many meanings and will have a different significance when occurring in the dreams of different people under different circumstances. There are conscious and unconscious identifications with people, animals, objects; in short, all kinds of external and internal stimuli produce dreams, all *individually shaded by the personality of the dreamer*. The interpretation of a man's sensual dream about a colored woman, for instance, will differ perforce from the interpretation of the same dream by a man who lives in a district populated mostly by Negroes. Generalizations are always a great mistake, but if applied when attempting to interpret dreams, they may become dangerous. The popularization of psychological dream-interpretation, supposedly revealing "deep-seated wishes" or reflecting character-attributes, can be confusing, sometimes ridiculous, and at other times pernicious.

Primitive as well as ancient symbols sometimes appear in dreams and their interpretive value can be most enlightening. Some of the manifold meanings embodied in these symbols are not yet quite erased from our unconscious, whereas others have lost their original meaning for us and the objects to which they refer have long ceased to impart any of their former significance to our emotions and our thinking. For example, the ancient peoples who offered up animals in sacrifice to their gods, ascribed great prophetic importance to the entrails of their sacrificial victims. But if we in our day happen to dream about animal intestines, it would hardly be accurate to evaluate the dream-material in terms of ancient symbolism, unless indicated by particular circumstances. If we believe exclusively in the dogmatism of Freud, then we interpret the twisted coils of intestines as the umbilical cord or as the thread of Ariadne leading out of the labyrinth! And there are other and rather involved analytical interpretations, which have nothing in common with the ancient significance of dreams about intestines. However, it is quite possible that our dream was merely the result of a memory retained after a visit to the butcher on the previous day.

A woman who tells of dreaming about snakes may find an amused expression on the faces of those listening to her. "Oho! so you dreamed about snakes," somebody is likely to chuckle. For anybody with a superficial knowledge of Freud's writings will immediately recall that the snake is a phallic symbol. Well, this is correct, but even in the ancient symbolic language, the image of the snake had various meanings. Therefore, when a woman dreams of snakes, she is not necessarily expressing a "naughty" thought in a symbolically disguised dream.

But if those who are listening to the woman telling her dream of snakes are more given to superstition than to psychoanalytical dream-interpretation, they may see in the same dream "suspected falsehood among friends" or the "foreboding of some evil" or whatnot! But even the superstitions of dreambooks are changeable. The older dreambooks tell us that dreaming of a loose tooth signifies the death of a close relative, whereas freckles on a woman's face announce the approach of "many displeasing incidents"! The more modern prophetic dreambooks inform us that a loose tooth means an impending airplane accident and freckles on a woman's face bluntly indicate "You drive too fast!"

If we were tempted to employ a similarly oversimplified technique in psychological dream-interpretation, then after dreaming about "pale pastry," we would only have to consult Freud to find that pale pastry means "nudity of the body"! Psychoanalytical dream-interpretation definitely overemphasizes and overgeneralizes the importance of sex in dreams, although dreams do provide a great variety of symbols by which our consciously inhibited instinctual drives may find release. But it is going to extremes to interpret dogmatically as symbols of the male sex organ all and any elongated objects dreamed of such as knives, tree-trunks, nail files, umbrellas, and so on, and to consider every dream about cavities, ships, boxes, cups and other open receptacles as symbolizing the female orifice. An attitude of mind which sees nothing but certain parts of the human body in all forms and shapes created by nature, by art, or imitated by craftsmanship, impresses one as almost pathetic and indicates regression to modes of thinking intrinsic to primitive peoples and small children. Both primitives and children are likely to seek a way to comprehend the outside world by identifying parts of their bodies with external objects. In children, this stage may sometimes continue into puberty, but in the course of normal development, it is superseded by more mature mental imagery and emotional reactions. To carry the attitudes of primitives and children into adulthood—and in an exaggerated form at that—would seem to indicate deviation toward a pathological form of thinking.

The interpreters of dreams say that we often reveal our instinctual drives by the kind of animals we see in dreams and by the way they behave toward us. If we dream of a dog who seems unhappy, it indicates, according to Jung and the Swiss psychiatrist Aeppli, that our emotional life is neglected, because the dog generally has a close emotional connection with us. Should a dog threaten us in a dream or warn us not to pass him, then we are "on the wrong track" in some way. When we dream that we are riding a horse, it may mean that we are on good terms with our instinctual drives and that we know how to control them—or, at least, that we are on the best way to regulate them. Very dark horses are said to signify anxiety and destructive sensual drives. White horses stand for psychical strength—but they may also reflect foggy thinking and too much fantasy. If we dream of snakes, it may indicate anxiety— but they can also be the announcers of wise ideas. The color of snakes is said to play an essential role in their symbolic significance; white and golden snakes have a favorable meaning according to Jung and so have snakes which we dream of as steel-blue. Yellow-black and black-red snakes point to unfavorable instinctual drives. If we see a great agglomeration of snakes, our emotions are quite confused, almost chaotic; and if a snake bites our heel, we are the slaves of our sexual desires.

As you can see, the interpretation of dreams may lead to endless contradictions, which is most unlikely to stop people from taking an enormous interest in this mystifying subject. Man has tried to interpret dreams long before their important role in the modern search for knowledge of the human mind was anticipated. Cicero had a great deal to say about dreams and some of the conclusions he drew are as apt in our day as they were in his. Cicero tells us of "a certain matron, who was very anxious to have children and who doubted whether she was pregnant or not. She dreamed one night that her womb was sealed up; she therefore asked a sooth-sayer whether her dream signified pregnancy. He answered: 'No, for the sealing implied that there could be no conception.' But an-other, whom she consulted, said that her dream plainly proved her pregnancy, for vessels that have nothing in them are never sealed at all." Cicero adds: "How delusive then, is the conjectural art of those interpreters! Or do these stories that I have recited, and a host of similar ones which the stoics have collected, prove anything else but the subtlety of men, who, from certain imaginary analogies of things arrive at all sorts of opposite conclusions."

All this emphasizes the necessity to abolish indiscriminate gen-eralization of dream-symbols, if dream-interpretation is to become what it actually can and should be in the words of Freud, "the royal road to the unconscious." Otherwise, dream-interpretation will be degraded to resemble the kind of ludicrous superstition we find in so-called prophetic dream-books.

29. ◆ DISGUISED AND UNDISGUISED DREAM-STIMULI

Dreams are stimulated in manifold ways; they may spring from many sources and embroider our sleep with a crazy-quilt variety of patterns. Dream symbols are often quite simple and sometimes there is no symbolic disguise at all. Other dream symbols are so complex that they cannot be successfully interpreted without a thorough knowledge of the dreamer's personality and of his life-circumstances and some dreams don't lend themselves to any form of interpretation.

If we consult Carl Gustav Jung and listen to a few of his thoughts about dreams, we learn that "the dream is the small hidden door in the deepest and most intimate sanctum of the soul. . . . The dream is apparently occupied with extremely silly details . . . we have always to overcome a certain resistance before we can seriously set about disentangling the intricate web . . . we find ourselves deep in the dreamer's secrets and discover with astonishment that an apparently quite senseless dream is in the highest degree significant . . . dreams contribute to psychological self-guidance . . . It is impossible to interpret a dream with any degree of certainty unless we know what the conscious situation is . . . My researches have clearly shown that the sexual language of the dream is . . . an archaic language . . . without necessarily referring to any recent sexual incident . . . there is no simple and generally known theory of psychic phenomena, either as regards their nature, their cause, or their purpose. We have therefore no general standard of judgement." (*Psychological Reflections.*)

These words indicate clearly the ambiguity of Freud's statement that "the dream is the hidden fulfillment of a repressed wish." Although Freud modified this viewpoint in later years, many of his followers still adhere to it. Consciously, of course, we cannot recognize the nature of a repressed wish as long as it remains repressed. Should anyone harbor the repressed wish to kill, that wish could manifest itself in the oddest physical and/or psychological symptoms as well as in disguised and undisguised dream images. Once this repressed wish to kill has come to be recognized (by means of analysis), it will be necessary to investigate whether the wish to kill is directed towards any one person or is an indeterminate drive. It must also be established whether the drive to kill, or to *destroy* in general, is continual, or only occurs at certain times under certain circumstances. Usually, the hidden drive to destroy remains repressed and only becomes apparent in occasional dreams.

But not all wishful dreams are based on repression. Let us assume that you love somebody very much, but you can not be with this person. Or, perhaps, you long to go to some particular place or country, and are unable to do so. The person you love, or the place you long to visit, may enter your dreams without any disguise and thus give you the satisfaction of a wish-fulfillment denied you in reality. Here we have neither a repressed wish nor a hidden wish-fulfillment, but the projection of a conscious wish into a dream.

Unfortunately, anxiety dreams are much more frequent than wish-fulfillment dreams. In anxiety dreams, justified or imagined fears and frustrations of the past or present, as well as those fears and frustrations which we apprehensively anticipate, show themselves in disguised and undisguised forms and images. Among these are the so-called typical anxiety dreams such as the dream of running to catch a train and missing it. The dreamer will feel excessive pressure and be in great haste to reach the railroad depot, but all sorts of happenings prevent him from catching his train. No doubt, our grandparents experienced similar sensations of catastrophe and frustration when they dreamed of missing the stage-coach. Well, sometimes that kind of dream can be based on a tangible apprehension. For instance, if a person who has never before left his small home town, is about to set out on the adventure of traveling to

New York, then we can understand his uneasiness. Consciously, he may be very happy about the trip, yet unconsciously he may be apprehensive of strange people and surroundings.

Another tangible reason for the "missed my train" dream may be a sick person's fear that traveling will entail physical discomfort and so he takes his more or less justified anxiety into his dream. But this type of anxiety dream may also occur when there is no past or projected trip involved and, like any other so-called typical anxiety dream, it may indicate *displaced* anxiety derived from a completely different source. The examination-dream, and most of us probably have known examination-jitters of some kind by experience, is a typical anxiety dream; strangely enough, the examination dream very often disguises anxiety unconnected with actual reasons for fear. Therefore, if somebody has frequent examination-dreams, it could indicate the indefinite form of *free-floating* anxiety not attached to any particular situation.

Other "typical" dreams are *flying* and *falling* dreams. In psychoanalytical dream-interpretation, certain types of motion such as flying and falling are correlated to sex. Flying-dreams are usually considered as pleasurable; but then again the sex-pleasure might be associated with the concept of the "forbidden fruit," thus instilling a component of anxiety into the dream. The psychic as well as the physical inciters of falling, flying, floating, swimming dreams are countless.

If anyone dreams of falling, a sensual longing may be expressed by his dream, but it may be coupled with fears, with taboos, conflicting with his desire. We can go a step farther and refer to the well-known generalized interpretation according to which women have "falling dreams," if their conflict involves "moral falling." But it cannot be stressed often enough that generalized interpretations of falling dreams as of any other dreams are only applicable if the personality of the dreamer and his life-circumstances substantiate this type of interpretation. The dreamer is just as likely to have projected residues of other actual events or emotions into his falling-dream. For instance, having seen somebody fall down might have kindled anxiety and, consequently, he may have identified himself in his dream with the person who fell. Somehow or other, most of us find it extremely funny to see a fellow human being fall down. The person who has a falling dream after having seen such an incident may be afraid of being ridiculed or may resent having been ridiculed in the past. Therefore, seeing a fall may have stimulated an unconscious association which later served as a pretext to express pent-up emotional discomfort in a dream. An uncomfortable position in bed affecting a person's sense of equilibrium can also bring on a falling dream.

Events of general interest are often woven into our dreams. Necessarily, the contents of dreams are stimulated by contemporary events. With all the new customs, inventions and discoveries of our times, even a period of a few years will cause changes in dream contents. During World War I, a soldier might have dreamed of the long-range cannon "Big Bertha"; today's soldier is more likely to dream of jets, missiles and atomic bombs. But not only the soldier's dreams may be influenced by the tools of war. As the evils of war are carried so very much more directly into everybody's life than ever before in history, the fear of powerful weapons will enter the dreams of the general population. Consciously, we may not register any particular signs of fear, yet this fear might show up in our dreams. Even the symbolical disguises of our dream-contents become modernized and emotions as old as mankind often assume attributes of the epoch we live in.

The following dream illustrates how the dream-inciter, in this case a draft-notice, stimulates the use of modern symbols. Having just received his draft-notice, the dreamer, a college student, Tom, told me: "I would prefer not to go into service until I finish college but if I admit this openly, I would be considered unpatriotic. I don't want people to think that I am afraid and I wonder whether I am! Quite often I dream of mushrooms and of atomic explosions in which the smoke bellows out in a mushroom shape." Well, it is quite natural that Tom is afraid of war, for people *do* dread war. But there are other aspects to his dream and among them are the "mushrooms," about which Tom dreams often and in different forms.

According to the accepted psychoanalytical interpretation, the mushroom is considered as a male sex symbol and an explosion serves as the symbolic disguise for sex-excitement. Thus, sex factors may have influenced this young man's dreams to a greater or lesser extent. However, his dreams were also a projection of images, nowadays strongly impressed on people's minds. We know that actual events will evoke different responses in different people and dreams are always affected by the individuality of the dreamer. It is for this reason that the aforementioned dream lends itself very well to demonstrate how strongly character-attributes may show up in dreams. The manner in which Tom expresses his fear of appearing "unpatriotic" indicates that he has not the courage to admit to himself: "I love my country—but I am not eager to die for it." Consciously, he is not worried about these conflicting feelings; he is merely afraid of how other people might interpret his action. This shows not only his tendency to attach too much importance to other people's opinions, but it also may point to a craving for sympathy. Tom may not get enough affection and love, or he may, as so many do, crave for more than he can reasonably expect. To show himself "unpatriotic" would, of course, make him lose people's sympathy and respect and, by the way, in a dream, *several* people may symbolize only *one* person and so Tom may be afraid to lose one specific person's sympathy and respect. But Tom's conscious attitude towards his dreams may also give an indication that he strives to be accepted by a certain group or class of people or, possibly, only by one particular person, and he is afraid of being rebuffed.

The subject of dreams is almost inexhaustible. The reader who wishes to avail himself of further information will find references in the "List of Books Recommended for Additional Reading."

3O. DREAM CONTENTS AND OUR HEALTH

The kind of thoughts which we take along into our sleep affects us deeply, because thoughts may stimulate our dreams or, to put it metaphorically, the bell-ringer has let go of the rope, yet the sound-waves created by the bell continue to reverberate through the air.

During sleep, we are affected physiologically and psychologically by the favorable or unfavorable qualities of our dreams. In accordance with them, we shall either benefit or fail to benefit from the physical and mental rest and regeneration which sound sleep supplies.

The unfavorable content of a dream may cause the same detrimental reactions to which we can be subjected while we are awake —reactions of fear and worry, jealousy, resentment and hostility, reactions to being under excessive mental-emotional pressure, and so on. The contents of our dreams may, in addition to their psychological effects on us, influence our heartbeat, our digestion, respiration, blood pressure, the secretion of our glands as well as other physiological functions and thereby cause all kinds of discomfort which we painstakingly try to avoid when awake. Yet, while we are awake, we have the advantage most of the time of being able to counteract unfavorable emotions and their injurious consequences by sound mental-emotional self-direction, whereas in sleep this ability is suspended. However, if we succeed in directing our thoughts and emotions positively while we are awake, then any harmful unconscious undercurrents which may lurk in the deepest depths of our mind, will become less and less active and infiltrate our dreams less and less frequently.

Positive thought-content which we encourage during our waking-condition cannot, of course, always warrant sound sleep and pleasant dreams. But more often than not, positive thoughts and constructive thought-direction will counterbalance beneficially the unfavorable undercurrents of the unconscious and prevent them from infiltrating our dreams.

The influence of dreams on our physical and mental well-being is made quite clear by the difference in how we feel on awakening after having had a pleasant or an unpleasant dream. Even if we don't recall the contents of a pleasant dream, it can, nevertheless, give us a distinct sensation of physical and mental well-being on awakening. What is more, we may not remember that we have dreamed at all, yet somehow we just *know* that everything will work out for the best. On the other hand, if we have had an unpleasant dream, we may be abnormally listless after waking up from sleep. And sometimes, although we don't remember what we dreamt or that we dreamt at all, futility may threaten to become the keynote of the day, in spite of our inability to realize what is bothering us.

How can pleasant or unpleasant dreams, the contents of which we don't remember, cause either well-being or distress? In his *Conversations with Eckermann,* the great German poet Goethe puts it this way: "Human nature possesses wonderful powers and has something good in readiness for us when we least hope for it . . . in my dreams the most charming forms have come to console and cheer me, and I have risen the next morning fresh and joyful."

But the real answer is contained in the fact that our conscious thoughts with their positive or negative contents extend their influence to our dream activities during sleep. Should a negative influence prevail, then this influence with its elements of confusion, discomfort and fear will continue to undermine and drain our physical and mental energies even while we sleep. As a consequence, our functioning during subsequent wakefulness will be seriously impeded. On the other hand, we may benefit on awakening from the strength and stamina engendered by pleasant dream-impressions, regardless of whether or not we recall them.

31. SCIENTIFIC AND ARTISTIC PROBLEMS SOLVED DURING SLEEP

Our mental processes do not cease during sleep and our mental faculties may attain a degree of skill and knowledge not at our disposal during wakefulness. Reverting to the form of atavistic mental functioning, our mental faculties acquire a different quality, one which prevailed during the struggle for survival of the species when reasoning faculties were merely potential and intuitive faculties superior.

It was this superiority to which the philosopher Immanuel Kant referred when he said in his *Dreams of a Spirit Seer:* "I rather suppose that ideas in sleep may be clearer and broader than even the clearest in the waking state." However, not only in deep sleep and in dreams, but also while passing through the deeper levels of the hypnoidal stage and approaching the levels of sleep, vague images may flicker across our mental vision and blend into so-called hypnagogic images which *resemble* dreams. These images are not considered to be real dreams, because their contents are often created by our own free volition, but intuition and creativeness are nevertheless intensified during these visions. Many of my patients have told me that, at times, they called forth hypnagogic fancies. Often they only remember that they experienced them but didn't recall of what they consisted, whereas, at other times, they retained a vague overall memory of the images.

One of my patients, a talented painter, who at that particular time was trying hard to determine the color schemes for an abstract composition he was working on, told me the following hypnagogic experience: "Yesterday, when I went to bed, I was really very drowsy, but my mind was wandering, in part freely, *in part slightly directed* toward a problem I am facing with my painting. Suddenly, I saw before my closed eyes a twilight sky. On the horizon were three extremely bright lights, all pointed toward me. The mental images of the lights were so extraordinarily brilliant that they left what seemed to be actual physical after-images when I turned my [mental] vision away from them. Immediately afterwards, I tried to re-induce the appearance of the brilliant lights, but could not do so. A little later, not called forth by my thoughts any more, mental images of color schemes and abstract compositions in color appeared before my closed eyes, vivid enough to let me think I would be able to remember and draw them later. But then I went to sleep and in the morning I could not remember the patterns or the color schemes."

This example shows that hypnagogic images and dreams alike should be fixated immediately on awakening. Otherwise you will be unlikely to recall the entire dream, or its memory may become erased completely. You need a pad and pencil on your bedside table and any time you wake up with a dream or hypnagogic images fresh on your mind, you should rouse yourself and make notes immediately. Of course, you should do this only if the dream is worth remembering, because this procedure might interfere with your going to sleep again.

In the aforementioned example of the painter's hypnagogic images, unfortunately by next morning his memory had retained no more than a vague impression. Could he have recreated the color schemes and abstract compositions as they had actually appeared before his mental vision, they might have amounted to a solution of the problem which was occupying his mind so intensely.

The range of creative ideas which can be freed in our minds by our intensified intuitive faculties during sleep and dreams is amazing. Poetry may be written in sleep and writers may conceive ideas for a novel or a play in precise detail and create it with a subtlety they wouldn't "dream" of while they are awake. Robert Louis Stevenson, for example, is said to have been able to charge the activities of his unconscious mind before lying down to sleep so that his unconscious would then evolve stories for him while he slept. Painters may have visions for a painting during sleep and musicians compose music. Thus, Richard Wagner conceived the theme for the *Rheingold Overture* in a dream. Wagner dreamed that he was drowning in a racing stream. When he awoke he still heard the torrent thundering over his head and, stimulated by the sound of the roaring waters, the theme of the *Rheingold Overture* arose from the depth of his unconscious.

While painting the fresco *The Last Supper* in the Church Santa Maria delle Grazie in Milan, Leonardo da Vinci lost himself in reveries over and over again, at least so it seemed to the indignant sexton who complained that Leonardo did more dozing than painting. Leonard would take up a brush and paint only a few strokes, then stop and gaze into nothingness for hours and hours. One can't blame the simple sexton for being greatly disturbed by Leonardo's "laziness," but undoubtedly the master used these quiescent hours to conceive and visualize the full splendor of the *Last Supper*.

This, of course, doesn't prove that all daydreams, all reveries, are fruitful; nevertheless, people's minds *can* be creatively stimulated during reveries and so-called daydreams.

Artistic activities, however, are not the only ones stimulated in this manner. Scientific problems also have found their solutions during suspended consciousness. One of the greatest discoveries in the field of modern medicine was made during sleep. In 1920, a Canadian physician, Dr. Banting, became engrossed in research on diabetes. One evening, his head buzzing with a host of contradictory theories and experiments, Banting felt too exhausted to continue working and went to bed. Suddenly he was wide awake. He lost no time trying to make sure whether he had been asleep, or only on the *verge of sleeping*. Taking up a notebook, he immediately jotted down the salient details of an animal experiment he had just dreamed of performing, or perhaps had seen himself performing in hypnagogic images. The following day, on carrying out the experiment according to his notes of the previous night, Banting found the long sought remedy for diabetes—he had discovered insulin!

A dream also led to another discovery, less important perhaps than insulin, but one which was to have far-reaching consequences

—it was the principle of the sewing-machine needle. Elias Howe, the father of the sewing-machine, had been racking his brain to find a suitable needle for his invention. One night he dreamed he was in Africa and trying to escape from hostile natives through caves which had two exits. He felt like a thread being twined through several openings when, suddenly, he stepped on a sharp nail. "If I drilled a hole in the nail beneath its point, I could draw a thread through the hole and extract the nail by pulling on the thread," he dreamed. Remembering this dream next morning, Howe realized in a flash-like association of ideas that he had found the basic principle of the sewing-machine needle.

Innumerable proofs attest to the ingenious mental faculties with which we are endowed in our sleep and dreams. Yet to most people it appears incredible and mysterious when they hear about artists finding inspiration in dreams, or scientists triumphing over problems they had been unable to solve before. Perhaps we would do well to ponder the words of the Swiss philosopher Amiel: "Let mystery have its place in you; . . . leave a little fallow corner in your heart ready for any seeds the winds may bring; and reserve a nook for the unexpected guest, an altar for the unknown God."

Sleep, the great healer, visits us every day. Whether sleep abides with us for hours, or only a few minutes, its potentials are unsurpassed and "it scarcely requires prophetic vision to foresee the time when the art or science of sleeping will be studied as systematically as the physiology of our nutritive and nervous systems." (Bigelow's *The Mystery of Sleep.*)

32. DON'T CONFUSE HYPNOIDAL
STAGE WITH HYPNOSIS

Have you ever had the rather odd sensation of losing your grip on yourself and drifting into a void as you were falling asleep? Or do you go to sleep the instant you lay your head down on the pillow?

And what about waking up in the morning? Are you fast asleep one moment and wide awake the next, ready to jump out of bed and tackle the demands of the day? Or could it be that you think: "Why, for heaven's sake, do I have to drag myself out of this wonderful, this protective haziness!" as sleep recedes and you struggle hard to re-establish identity with your waking self?

Most people will be able to answer these questions with an unhesitating "Yes" or "No." But whatever your answer may be and whatever individual sleep-characteristics you may have, each time you fall asleep or awaken, you pass through a stage of transition from *being awake into being asleep,* or from *being asleep into being awake.* This transition stage, during which various mental changes are taking place, is the hypnoidal stage. You may or may not ever become aware of the peculiar transition stage you are in, and you may or you may not remember it later on. This depends on whether you "dawdle" or "race" through the hypnoidal stage and whether, accordingly, you have sufficient time to become aware of it. Those who race through the hypnoidal stage may receive the deceptive impression of falling asleep or waking up without any transition period.

In any case, the exact point of intersection at which actual sleep sets in, is never consciously experienced and has not been determined as yet by experimental measurements. But this is of no importance in making use of the hypnoidal stage for the purpose of self-development. It is important, however, to know whether or not the hypnoidal stage is some form of hypnosis. The following questions and answers will clarify this point.

QUESTION: If the hypnoidal stage is the natural falling-asleep stage, why do so many people think that *hypnoidal* means a light form of hypnosis?

ANSWER: This error goes to show how the inaccurate use of words and faulty understanding of their meaning contribute to or cause muddled thinking. In the Greek language, *hypnos* signifies *natural sleep* and nothing else. But words taken from Latin and Greek, the classic languages, have always appealed to people, because such words appeared to them more "learned." This fact may have motivated the English physician James Braid to introduce the term *hypnosis* (1841) by which he described a strange and abnormal condition, the phenomena of which have been known under various other names throughout the ages far back into antiquity.

Hypnosis has been revived and modernized from time to time and Abraham Myerson has hit the nail squarely on the head by quoting an old teacher of his who once said that "hypnosis is like the proverbial woman in the streets—every so often she becomes respectable, but soon relapses into her old status."

The phenomena of hypnosis have nothing to do with natural sleep. However, in some instances the hypnotic state may *resemble* sleep and this deceptive appearance probably accounts for the inaccurate choice of the term *hypnosis*.

The term *hypnoidal,* however, is justifiably derived from the word *hypnos,* meaning natural sleep; *hypnoidal* refers to a very light form of natural sleep, namely, sleepiness. On the other hand, the term *hypnosis* is unjustifiably derived from the word *hypnos,* because the phenomena of hypnosis are not related to the phenomena of hypnos or natural sleep.

QUESTION: Is there any other proof that the hypnoidal stage is natural sleepiness or drowsiness?

ANSWER: Yes, there is. Nobody can claim that we have to pass through *any degree of hypnosis* whenever we take a nap, or each night when we go to sleep. Yet, before falling asleep, or waking up, we all go through a momentary or a long drawn-out stage of drowsiness. This drowsiness, the hypnoidal stage, is a forerunner or a follower, as the case may be, of our daily natural sleep. We know that sleep is necessary for the upkeep of our physical and mental health; sleep is a normal function of living and the hypnoidal stage, being a phase of natural sleep, is a part of this normal function.

On the other hand, hypnosis is not a normal function of living like our daily natural sleep. Hypnosis is always induced artificially by various methods and means. Consequently, hypnosis is in contrast to natural sleep with its physical and mental restorative powers and its tide-like rhythm of alternating sleeping and waking periods throughout life. The psychiatrist Boris Sidis, author of many books dealing extensively with research in the field of hypnosis and natural sleep, was the first to describe natural drowsiness as the *hypnoidal stage*. Sidis was careful to point out that the hypnoidal stage has nothing to do with hypnosis and emphasized this by adding "not even with light hypnosis."

QUESTION: Are there any tests which prove the difference between natural sleep and the *hypnotic* stage?

ANSWER: Experiments with the electro-encephalograph, conducted with persons while they slept normally and again when they were under hypnosis, have conclusively demonstrated the vast difference between the hypnotic state and natural sleep. One of the outstanding authorities in the field of electro-encephalography, W. Grey Walter, states that: "hypnosis shows none of the electrical features of natural sleep; indeed, the more carefully we consider the subject's state, the less it seems to resemble anything we know of sleep."

QUESTION: Would it not have been preferable to have chosen an appellation other than hypnoidal in order to avoid the misunderstanding to which the term *hypnoidal* lends itself so easily?

ANSWER: Yes, it would have been preferable, if only an expression existed which, like the term *hypnoidal,* would indicate in a single word one of the main factors in my specific technique of psychotherapy and in self-development.

Unfortunately, I have failed to discover any other term, just as

Boris Sidis himself, when coining the expression *hypnoidal,* remarked that he did so for lack of a better term.

Speaking for myself, I considered it more exact to speak of "hypnoidal psychotherapy" or "hypnoidal self-development" and not, for example, of "sleepiness-" psychotherapy, or "near-sleep" psychotherapy, to borrow Aldous Huxley's term *near-sleep* for the hypnoidal stage. And in formulating and administering suggestions in a form specific to the method of hypnoidal self-development, here too it seemed to me descriptively more accurate to call these suggestions: *hypnoidal suggestions.*

QUESTION: Is there a difference between hypnoidal suggestions and hypnotic suggestions?

ANSWER: Yes, there is. In fact, there are various differences and one of them is decisive. *A subject in hypnosis has no option but to obey the hypnotic suggestions being imposed on him;* he can be forced to accept, or to act upon, any kind of suggestion and he will even submit to those with which he would refuse to comply were he *not* under the hypnotic spell. To give an illustration: if I take a glass filled with ordinary drinking water and tell the person I have hypnotized, that the glass contains an extremely bad tasting medicine and command him to swallow it, he will exhibit distinct signs of reluctance, or even of disgust, but in the end he will drink the alleged medicine.

To make somebody drink water and have him believe that it is a nauseating medicine is probably quite a harmless suggestion. But it is not harmless to *impose hypnotic suggestions of any type* on a subject against his will or his inner feelings or convictions. This may induce dangerous emotional conflicts, or add to the subject's already existing conflicts. It is utterly misleading to claim, as many hypnotists do, that a subject in hypnosis will only accept those suggestions which are not opposed to his true character-traits. Very often we are completely in the dark about the innermost drives and impulses of a person. Once he is actually in the hypnotic condition, a subject will rarely balk at obeying a suggestion. An experienced hypnotist will usually be able to impose a suggestion on his subject even if this suggestion is contrary to his obvious character-traits.

Hypnotic and post-hypnotic suggestions as well as auto-suggestions, regardless of whether their contents are beneficial or not, may stir up overt or concealed conflicts and thereby cause a chronic condition of dangerous stress. Although hypnotic suggestions with beneficial contents may achieve quite dramatic temporary surface-effects, in the long run they don't amount to more than masking skin blemishes with heavy make-up. The skin may look considerably better so long as the make-up stays on, but the blemishes remain underneath.

Contrariwise, hypnoidal suggestions have no dramatic immediate effect, because their contents are only gradually absorbed by the unconscious. They will, however, make it increasingly easy for a person to transform his constructive intentions and aspirations into action; thus they will aid him to develop his inherent faculties and talents to their full extent. Hypnoidal suggestions can never be imposed on an individual; they will never mislead or deceive. The stunt of making somebody swallow water as a distasteful medicine would never succeed by hypnoidal suggestions. Usually, the person who is in the hypnoidal stage will awaken the moment his unconscious does not accept the contents of hypnoidal suggestions.

QUESTION: But if I *want* to give myself auto-hypnotic suggestions and approve of their contents, could they cause inner conflict in that case also?

ANSWER: Auto-hypnotic suggestions, even with beneficial contents, can cause conflict, because you may agree only theoretically with their meaning. This meaning may therefore remain in sharp contrast to your actual and sometimes undesirable drives. Consequently, you would be imposing a deception on your unconscious by auto-hypnotic coercion.

QUESTION: Couldn't the *preparatory work* be combined with auto-hypnotic suggestions just as well as with hypnoidal suggestions?

ANSWER: The effect of combining *preparatory work* with hypnotic suggestions *differs* radically from the effect of combining it with hypnoidal suggestions. Hypnotic suggestions are always coercive and amount to making somebody comply at gunpoint. This is probably one of the main reasons why corrective hypnotic suggestions usually wear off after a certain time, whereas hypnoidal suggestions are cumulatively effective.

Hypnoidal suggestions penetrate gradually into the unconscious and thus their beneficial meaning has time to become integrated naturally and thereby to result in genuine corrective personality-development.

Even in ordinary everyday activities, if you have to force yourself continually to do something you don't want to do, although it may be a very useful activity, or if you assume an attitude which you resent having to assume, although it may be a desirable attitude, this continual coercion causes conflict and resentment and therefore results in chronic stress. It is obvious that the coercion of hypnotic or auto-hypnotic suggestions will merely transform conscious conflict into concealed conflict and may deprive you of your last shred of conscious self-directional ability.

But there is an additional danger in auto-hypnotic suggestions. A hypnotic condition induced by an operator is under the operator's controlling direction, despite the fact that his personality and "willpower" need not be stronger than your own. But while you *are* in hypnosis, or under the effect of post-hypnotic suggestions, the operator controls and directs you by means of the hypnotic suggestions which he is, or has been, communicating to you. On the other hand, while you are in a self-induced hypnotic state, there is no operator present to direct the suggestions; and while you *are* in the hypnotic state, your capacity for voluntary self-direction is in abeyance. As a consequence, and regardless of the means by which you have induced self-hypnosis, the undesirable instinctual drives you are seeking to dispel may take over control and reverse the corrective meaning of the auto-hypnotic suggestions.

Because of these obvious disadvantages and because of the detrimental effect the hypnotic condition itself may exert on certain personality types, the practice of self-hypnosis is of dubious value. Although fabulous results are often claimed by the "inventors" of self-hypnotic methods, Dr. J. H. Schultz, one of the foremost advocates of *auto-conditioning by self-hypnosis,* recognized the dangers connected with self-hypnosis and recommended strict supervision by a physician well trained in this method.

QUESTION: Is the hypnoidal stage the same as deep relaxation?

ANSWER: No, it is not. The natural drowsiness of the hypnoidal stage is not relaxation per se; yet some form and degree of relaxation are necessary *to lead into* the hypnoidal stage and on into natural sleep.

33. THE HYPNOIDAL STAGE CAN BE ENEMY OR BEST FRIEND

Although we have no precise answers regarding the query "What causes sleep?" and related questions, one fact has nevertheless been determined. It has been ascertained that the pattern of electrical brain activity during the period of falling asleep *differs from both the brain activity pattern during wakefulness and from that produced during sleep.*

In *The Living Brain,* W. Grey Walter enumerates three stages of sleep which can be recorded with the electroencephalograph and I urge everybody to read this fascinating book. Here are important passages:

"When a subject begins to feel drowsy, the first sign is usually a *reduction* in alpha rhythms and their gradual replacement by something more like the theta activity, mainly at the back and sides of the brain but spreading occasionally to all regions. At this stage the subject is easily roused and not yet really dozing; it is the beginning of that delicious state in which consciousness is consciously waning.

"If the subject is trying not to shut his eyes, he will find himself seeing double; if reading, he will go over a paragraph time and again without getting its meaning . . . At this stage the brain can still respond electrically and functionally to incoming signals, but the electrical response begins to show a prominent slow component, and the spread of the faster excitatory effects is more limited and more transient . . . The reader's eyes can follow the lines of print but the *meaning of the words escapes him* and, merging into private fancy, his bedtime story becomes a dream. . . .

"The electrical changes in the first stage of drowsiness are clear enough to be exploited as a selective warning device for those who are liable to doze in dangerous situations . . . Worn by hard-driving motorists, *theta* warning-sets would probably save more lives than do motor horns; and they might assist self-knowledge and self-control.

"If we follow a drowsy subject further along the path to oblivion, we soon see other changes; slow irregular waves appear, and with them, from time to time, bursts of smaller, faster, spindly waves . . . The subject is now asleep and if we waken him suddenly will start and look confused; he may deny that he was sleeping, or he may say that he has just had a dream.

"As slumber deepens, its characteristic patterns become more pronounced in the EEG (electroencephalogram). . . .

"The length of each stage of sleep and the patterns of awakening, the form and extent, the abundance and efficacy of 'complexes'—the frequency of the spindle-waves of dozing—all these features are assembled in the nocturnal rhythms with as personal a character as the waking ones . . . There is still a great deal to learn about the physiology of sleep and its relation to brain functions as a whole."

We will try now to translate W. Grey Walter's description of the electrical changes in the brain into an actual happening by setting the stage for a sample illustration. Let us visualize a lazy Sunday afternoon. Rain is pouring down. In the fireplace of your room the burning logs crackle in cozy contrast to the monotonous tapping of raindrops against the windows. A chair near the fire invites you to sit down, read, and perhaps take a nap after a while. You select a book and begin reading. But little by little you find it more difficult to concentrate, until finally increasing drowsiness closes in on you like fog rising from a river on the evening of a warm day.

One of several things will happen to you now. Either the book may slip from your hands while you doze off from one second to another without being able to register the transitional hypnoidal stage. Or, sleepily, you may lay aside the book, change to a still more comfortable position and glide slowly into sleep. But, as you do so, you may become aware that your senses are gradually losing contact with reality as your faculty of selective thinking becomes more and more impaired.

During this unique condition of falling asleep, your faculties, although still functioning, no longer have the same full capacity as during complete wakefulness. You sway like a child on a swing between closeness to actual sleep and the brink of being awake, doing this either slowly, or more or less rapidly, sometimes unaware of this oscillation, at other times with an accompanying sensation of going in-and-out and in-and-out again.

Shallow levels of the hypnoidal stage are closer to consciousness and may lead us gradually, or rapidly, back into complete wakefulness. When we reach the deeper levels of the hypnoidal stage, we are closer to sleep and are likely to glide into the still deeper levels of actual sleep. In his *Interpretation of Dreams,* Freud speaks of this condition as "the fluctuation between sleep and waking." This *fluctuation* may bring into play deep-seated impulses, often tinged with frustrations and fears, but also with yearnings, which surge up from the depth of the unconscious. Often, they blend with thoughts and emotional impressions lingering on from everyday experiences. It is then that they form in the words of Alexander Pope:

> The last image of that troubled heap
> When sense subsides, and fancy sports in sleep,
> Though past, the recollections of the thought,
> Becomes the stuff of which our dreams are wrought.

In the condition of falling-asleep, in the hypnoidal stage, the *non-controlled* and intensified emotional impact of thoughts and images may dissipate our drowsiness and for that reason it may happen that we don't reach the deeper levels of actual sleep. Instead we awaken again, at times with a startling jolt, as we emerge suddenly out of deep somnolence back into wakefulness.

But should the fluctuation between waking and sleeping have carried us close enough to the border of sleep, then the thoughts and images which populate our mind during the hypnoidal stage are not likely to awaken us any more and so we shift from falling asleep into being asleep. At this point, thoughts and images may be transformed into almost self-directed hypnagogic images and then lose themselves in the non-directed and manifold disguises and distortions of dreams.

Just as sleep itself fluctuates between light and deep sleep lasting, at any of these levels, from a few seconds or minutes to many hours, so does the hypnoidal stage as such last from a split second to a couple of minutes up to a full hour. Freud was well aware of the effects of the falling-asleep stage when he put his patients on a couch in order to have them relax and come closer to the drowsiness of the hypnoidal stage. For, at shallow levels of the hypnoidal stage, mental inhibitions diminish and, as a consequence, the stream of free associations which is so important in psychoanalysis, may flow more abundantly.

Still more important than the diminished inhibitions is the easier access to the unconscious which *during the fluctuations of the hypnoidal stage* permits the unconscious to absorb the *sense* of words and thoughts. But not only may the quality and contents of the thoughts which we take over into sleep infiltrate our dreams, their influence on us during the hypnoidal stage may go far beyond providing dream-material. They affect our personality favorably or unfavorably to a lasting degree. Therefore, the hypnoidal stage, if made use of in the proper way, can be a most efficacious instrument with which to achieve satisfactory results in psychotherapy and psychological self-help.

As we know, even during wakefulness a habitually positive and constructive manner of thinking produces a wholesome auto-suggestive effect, whereas a chronically defeatist attitude, frequent brooding on fears or other negative thought-contents have unfortunate and often very harmful auto-suggestive effects.

Because suggestibility and auto-suggestibility are considerably heightened during the hypnoidal stage, it is decisive whether we dwell repeatedly on favorable, or harp on unfavorable thought-contents during extended periods of the hypnoidal stage. For these thought-contents will amount to extremely powerful forms of auto-suggestion and therefore almost inevitably make desirable or undesirable mental imprints on our personality. These mental imprints can also be produced and intensified by hypnoidal suggestions while you are in the hypnoidal stage. Thus you can see clearly that the hypnoidal stage may become your enemy or your best friend.

34. WORDS AS STIMULI
IN HYPNOIDAL SUGGESTIONS

Doubts are often expressed as to whether suggestions can really do any good. "How can they be effective?" people sometimes ask. "After all, suggestions consist of nothing but empty words!"

Unfortunately it is true that some people's minds are so barren that words evoke almost no mental or emotional echo in them, just as they themselves merely parrot phrases and opinions they know are acceptable or are expected of them. But thoughts and words can and do transmit a wealth of meaning and exert a considerable degree of influence.

It is mainly by words that the human mind manifests itself and reveals its quality. Words kindle our imagination, stir up our emotions and express or disguise our innermost thoughts and feelings. Words are powerful tools; they enable us to absorb and to convey knowledge, they fill us with joy and allow us to share the poet's inspiration. Words may threaten and frighten us, cause us grief, or bestow on us soothing balm offered by a compassionate heart. To accomplish all this, words as a rule will have to depend on the tone of voice in which they are spoken and on their arrangement into meaningful sentences. Then words can assume myriad subtle shades of meaning and open new worlds of thought.

At times, even a single word can take on tremendous significance. Imagine a ragged little boy standing before a store-window, proudly clutching two pennies in a grubby hand. After lengthy deliberation, he enters the store, points to the candy of his choice and asks: "How many cents?" "Five," answers the clerk and this one short word "five" makes the child's wish unattainable.

It is amazing what world-shaking consequences may be enclosed in the digits from zero to nine and combinations of them, or in any other single word or combinations of words. "Perhaps all living is just learning the meaning of words . . . 'work and play' . . . 'joy and pain' . . . 'peace' . . . 'love' . . . 'life' itself . . . their meaning, we master too late to employ completely. The learning is all." (Ferris Greenslet in *Under the Bridge*).

There are people who only respond, or claim that they can only respond, to so-called concrete words which refer to tangible facts and objects, such as tree, chair, bottle, or to words which describe tangible qualities such as bitter, sharp, hard, warm, cold, and so on. Yet even these concrete words permit a wide divergence of interpretation. Physiological handicaps or peculiarities may impair and sometimes erase an individual's ability to realize the meaning of these words. Color-blindness, loss of taste, to name only two, may alter the meaning of certain concrete words. Besides, personal tastes and inclinations also affect the meaning of concrete words, since the same object may delight one person, but prove obnoxious to another. Clearly, then, concrete words do not always convey a precise meaning.

Abstract words, on the other hand, may assume extremely tangible meanings and have far-reaching concrete results. Interpretation of such abstract terms as goodness, reverence, loyalty, justice, power, and countless more, has been a subject of controversy among philosophers and theologians of all tongues and ages. Shakespeare speaks of the tangible consequences of abstract terms when he describes them in *The Tempest:*

> O, when degree is shak'd,
> Which is the ladder to all high designs,
> The enterprise is sick! . . . Take but degree away,
>   untune that string,
> And hark, what discord follows . . . right and wrong,
> Should lose their names, and so should justice too.

Then everything includes itself in power,
Power into will, will into appetite;
And appetite, an universal wolf,
So doubly seconded with will and power,
Must make perforce an universal prey,
And last eat up himself.

In science too, abstract terms are used to describe very concrete and powerful things. Physicists, for instance, employ the term *energy,* although they don't quite know the exact nature of what they identify as energy. And psychiatrists as well as psychologists speak alternately of nervous energy and of psychic energy, yet the nature of these forms of energy also remains somewhat obscure. But there is consolation in the fact that here, as in other provinces of science, lack of a comprehensive explanation by no means prevents the functioning and the profitable utilization of the designated phenomenon—and this goes also for the phenomenon of suggestibility.

But regardless of whether words imply a concrete or an abstract meaning, they exert a tremendous influence on our mental, emotional and physiological functioning throughout life. This influence becomes all the more pronounced and intensified when our normal suggestibility is transformed into heightened suggestibility. Powerful mental and physiological processes can then be set in motion by suggestions and our mental attitudes will be benefited considerably by the right kind of suggestions. The contents of words and sentences becomes even more intensified in meaning and weight when the stage of heightened suggestibility, the hypnoidal stage, coincides with the specific formulation and rhythm of hypnoidal suggestions.

During the hypnoidal stage, our thinking turns into a *sensing* rather than thinking. This contributes to transform our normal suggestibility into heightened suggestibility. The effect which the hypnoidal stage has on the meaning of words is comparable to the effect sleep has on dream-inciting stimuli; they become magnified and intensified during a dream. For instance, the sound of falling rain may stimulate a dream about a torrent, while an uncomfortable position assumed in sleep might make us dream about physical torture. In a similar manner, the meaning of words and sentences becomes intensified and gains in suggestive impact during the hypnoidal stage. Charles Dickens observed the characteristics of the hypnoidal stage with striking accuracy when he wrote: "It was late next morning when Oliver aroused himself from sleep; he was not thoroughly awake. There is a drowsy state, between sleeping and waking, when you dream more in five minutes with your eyes half open and yourself half conscious of everything that is passing around you, than you would in five nights . . . At such time a mortal knows just enough of what his mind is doing, to form some glimmering conception of its mighty powers . . . words, which are really spoken . . . at the moment, accommodate themselves with surprising readiness to our visions, until reality and imagination become so strangely blended that it is afterwards almost a matter of impossibility to separate the two . . ."

We find another reference to the significance of words in semisleep, in the hypnoidal stage, in the *Road to Xanadu*. Speaking about Samuel Taylor Coleridge, John Livingstone Lowes says: "Things actually seen and things only read undoubtedly coalesced during their strange sleep in his brain . . . his imagination sprang habitually to creative activity on the spur of words."

But the effect of words is emphasized by others than novelists and poets. The psychiatrist Dr. Emil Gutheil refers to word-absorption during the hypnoidal stage by telling about a patient's experience. Dr. Gutheil says: "The patient is a thirty-two-year-old physician. He reports 'I dreamed that I was in a store where Persian rugs were sold. My mother and my fiancee were also present.' Upon awakening, the patient was asked by his mother whether he had seen anything the night before. When the patient answered in the negative, his mother revealed to him that the day before, as a surprise, she had bought a Persian rug. He remembered his dream about the rug only when his mother questioned him . . . We had to investigate the possibility that the Persian rug was mentioned at a time when the patient was in a state of decreased consciousness; for example, if he were falling asleep or just awakening, the feeling of re-appearing consciousness could have absorbed the words, yet not to such a degree they could be remembered." (*The Handbook of Dream Analysis*).

This example illustrates how the fluctuation between waking and sleeping facilitates access to the unconscious by permitting words, not consciously registered, to reach our auditory senses and to penetrate into the unconscious.

The basis for inducing dreams artificially by whispering into the ear of an apparently sleeping person is based on this principle and it is also fundamental for the "Learn while you sleep" method which was originated many years ago. The usefulness of this method has been doubted by some psychologists, whereas others have conceded that it is effective. The reasons for this disagreement are the following:

a) So long as a person *is* and *remains* in actual sleep, the meaning of words spoken to him, live or recorded, is quite unlikely to have access to his unconscious. Therefore, no one can assimilate the material he is supposed to learn when it is played back to him on records while he is fast asleep. Neither can anyone absorb the meaning of spoken suggestions or the contents of a dream whispered into his ear, while he is really asleep.

b) A person may have been actually asleep, but the sound of a voice has reached his auditory senses and recalled him from deeper levels of sleep to shallower ones and back into the fluctuation of the hypnoidal stage. Once he *is* in this stage, and provided that his mind has been adequately prepared during his waking condition, he will then absorb the meaning of spoken words.

c) A person is about to fall asleep. If the sound of spoken words reaches him then, he may be prevented from actually going into deep sleep. Consequently, this person remains in the hypnoidal stage and will absorb the meaning of what is spoken to him. All this may happen without fully awakening a person; in fact, he may give the superficial impression of being continuously fast asleep.

Once access to the unconscious has been facilitated by the use of the hypnoidal stage, subsequent deep natural sleep, even if it lasts merely a couple of minutes, will contribute additionally to a gradual integration of the meaning contained in thoughts and words. But it should be kept in mind that thoughts and words carry their meaning effectively into our unconscious only while we are in one of the various phases of the fluctuating hypnoidal stage.

It is always easier, of course, to absorb impersonal learning material than the meaning of suggestions aimed at personality-development or the correction of personality-shortcomings. In the latter cases, deep-seated emotional inclinations and often instinctual resistance may have to be overcome, before the beneficial meaning of suggestions can be absorbed and successfully integrated.

35. ◆ OUR NORMAL SUGGESTIBILITY

Possibly you have never given much thought to the nature of suggestibility. Or, as many people do, you may have associated suggestibility mistakenly with being influenced too easily and being talked into the acceptance or rejection of something, regardless of its actual value or consequences. Should you feel that way, then what you have in mind is not normal suggestibility at all; it is rather a deterioration of normal suggestibility into gullibility. But normal suggestibility and gullibility are by no means identical.

Normal suggestibility and normal auto-suggestibility are an integral part of our mental mechanism and play a decisive role in whatever we think, feel and do.

Normal suggestibility manifests itself in our psychical, mental and physical responses to all kinds of stimuli conveyed to us by our senses, our emotions and our thought-processes. An audible stimulus such as the song of a bird may suggest joy to us; the sound of a shot may, by association, suggest fear to somebody who has witnessed a shooting accident, or it may suggest grief to someone who has lost a loved one in the war. Visible stimuli, for instance the design of a piece of furniture, may suggest comfort, beauty, or exactly the opposite; or they may not make any impression at all. Then again, a painting, representing a particular landscape, may have an elating or a depressive effect, because we may associate the painted landscape with one familiar to us and reminiscent of some pleasant or unpleasant experience. Or we may have no conscious association at all with this landscape, but for no explicable reason, it suggests a particular mood.

The quality and degree of our responses to stimuli depends on their general and individual meaningfulness to us; consequently, one and the same stimulus may have different suggestive values for different people. For instance, "A" and "B" see an airplane. This visual stimulus may convey to "A," who was in the Air Force during wartime, a suggestion of danger and death, whereas to "B," who has never left his small home-town the same airplane may suggest the pleasurable excitement of flying to interesting new places. Even simple questions like "Shall we go for a walk?" or "Would you like a cup of coffee?" amount to stimulating suggestions to which we respond in one way or another.

In accordance with the general and individual meaningfulness of a stimulus, we will either accept or reject whatever the stimulus stands for. Our acceptance may range from a slight inclination to an ardent desire to get or to accomplish what the stimulus suggests to us. Rejection may equally range from mild unwillingness to violent refusal to take or do what the stimulus suggests. All these are well-known facts, yet they have to be enumerated here in order to impress on the reader how simple in its functioning the mechanism of suggestibility can be and, at the same time, how complex.

There may also be indifference toward stimuli, and this indifference may stem from a certain form of laziness which prevents some people from responding positively, whenever they anticipate an effort will be required of them. Even when anticipation of this effort is not registered consciously, their defence-mechanism provides them with a pseudo-excuse in the form of lack of interest. But genuine and overall lack of interest and an excessive or chronic fatigue may be conditions of temperament and close to being pathological. This applies also to mental attitudes which condition people into perpetually resenting what they have to do or into feeling constantly discontented with their life-circumstances; no wonder these people are overwhelmed by fatigue and disinclined to do much of anything.

Laziness interferes to a great extent with our responsiveness to constructive suggestions and, very often, a certain type of laziness can also be based on a defence-mechanism derived from a conditioned reflex-reaction. This laziness is apt to increase if left uncorrected and may extend to various forms of activity. The following case is a good example. Harry, a boy of sixteen, whose parents require him to mow the lawn around their home, dislikes the chore and finds excuses every time he is reminded to do the job. Finally, he has come to regard his own excuses as facts and thus as valid reasons for his increasing resentment; by now, his resentment has tended to make him less cooperative about other things as well.

It is difficult to draw the line between degrees of psychological response and it is also difficult to detect at what point laziness and resentfulness combine to produce a most unfortunate mental attitude that occurs rather frequently. Housewives, for instance, may abhor their household work and protest against it in word and thought. In the long run, these women may develop almost a psychological block against their chores and, sometimes, against other duties also.

While we are on the subject of suggestions, let us take into consideration their effect on certain individuals who offer very limited response to normal suggestive stimuli. Feeling satisfaction at doing good work in some field, enjoying pleasant company, an interesting book, a game of golf, a stimulating discussion and, despite our diet-conscious minds, relishing a well-prepared meal, these find no echo in unresponsive persons. An emotional blindness or a general dullness and, sometimes, an attitude of chronic discontent interfere with their positive mental and emotional response. It is not always easy to determine whether these people are unamenable to normal suggestive stimuli, or only appear to be unresponsive. Under certain circumstances, appropriate use of the hypnoidal stage and hypnoidal suggestions may awaken even in these unresponsive people an inherent faculty for increased mental and emotional response, thereby enriching their lives. Normal suggestibility in response to stimuli permits us to live our daily lives efficiently and satisfactorily.

But should we react to stimuli without applying our selective and directive mental faculties as brakes, then, instead of arousing normal suggestibility, the stimuli let us succumb to *abnormal* suggestibility, to gullibility. The latter is most likely to occur when the stimulus suggests to us a reaction which coincides with our wishful thinking and daydreaming. In that event we succumb without questioning and reasoning, or we are too weak to restrain our hopes of or desires for anticipating pleasure, comfort, or profit. These attitudes reveal a suggestibility intensified beyond its normal extent because, for one or another reason, our selective and directive faculties are or have become more or less impaired.

36. HEIGHTENED SUGGESTIBILITY

Our selective and directive faculties may become impaired from various causes and to different degrees. One cause is the condition of falling asleep, during which our awareness of the realities around us gradually becomes blurred. The condition of falling asleep heightens our normal suggestibility, because a slight dissociation in consciousness sets in while we are falling asleep. This *natural* dissociation in consciousness becomes more pronounced, the closer we come to actual sleep, until consciousness blanks out completely.

Drifting off to sleep is a natural cause for dissociation in consciousness. It can also be induced artificially by drugs, hypnosis, or the intoxicating effect of alcohol. Besides, there are pathological forms of dissociation in consciousness such as occur in psychotic conditions, or because of a very high fever. The temporary delirium which high fever often entails may resemble the erratic manifestations of a psychotic dissociation. And driving an automobile over long, monotonous stretches of highway can create a dissociation in consciousness known as "highway-hypnosis."

But our present interest is in the particular form of natural dissociation in consciousness which is part of our nightly falling-asleep; it sets in as soon as the fluctuation between waking and sleeping begins and ego-consciousness becomes less and less distinct. It is during this hazy, half-conscious condition that you may hear a dog barking and only register a vague irritation, sometimes not even associated with the barking. Or you may hear the doorbell ring, but don't instantly connect the sound with the necessity to rise and find out who is at the door. And should anybody ask you: "How much are two and four?" while you are on the verge of falling asleep or of waking up, you will answer hesitatingly: "Two . . . a-and . . . four . . . are . . . s-six." Although with great probability you will answer correctly, it will cause you some effort, because of your sloweddown reactions and actions while you glide through the hypnoidal stage before you are really asleep or are not yet quite awake. But whenever our perceptive and selective mental faculties are impaired by a temporary dissociation in consciousness, the power of suggestion takes over and fills the mental vacuum left by the absence of conscious direction.

As we nod off to sleep, our emotional responses become less controlled and less directed by reasoning; at the same time, the impending dissociation in consciousness facilitates access to our unconscious. This means that stimuli, especially audible ones, affect us with tremendous impact, and thought-stimuli become forceful autosuggestions. To further clarify this subject-matter, the question-and-answer method will be helpful again.

QUESTION: If it is dissocation in consciousness which increases the power of suggestion, is it not contradictory to say that repetition of negative thoughts has an extremely strong auto-suggestive effect? We may repeat negative thoughts such as "I am incapable of doing this or that!" or "Everything is hopeless!" while we are fully conscious; consequently their auto-suggestive effect cannot be ascribed to a dissociation in consciousness—isn't that correct?

ANSWER: No, it is not correct, as you will find if you examine closely what actually happens when you indulge in apprehensive, despondent, resentful, or angry and hostile thoughts. They show an electro-encephalographic pattern of brain waves which indicates a dissociation in consciousness. Besides, except in hypnosis, where a response can be artificially created and imposed, suggestions are only as powerful as the response they are able to awaken. To be effective, suggestions must fall on well-prepared and fertile soil. However, hardly anything intensifies the receptivity for negative auto-suggestions more strongly than anxiety, resentfulness, anger, hostility and defeatism.

Auto-suggestions often have a heightened effect when they coincide with some physical sensation. If you wake up with a slight headache and are afraid that the headache will become worse, it *will* become worse. If you are inclined to be over-afraid, then the slightest pain may activate fear- and anxiety-laden psychic contents. As a result, you may worry disproportionately about possible consequences of this pain. Undeniably, any discomfort might, to some degree, interfere with one's normal efficiency to perform a difficult or an important task. Therefore, if you are faced with a demanding task on the same day you wake up with a slight headache, it seems to be quite natural that you should be somewhat concerned. But you have to realize that anxiety may prove far more detrimental to your efficiency than the original physical discomfort.

Negative auto-suggestions frequently trigger an upsurge of unpleasant memories which may lead to all kinds of mental and emotional associations. Frustrated desires, worries and fears, or feelings of guilt, resentment, hate and many other combinations of harmful emotions, form a receptive soil in which the seeds of negative associations will thrive. In this manner, amazing emotional chain-reactions may develop, the original cause of which is often extremely hard to discover. I can cite a very simple chain-reaction of this type from my own experience. I had been suffering from an excruciating toothache for over a week. After the dentist had done the necessary work, the pain finally stopped. Several days afterwards, I drove to the beach; it was a lovely day and I was enjoying the drive. All of a sudden the thought came to my mind how wonderful it was to be without a toothache. A few seconds later, my tooth began to ache again. It didn't last long, only a minute or two, then the pain ceased and did not recur. Recalling the recently endured pain had stimulated an associative return of the toothache.

QUESTION: This is not a pertinent example, because there was no negative thinking involved on your part. On the contrary, you were thinking positively when you told yourself how pleasant it was to be without pain! You didn't even feel apprehensive that the pain might return; where then did the negative auto-suggestion come in?

ANSWER: You are partly right; consciously I was very far from feeling apprehensive. However, certain types of positive thinking often are characterized by a Janus head. On the one side, everything seems to be all right, but on the other side lurk painful surprises, fear and trouble. Even a pleasant and positive thought like "How glad I am that I am feeling no more pain" may, under certain circumstances, set off unconscious associations—an unconscious fear-reaction, because the temporary remembrance of the past pain may be linked to an unconscious anxiety complex. In other words, our unconscious recalls the actual pain and our own thoughts, or any other stimulus that can mentally revive this memory in the unconscious, may cause a recurrence of the pain, if only for a split second. In fact, we never know exactly what might act as a stimulus to set off a chain-reaction of unconscious and conscious associations. It is well-known that people whose arms or legs have been amputated often feel discomfort in their artificial arm or leg, or may dream of feeling the exact suffering they went through before the operation. In either case, these people will feel the same kind of pain they would have felt if they still possessed the amputated limb. There are neuro-psychiatrists who think that this pain may come from some nerves which formerly conveyed the particular sensation of pain to the brain. But the pain could have been stimulated also by associations with psychic contents which became affected with the fear and pain this person experienced before the amputation.

QUESTION: You speak of *psychic contents* and also of *unconscious associations*—what do you mean by them?

ANSWER: Psychic contents can be considered as a blending of conscious and unconscious residues of our own individual experiences together with those transmitted to us from our forebears. According to Jung, these vestiges of composite experiences of the human race as such are stored up in the *collective unconscious*. The concept of the collective unconscious is paramount for the psychological structure of the human personality. It is, nevertheless, misunderstood at times, or not understood at all, especially by those who, with the self-assurance of ignorance, attack Jung as being "obscure." However, the poet Rainer Maria Rilke seems to know more about the collective unconscious than some professionals. In his "Tenth Elegy," Rilke says:

> . . . You mortals
> sometimes retain a fragment of primeval sorrow
> or a slag of old anger out of an ancient volcano

and these words may give you a good idea of what is meant when you speak of the collective unconscious and of psychic contents.

Although Rilke refers in his "Tenth Elegy" merely to negative psychic contents when he speaks of "primeval sorrow" and of "old anger," there are positive psychic contents stored up in the collective unconscious as well, such as a predisposition for ethical concepts, for reverence, for genuine dignity, to mention but a few potential assets in the human personality. Psychic contents are stirred up by suggestive stimuli and then cause unconscious and conscious associations. There is a difference, however. If a *conscious* stimulus, a word, a melody, a landscape, stirs up some pleasant or unpleasant emotional reaction or idea or some feeling of comfort or discomfort, we are aware of what is happening to us. On the other hand, when we are dealing with *unconscious* associations, we cannot trace consciously what kind of stimulus has caused our specific reaction. This is comparable to having had a dream which we don't remember, but which nevertheless produces pleasant or unpleasant after-effects.

An associative stimulus may bring back into our consciousness long forgotten experiences of greater or less import. We find an eloquent illustration of unconscious and conscious associative stimulation in *Swann's Way* by Marcel Proust. He describes how Swann dips a bun into a cup of tea and how the taste of the crumbs mixed with tea, makes him "aware of something taking place in his unconscious . . . An exquisite pleasure had invaded my senses, but . . . with no suggestion of its origin . . ." This is an example of an unconscious association which, however, is turned into a conscious one when Proust goes on to remember that, as a child, he was given a piece of bun dipped in tea by his aunt Leonie. As soon, as he has "tracked down the origin of the flavor, his whole childhood swims back into consciousness." Again, and more vividly than the most erudite professional explanation, the poetic genius of Proust reveals the essential meaning of associations.

QUESTION: Does not all this indicate that we remain the playthings of our unconscious associations, whether or not we train ourselves to think logically and positively?

ANSWER: Not quite. You must keep in mind that the terms *unconscious* and *conscious* are only descriptive. The human mind does not consist of isolated compartments—the human mind is an entity and the functions of the unconscious are reflected in our conscious behavior. But then again, our conscious behavior is reflected also in the functions of our unconscious. These functions can be made obedient and helpful servants, if they are well coordinated to sound conscious attitudes. There is an interaction between our conscious and unconscious functions. If our conscious behavior is composed of harmful attitudes, then the unconscious is incited to play exceedingly unfortunate tricks on us in the form of disproportionate anxieties, frustrations, resentments and unconscious associations of a most harmful and disturbing nature.

Only by the practice of healthful attitudes can we check potentially negative psychic contents and disturbing unconscious associations. If we thus abstain from fostering negative conscious attitudes, the likelihood of their being stimulated and activated will decrease accordingly.

The far-reaching consequences of unwholesome mental attitudes are also brought to light by W. Grey Walter's encephalographic findings. He states that *electrical brain-rhythms of drowsiness resemble the electrical brain-rhythms of anger and frustration.* This similarity indicates that in both instances a dissociation in consciousness takes place which impairs our reasoning faculties. Often, we hear hyper-emotional people say after a bout of anger or of excessive frustration and despair: "I just didn't know what I was doing!" In this condition, people may talk themselves with mounting vehemence into a rage or into intensified frustration, anxiety, despair and self-pity. In short, angry and frustrated people lose directional control over their selective mental faculties and therefore succumb much more easily to their negative thoughts which, in turn, operate as destructive auto-suggestions. When our mental faculties are caught in a fog conjured up by hyper-emotional reactions to negative thoughts and associations, every type of apprehensive or of aggressive thinking can amount to a very strong auto-suggestive stimulus and cause most unfortunate psychological and physiological chain-reactions.

Regardless of whether our selective and directive mental faculties are impaired by natural drowsiness, or by anger, frustration, or despair, this impairment opens the door to heightened suggestibility and auto-suggestibility.

But a sharp distinction has to be made here. Although the electrical brain-waves in the hypnoidal stage *resemble* those registered in anger, frustration and despair and, although they all indicate a slight dissociation in consciousness, *there is a difference in the quality of the dissociation.* The dissociation in consciousness caused by anger, frustration, or any other negative mental state, *seems to carry in itself the specific negative quality of these negative mental attitudes.* As a consequence, the ensuing impairment of our mental faculties is affected by this negative quality which automatically transforms our angry or frustrating thoughts into negative auto-suggestions.

In contrast to this negative auto-suggestibility, the dissociation brought on by *natural drowsiness* in the course of the normal life-function of natural sleep is in itself *neutral* and therefore seems to produce a *neutral type of suggestibility and auto-suggestibility.* This neutral suggestibility intensifies our receptivity for whatever negative or positive thoughts we may harbor while we are falling asleep.

Our receptivity for positive thought-contents is further increased, when beneficial suggestions are thought of in silence, or are verbally expressed on records, in certain patterns of repetitious rhythm. There are various patterns of these rhythms; I call them *hypnoidal monotony-rhythms.*

Like anything else, intensification of the meaning of words by coupling them with certain patterns of rhythms can be made to serve an undesirable as well as a desirable purpose. The effect produced will depend on the meaning contained in the words and the rhythm-pattern which accompanies them.

37 ♦ HYPNOIDAL SUGGESTIONS

Up to this point, the expression *hypnoidal suggestions* has been brought to your attention several times and, probably, it has occurred to you just as often to ask "What are hypnoidal suggestions?" Here is the answer to your question:

1) Hypnoidal suggestions consist of words and sentences chosen and grouped with profound regard to their beneficial impact on the unconscious. The sentences are broken up into varying and specific forms of rhythmical repetition in order to form hypnoidal monotony-rhythms.

Rhythmical repetition of ritual sounds and words are found in devotional practices of the East since ancient times, because rhythmic repetition "produces an effect ten times greater than other ritual practices. If it is practiced in secret and silence, the effect is a hundred times greater." (Manava-dharma-shastra II.) It is also mentioned that "the lips move, the sounds are articulate, but so low as to be inaudible. They are really turned inward." Then it is added that "nothing is any longer pronounced . . . all remains in the mind. Its practice confers immense powers." ("The Principal Yogas" by Jacques H. Masui in *Forms and Techniques of Altruistic and Spiritual Growth.*)

The principle of repetition and rhythm is adapted in hypnoidal suggestions to the requirements of the Western mind and the hypnoidal monotony-rhythms are specifically designed to:

a) intensify the meaning of the words and carry this meaning far more deeply and effectively into the unconscious than is possible by reciting or thinking the usual kind of suggestions in the usual manner;

b) stimulate all kinds of favorable impulses and incentives as well as latent faculties and talents. This stimulation is immensely heightened by the hypnoidal monotony-rhythms;

c) facilitate self-administration of hypnoidal suggestions during the hypnoidal stage. The combination of rhythmical repetition and the hypnoidal stage results in a technique which has never before been employed in psychotherapy, in psychological self-help, or while administering suggestions.

d) It cannot be stressed enough that *preparatory work* is indispensable to accomplish your goal; it equals the ploughing of the soil in order that the seeds, the suggestions, planted therein may bear good fruit.

The hypnoidal suggestions you find later in this book are *generalized* hypnoidal suggestions. They are sufficiently potent to stimulate whatever slumbering faculties and positive character-traits you may possess, but they are not designed to touch on any *personal* problem a reader may have. Those readers who during their self-educational preparatory work feel the need of *individualized* hypnoidal suggestions are invited to consult a trained hypnoidal therapy expert. Thereupon, on the basis of additional information, *individualized* hypnoidal suggestions can be formulated so that they can meet the reader's specific requirements. In some cases, "custom-made" *individualized* hypnoidal suggestions will have to differ appreciably from *generalized* hypnoidal suggestions, whereas in most other instances grouping words and sentences differently, or changing the hypnoidal monotony-rhythm of the suggestions is all that is required to accomplish the desired results. But whatever changes are necessary, they should never be made by you or any other person who is not thoroughly trained in my specific hypnoidal technique.

Those who wish to avail themselves of the benefits of hypnoidal self-development in order to improve their overall psychological functioning rarely need *individualized* hypnoidal suggestions, because *generalized* hypnoidal suggestions will:

a) stimulate beneficial emotional reflexes which are essential to the development of sound mental attitudes;

b) stimulate and condition the inner strength needed in handling everyday-life responsibilities and problems. Inner strength is also needed to enjoy life. On the other hand, lack of or thwarted inner strength may at times cause a person to fail quite unnecessarily at some task or in some situation. This again may contribute to a lack of self-confidence which could be a stumbling-block to success;

c) stimulate your good reasoning abilities and your intuitive faculties;

d) coordinate your feeling with your constructive thinking;

e) stimulate your ability for satisfactory self-direction;

f) stimulate dormant talents in general;

g) further mental and physical relaxation;

h) further the integration of the stimulated faculties into your personality.

In the following section you will become familiar with certain basic rules which must be observed for hypnoidal suggestions to be successful.

38. ◆ NEVER LIE TO YOUR
UNCONSCIOUS

The unconscious will not integrate a suggestion which conveys a lie to it; the unconscious will absorb only what it is prepared to absorb, either by your individual disposition or after systematic preparation. It is imperative to consider this fact when you attempt to tackle any problem you wish to solve. I remember the tragicomic case of a housewife who disliked housework and finally had to consult a psychiatrist. The latter advised her to use positive thinking in order to counteract her negative mental attitude and to say or think "I love to dust and clean" while she worked.

Positive auto-suggestions can be most helpful; in this case, however, the housewife, not having previously gone through adequate mental-emotional preparation, was using a lie as an auto-suggestion, namely "I love housework!" although she hated it. Consequently, her unconscious rejected the meaning of an auto-suggestion which was in sharp contrast to her actual feelings.

QUESTION: Is it true that one should beware of so-called negative suggestions such as "I am *not* worried"—"I am *not* afraid"—"I will *not* smoke any more"—"Cigarettes taste horrible," and so on?

ANSWER: Yes, it is true, because you lie to your unconscious if you say "Cigarettes taste horrible." Obviously, you are trying to convince yourself of something that doesn't concur with what you actually feel. Although you want to give up smoking, the cigarette doesn't taste horrible to you, instead you like it too much, otherwise there wouldn't be any necessity to give yourself suggestions to the contrary. It would be much better if, for example, you were to impress on your mind "I can and I do refrain from smoking, because it is harmful to me!" Don't ever lie to your unconscious; face the facts squarely during your preparatory work! As for negative suggestions such as "I am *not* afraid," they are not only ineffective, they may be dangerous.

The unconscious doesn't think or reason the same way we think and reason consciously. Freud observed this peculiarity of the unconscious mind: "The attitude of dreams towards the category of antithesis and contradiction is most striking. This category is simply ignored; the 'No' does not seem to exist for a dream."

The same is true regarding suggestions; for them too, the words "No" and "Not" do not seem to exist. Since the meaning of words used in suggestions has to be absorbed by the unconscious in order to make the suggestions effective and since the unconscious ignores the meaning of the words "No" and "Not," negative suggestions do not accomplish anything. For instance, in a suggestion such as "I am *not* afraid," the unconscious absorbs only the meaning of the word "afraid," because this is the word that stirs up psychic contents in which your possible reaction of fear is anchored. After all, you wouldn't wish to suggest to yourself that you shouldn't be afraid, if you weren't afraid, or you wouldn't wish that you shouldn't worry too much, if you didn't worry too much. And because this is so, your unconscious is *prepared* to respond to the meaning of the words *afraid* and *worry*. As a consequence, thoughts and emotions of fear and worry are stimulated, instead of weakened, by these words. It is obvious, therefore, that suggestions containing words which have a negative connotation for you, will not bring improvement. In fact, they may even contribute to the increase of fears, or aggravate other negative tendencies.

QUESTION: How do hypnoidal suggestions avoid lying to the unconscious?

ANSWER: Hypnoidal suggestions don't directly attack emotional problems, negative emotional attitudes, bad habits, and so on, at least not at the beginning. The "take the bull by the horns" method may be successful at times, but only if the attitude to be improved hasn't had time to become too deeply ingrained in the structure of our personality. In other words, only if it is not too weighty a problem will the direct approach be likely to succeed.

But in general anyone approaching negative emotional attitudes and difficulties by direct suggestions would be comparable to a traveler who considers a beeline to his destination the quickest route to take. But this reasoning could be deceptive because by following a straight line from one place to another, he might find himself stopped by an impassable mountain range or drowning in a lake. When attacking emotional problems directly, our own emotional vulnerability may take the place of the lake in which we drown, while our resistance, like the impassable mountain range, may block any further progress. Consequently, a detour, even though tedious, will be more likely to lead us to our goal.

39. GET ON GOOD TERMS
WITH YOURSELF

In every form of development, of learning, of training, we progress by steps and degrees towards proficiency. This refers also to the development and use of our mental resources. But before we can deal satisfactorily with the tasks and pleasures of living, our mental-emotional qualities have to be developed properly and this principle applies also to all attempts to remedy negative mental attitudes. It is essential, however, to have a genuine wish to develop our positive or to correct our negative traits and qualities. This wish, like any other, has its more or less strong motivation. If the motivation is a constructive one such as a desire for achievement or a desire to overcome unfortunate mental attitudes, it is this motivating drive which should be stimulated by hypnoidal suggestions and *then* made use of toward fulfillment of the wish. But this final step can be undertaken successfully only if the preparatory groundwork has been laid.

QUESTION: Of what would this groundwork consist, if, for instance, I am troubled by lack of self-confidence?

ANSWER: You should begin by finding out *why* you think you lack self-confidence. Ask yourself whether you are afraid of displeasing others, of appearing awkward, of being ridiculed, or of being rejected.

Maybe you fear that your educational background is inadequate, or that you are not efficient enough at your work or in your life-situation. Perhaps you feel that your appearance is unappealing or you have an exaggerated tendency to compare yourself with others. When you examine these fears more closely, you will probably come to realize that you have been judging yourself too harshly by under-estimating your personality-assets, while overestimating your personality-liabilities. Maybe, when you were a child, your constructive urge to accomplish something was constantly interfered with and, as a consequence, your timidity and lack of working-skill increased, whereas your self-confidence decreased.

Lack of self-confidence may also stem from having been over-protected as a child, although it is rather difficult to draw a clearcut demarcation between the parent's possible over-protectiveness and genuine parental love, care and concern. There are many factual as well as imaginary reasons for lack of self-confidence and there is always some degree of anxiety present which contributes strongly to undermine feelings of security and self-confidence.

Although fears, lack of self-confidence and frustration may be entirely imaginary sometimes, the person who is harassed by them will derive little comfort from being told there is no actual justification for his negative feelings. A Moorish proverb says "He who is afraid of a thing, gives it power over him." Of course, he does! But the attempt to orient oneself more realistically and to figure out clearly the possible reasons for one's anxieties are, in most cases, not sufficient to conquer them. And yet this attempt is essential, because without conscious understanding of one's trouble, the subsequent coordination of emotional response to constructive thinking is hardly possible.

The case of one of my patients will serve as an example. Robert X, an electrical engineer, felt that he was hampered in his career by an excessive slowness. The conviction "I am too slow and cannot compete, or succeed in anything I do!" constantly haunted him; consequently his negative attitude turned into a conditioned emotional reflex-reaction. As a result of his negative and auto-suggestive thinking, he actually slowed down considerably; this, of course, diminished his self-confidence more and more. Finally, he followed the counsel of his physician who gave him the well-meant and popular but often misunderstood advice to replace his negative approach by a positive one. But this is not quite as simple as it sounds. In order to overcome a feeling of lack of self-confidence, this type of *direct* and *positive* approach usually consists of mere empty words to which the unconscious does not respond. It is quite natural, of course, that one wishes one were self-confident; however, the wish to react or not to react in a certain way, does not of itself bring about fulfillment of the wish.

When Robert X tried to convince himself by the positive auto-suggestion "I am just as quick and efficient in my work as anybody else!" he found not only that he derived no benefit from forcing himself to smother his negative feelings in positive suggestions, but also noticed a gradual increase in his emotional discomfort and insecurity. This is understandable, because there is no sizable difference in the effect of talking oneself into or out of one's discomfort. In both cases one exerts over-concentration on them. A mere theoretically positive approach is too weak to counteract successfully the negative emotional undercurrents which continue to function, because they remain unaffected by these pseudo-positive thoughts.

Before Robert X could change his negative attitude, he first had to acquire the *habit of thinking things through* and thus gain better judgment of the overall situation and of his own abilities. Robert X had to come to the point where he stopped giving mere lip-service to the betterment of his condition by saying: "I am just as quick and efficient as anybody else," while actually he *felt* his efficiency diminishing. It was true that he was somewhat slower than the average person and he had to begin to realize that some people have an inherent disposition to be slower than others and that there are considerable differences in the tempo of people's actions and reactions, ranging from extreme slowness to unusual swiftness. Slowness has its disadvantages, but may also have advantages—and so has swiftness. The quality of work done by a person who is on the slow side is often more thorough and his thinking more accurate than that of somebody who prides himself on being extremely quick. Robert X came to realize this fact in the course of his preparatory work; he also succeeded in remembering the circumstances which had caused his original slowness to become excessive. Finally, by means of hypnoidal suggestions, his conscious realizations became synchronized with his emotional reactions and he was able to build up genuine and well-justified self-confidence.

If you suffer from lack of self-confidence and want to get rid of this, or any other negative emotional attitude, you would do well to follow these steps:

1) Develop your ability to reason well and acquire the habit of thinking things through objectively. This practice will improve your judgment in reference to people, to ideas, to many subjects and objectives; most important of all, it will improve your ability for constructive self-evaluation.

2) It is almost impossible to be one hundred per cent objective about anything and, least of all, about oneself. Nevertheless, one has to endeavor to reach the highest possible score in objectivity. Your ability to do so will progress, provided that you keep up your efforts to be objective; making sporadic efforts will prove ineffectual.

3) Try to find out *what* causes your negative emotional attitude; then you should determine whether your negative feelings occur often or only in connection with specific circumstances. This soul-searching presupposes your ability to appraise yourself objectively and this ability will help you in many ways. For instance, it will prevent you from catering to an unfortunate overawareness of self as a result of comparing yourself too often and too intensely with other people. Strange as it may sound, overawareness of oneself is often based on vanity. In turn, vanity may become a main cause for inaccurate self-evaluation; this may lead either into feelings of exaggerated self-confidence, into cockiness, or into lack of self-confidence; most of the time, cockiness is merely a disguise for lack of self-confidence.

QUESTION: Why does comparison with other people interfere with adequate self-evaluation?

ANSWER: If you tend to compare yourself with other people, you feel a motivation to do so. Usually this motivation is based on inaccurate self-evaluation and dims your ability to judge yourself objectively; it is simply a vicious circle. It is clear that self-critical appraisal should never consist of moralizing, or of belittling self-accusations, nor should it be self-complacent. Only when self-appraisal is as objective as possible, does it amount to sound self-evaluation.

Continual comparison with others also involves the danger of imitation and, all too often, an inadvisable form of identification. By creating imitative images within ourselves, we apply a type of positive or negative auto-suggestion, which powerfully affects our personality. Very often, imitative images are created by comparing ourselves with others; this may have consequences which will depend on what we consider to be desirable or undesirable qualities in the model we have chosen to imitate. Unfortunately, our faculty to judge these qualities correctly may be clouded by our very desire to imitate them! For example, a man may feel that he lacks sufficient masculine strength and therefore likes to compare and identify himself with the so-called "tough guy" in the movies, whose brutality he mistakes for masculinity. Or a woman may tend to identify herself with immensely wealthy movie heroines. If the woman dreams only occasionally of wearing precious jewels and furs, it might give her spirits a lift! But if she sees herself continually in life-situations which are completely alien to the reality of her own circumstances, she may easily develop feelings of envy, resentment and frustration. Countless other examples could illustrate how badly our personality may be affected by wrongly directed imitative and auto-suggestive images. Children, as we know, imitate habitually; however, in a child imitation may serve as a natural stepping-stone to learning and development. The opposite is true of adults; they arrest their development by imitation.

There is a great difference between *learning* and *imitation*. An adult may imitate ideas without learning from them, or he may fail to derive real benefit from imitating desirable character-traits, because his behavior remains a mere surface-mimicry and his "noble gestures" have no basis in noble motives.

Adults imitate fashions, customs and tastes; they may imitate moral conduct and parrot opinions and slogans regarding politics, philosophical concepts, art and literature. Our imitative tendencies are almost limitless and often are brought to a halt only by the measure of our genuine desire to give up superficial imitation. It is not possible to *imitate* kindness, integrity, reliability, consideration, emotional generosity; instead we have to endeavor to live up to these human attributes. Nor can we imitate a sense for ethics, a sense of humor, good taste, or tact. We can, however, come to appreciate and consequently to emulate desirable personality- and character-traits in others; then it is no longer superficial imitation, but a process of shaping our own personality. And yet a peculiar distinction exists between our endeavors to live up to *positive* forms of personality-development and our *negative* imitative tendencies; to develop negative tendencies gives us considerably less trouble than the often very strenuous striving for positive gains.

However, by improving your ability for adequate self-evaluation and constructive self-direction, your striving for positive gains will cost you less and less effort and, besides, this improvement will provide you with a source of genuine self-confidence.

QUESTION: Is it possible to overcome bad habits by the method of hypnoidal self-development and how does one go about it?

ANSWER: Bad habits can be overcome by the method of hypnoidal self-development. But in order to succeed, you have to consider first whether you are inclined to acquire habits all too easily and then cannot find the strength to shake them off again, or whether there are additional reasons for your inability to overcome a bad habit or habits. These additional psychological reasons may merely contribute to the bad habit, or they may be at the root of it. The habit of excessive drinking, for instance, is usually linked to deep-rooted personality-malfunctioning; of course, excessive drinking is often an addiction, but many addictions start out as habits.

Either one or several psychological factors may be responsible for a person's lack of desirable and desired self-direction. If this lack is complicated by personality-shortcomings, these may have to be dealt with before the habit itself can be overcome. But whatever the case, the following questions are specifically designed to advance the preparatory work needed to overcome an undesirable habit:

1) Is the habit in question the only one you wish to break?
2) Do you recall how you acquired this one habit or others you may have?
3) Do you function well only if everything is on an even keel and going along smoothly?

4) Do discomforts or complications in your everyday life throw you off balance easily?

5) Are you capable of constructive mental-emotional self-direction and constructive self-discipline: (a) most of the time? (b) only under certain circumstances? (c) practically never?

6) Is it difficult for you to deny yourself anything in general or only under some particular circumstances?

7) Is it difficult for you to deny yourself one or another thing, but only under certain circumstances? For instance: Do you smoke, or drink too much either when you (a) are under mental-emotional strain and pressure? (b) feel sorry for yourself? (c) are under tension, especially when you are alone?

8) Are the circumstances which irritate you, such as an unpleasant situation in the office or too much friction at home, within your control: (a) by changing your own attitudes? (b) by changing your attitudes to a certain extent? If either (a) or (b) is the case, do you intend to change your attitudes and will you attempt to do so immediately?

9) Could you influence the circumstances which irritate you for the better if you were to try and do so?

10) Are these circumstances beyond your control or do you only take this for granted? Could a serious effort on your part bring about a favorable change?

11) Do you shrink from the effort because of indecision or indolence, or because of fear that you will not succeed?

12) If you *want* to make an effort, do you feel sufficiently resolute and able to make this effort or do you feel you would need greater mental and emotional strength?

Let us transpose question 12 into the physical sphere and immediately you will realize that there are weights which even the strongest man cannot lift. He might nevertheless be able to lift the weight, if he knew *how and at what point* to apply his strength. The same principle holds true in reference to emotional difficulties.

Write down your answers to these twelve questions; then read your answers through and you will recognize the point where you function least well and where you should apply your strength.

Practice psycho-gymnastic exercises in order to improve your self-directive ability. Later on, use hypnoidal suggestions; they will stimulate your mental-emotional strength and enable you to cope with your difficulties successfully.

Certain forms of thinking can also become a matter of habit; for example, the habit of worrying too much or the habit of permitting oneself to be discontented with almost everything. These habits should be remedied in approximately the same manner as other undesirable habits. Often we find that thoughtlessness and inconsiderateness are nothing but bad habits, although at the same time they may be the consequence of a specific character-disposition on which these habits thrive. *Training* oneself to a different way of thinking and reacting emotionally has, in many cases, a very good effect on improving an unfavorable character-disposition. In any case, conscious conditioning in sensible self-discipline by means of both psycho-gymnastic exercises and suitable hypnoidal suggestions, will be most helpful.

QUESTION: How does one go about activating latent faculties and talents?

ANSWER: Latent faculties and talents can be activated when the contents of hypnoidal suggestions, aimed at the awakening of these faculties, penetrate into the unconscious. But kernels of the faculties to be awakened have to be in you, although consciously you may not have the faintest notion that you possess them. However, stimulated by adequate hypnoidal suggestions, all of a sudden you may become aware, let us say, of an urge to write or to paint, play an instrument, study languages, and so on. It cannot be foreseen in which of many different directions each reader's potentialities may lie and be materialized. Therefore, this book contains *generalized* hypnoidal suggestions sufficiently strong to activate any of your latent potentialities.

QUESTION: Is it possible to further more practical faculties besides artistic talents?

ANSWER: Certainly. Hypnoidal self-development brings out and improves any constructive faculty you may possess and wish to develop. This method fertilizes your mind to make your ideas more abundant and productive; it intensifies your ability to organize your activities in the most lucrative way; it increases your working-power and your efficiency in business or profession and in other matters important to you. But to awaken and develop *specific* faculties, hypnoidal suggestions have to be adapted in content as well as in formulation to individual requirements.

QUESTION: How does one go about developing specific faculties or talents, for instance, as a writer?

ANSWER: In order to develop your writing talent, several factors have to be ascertained first. For example, if you feel that you have a talent for writing and if you want to stimulate this talent, it has to be ascertained what type of writing you prefer, whether it is fiction, scientific writing, mystery stories, essays, poetry, theatrical plays, or, perhaps, journalism. The effect of hypnoidal suggestions becomes intensified, if their contents are directed towards the stimulation of a specific faculty. Next, it should be determined what has prevented you so far from either using your talent at all, or from being as successful as you could be.

However, maybe you are quite successful already, but want to further improve the quality of your writing, or wish your imagination were more prolific, or that you could express yourself more succinctly and originally. These and many other factors have to be considered before *individualized* hypnoidal suggestions can be designed for successful use.

QUESTION: Does one self-administer *individualized* hypnoidal suggestions in the same manner as *generalized* hypnoidal suggestions, or does one proceed differently?

ANSWER: The procedure is the same. The difference between *generalized* and *individualized* hypnoidal suggestions consists only in their contents and formulation, but *not in the manner of application.*

The instructions in the next section give ample information on how to self-administer hypnoidal suggestions. The benefits you can derive from hypnoidal suggestions will be the greater, the more earnestly you comply with the instructions. At first, this may seem rather uphill work, but soon you will find that practice enables you to carry out the instructions with increasing ease. Ultimately, you will experience a distinct change for the better in your everyday spontaneous emotional reactions, in your attitudes and in all your activities.

40. INSTRUCTIONS FOR USING THE HYPNOIDAL STAGE

Two different steps are required, both essential to ensure full success in hypnoidal self-development.

STEP ONE consists in the training for, and practicing of concentration and meditation.

STEP TWO consists in using the hypnoidal stage in a specific manner that permits the complete absorption of meaningful thoughts, stimulated by preceding meditation. Step Two also consists in *self-administering* hypnoidal suggestions by reading, or reciting them silently in hypnoidal monotony-rhythms according to the directions on pp. 219-227. In addition, hypnoidal suggestions are *recorded* in specifically designed monotony-rhythms to be played back to you while you are in the hypnoidal stage.

Don't be concerned about the amount of time you have to devote to the necessary exercises. They don't take up more than about fifteen minutes a day; this is possibly less time than you might expend on daily physical exercises to keep fit. It is obvious that it is at least as important to attend to fitness of mind as it is to attend to fitness of body.

The effect of concentration and meditation on personality-development is a known fact. If you practice concentration and meditation properly, you avail yourself of a forceful instrument which will aid you to achieve your goals.

Within the method of hypnoidal self-development, the beneficial effect of concentration and meditation becomes considerably intensified. *Their interaction* with the hypnoidal stage, hypnoidal suggestions, and monotony-rhythms produces a unique impact on the development of our personality.

CONCENTRATION as used in hypnoidal self-development consists of:

1. Training and applying your ability to focus your attention on one particular subject or object or part of an object to the exclusion of all else. This type of concentration is the *impersonal* form.

2. Training and applying your ability to direct your *feelings* and *sensations* deliberately towards certain imagined actions and situations and to project yourself into experiencing these feelings as if you were actually participating in those actions and situations. This type of concentration is the *personal* form.

MEDITATION makes use of the acquired skill of both *impersonal and personal* forms of concentration. During meditation, you need to use the *impersonal* form of concentration in order to focus your exclusive attention on *thinking through* the aspects of some worthwhile personal aspiration, objective, or idea. For example, you might meditate on the meaning of *patience* or of *compassion* by thinking through what these character-traits stand for and what they mean to you. But here you need the additional skill of using *personal* concentration, because you have to *feel* yourself into *being* patient, or compassionate, or whatever you may have chosen to meditate on.

You may meditate also by *thinking through* aspects of some artistic or scientific problem; and you may meditate on how to tackle one or the other of your professional or business problems. In fact, you may meditate on any activity, idea, or interest in your everyday life, in order to become more efficient generally, or to attain greater proficiency in some specific field.

You may meditate on the contents of a meaningful sentence you have read somewhere or on the applicable truth of a wise axiom. You may meditate on a poem which captures your imagination by its beauty and depth of thought. But within hypnoidal self-development you have to meditate, first of all, on the contents and meaning of hypnoidal suggestions. Meditate especially on the paragraph(s) of the hypnoidal suggestions which you intend to self-administer later on that same day, while you are in the hypnoidal stage.

The method of hypnoidal self-development doesn't use meditation in the theological sense or in that of Yoga practices; it doesn't strive for mystical experience or for Indian Nirvana. *Hypnoidal self-development simply takes advantage of a few basic rules contained in the mental techniques of concentration and meditation, because they facilitate the disciplining of the mind for constructive purposes.* In other words, the method of hypnoidal self-development requires a *personal form of meditation.*

The *personal* approach to meditation is not in opposition to the customary concept of meditation. The Swiss Buddhist monk Hans-Ulrich Rieker points to this: "Far be it from me to wish to dictate how you must follow the path to your inner strength. The ways to meditation are as manifold as are the faces around us . . . What is important is the cause within . . . It is always best not to occupy oneself intellectually with meditation . . . it is . . . intuition which moulds our 'inner attitudes' . . . Once we realize that certain truths can only be understood intuitively and that our intuition is near to the miraculous, then we have already taken the first step towards developing it." (*The Secret of Meditation,* 1957.)

Intuition, as it is understood in these words, does not constitute guesswork and hunches, neither does it infer that intuition is inferior to rational thinking. Rather we must be mindful of Thomas Aquinas' interpretation which affirms that intuition may transcend the efficiency peculiar to our rational thinking. It is when we immerse ourselves in meditation that this form of intuition may take over and bring us closer to the fulfillment of our aspirations.

And now let us begin with the directions of STEP ONE (A) Concentration and (B) Meditation.

STEP ONE

"Concentration means occupying oneself with one object exclusively; so exclusively that even the intention to concentrate is forgotten

... it is not only advisable but absolutely essential to be concentrated before entering meditation."

Hans-Ulrich Rieker

(A) *Concentration*

While you are concentrating or meditating, your mind must not be concerned with time. Therefore, all future references to time and time-limits to be set for concentration and meditation should be handled as follows: Just before you begin to concentrate or meditate, *verify the time.* If it is, let us say, 8.30 A.M., then set the alarm-clock for 8.40 or 8.45 A.M., making the limit ten to fifteen minutes, never longer. Whenever you stop concentrating or meditating before the alarm-clock goes off, one glance at the clock will show you exactly how long you have concentrated or meditated.

Whatever subject or object you may have chosen as a concentration-exercise, keep your attention fixed on it exclusively. It may take several weeks before you can keep your attention focused exclusively on your exercise for a certain length of time. If, after two or three weeks, you are able to keep your attention fixed on your concentration-exercise for about *two* minutes, you will have accomplished a great deal.

Nevertheless, try to increase the length of time your attention remains focused on each concentration-exercise up to between three to five minutes.

Concentration-exercises in the form of puzzles or brain-teasers may require somewhat more or somewhat less than the time-limit for the usual concentration-exercises, i.e., five minutes. However, the length of time you can keep your attention focused exclusively on one particular subject or object is less important than to establish the habit of practicing regularly. *Practice every day!*

The following few examples of concentration-exercises lead to concentration in an *impersonal manner:*

1) Concentrate on counting up to twenty, let us say, not too fast and not too slowly, in more or less the same rhythm. Or count up to twenty and back again; in both cases *without thinking of anything else.* As soon as you master this exercise, you may, while you are counting, *visualize yourself* slowly tracing the

numerals, either in the air with your finger, or with chalk on a blackboard. Or you may trace the numerals in your imagination *without visualizing* yourself using any means of doing so.

2) Concentrate on tracing the lines of an intricate abstract drawing such as you may find in some advertisements or, for instance, in books on calligraphy. A very good exercise is to concentrate on the pathways of maze-puzzles, at first, for a minute or so, then, later on, up to three and four minutes.

3) Choose an object or part of an object, such as the hands of a watch or a door-knob. Concentrate on the object, or part of it, exclusively, without blinking your eyes for about twenty seconds. Or concentrate on an object or some part of it without blinking your eyes and, in addition, count up to twenty, or up to twenty and back again.

4) Attempt to solve in your mind one of those brain teasers or puzzles, which are not too hard to solve, but require some abstract thinking. For example: "In a certain bank in Fargo, North Dakota, the positions of cashier, manager and teller are held by Brown, Jones and Smith, though not necessarily in that order. The teller, who was an only child, earns the least. Smith, who married Brown's sister, earns more than the manager. What position does each man hold?" (*Puzzles in Thought and Logic.*) In the "List of Books Recommended for Additional Reading," you will find titles of several books which will supply you with material of this and other types of *impersonal* mental exercises.

Now you may turn to the *personal* form of concentration exercises. This personal form of concentration *easily merges into meditation.*

Regardless of whether you meditate directly on your individual problems or aspirations or whether you meditate on hypnoidal suggestions, you must be able to grasp the meaning *not only intellectually,* but also *with your feeling!* In order to accomplish this, it may be necessary for you to begin by using specific training-exercises.

These training-exercises will condition you to *direct* and to *project* your feelings at will. The training-exercises are quite simple and don't consume more than three to five minutes a day. Discontinue these specific training-exercises as soon as you have acquired the faculty to project yourself into *experiencing* certain imaginary situations and activities and have also learned to reactivate or create constructive feelings at will.

To direct and project your imagination and your emotions at will is an indispensable prerequisite to meditating successfully, before subsequently applying hypnoidal suggestions while you are in the hypnoidal stage.

EXAMPLES OF
SPECIFIC MENTAL TRAINING-EXERCISES

While practicing the exercises, *do not merely describe* the object you visualize or the situation you imagine yourself to be in or the activity in which you imagine yourself engaged, such as watching a baseball game, painting a room, and so on. Instead try actually to *feel yourself experiencing* the situation you have selected and *feel yourself into doing certain things. The necessity for this cannot be stressed too often.*

Imagine Yourself . . . . washing dishes
    "   " . . . . dancing
    "   " . . . . watching the ocean-waves
    "   " . . . . flying an airplane
    "   " . . . . walking in the rain
    "   " . . . . rowing a boat
    "   " . . . . planting flowers
    "   " . . . . climbing a hill
    "   " . . . . meeting interesting people
    "   " . . . . driving in heavy traffic with consideration and not being irritated

Imagine Yourself . . . . writing about a subject which intrigues you
    "   " . . . . disentangling some confused situation
    "   " . . . . inhaling the fragrance of carnations or other flower

Imagine Yourself . . . . outlining characters for a story or play

"   "   . . . . doing a good job of selling something or other

"   "   . . . . engaging in some difficult activity successfully

"   "   . . . . speaking in a relaxed but efficient manner to a superior in your office

"   "   . . . . engaging in some sport, for instance: playing a game of golf, a game of tennis, and so on.

Visualize . . . . the arrangement of a room in which you have been only once

"   . . . . the colors of a sunset

"   . . . . antique furniture (in detail)

"   . . . . yourself applying for a job

"   . . . . yourself succeeding in some contest

"   . . . . driving through scenery which appeals to you. Recall those spots which you found especially attractive

"   . . . . modern furniture (in detail) and so on.

Evoke the sound of . . . . a dog barking; a train whistling

"   "   "   "   . . . . bells chiming; rain pouring down

"   "   "   "   . . . . walking on a path covered with snow

"   "   "   "   . . . . and so on.

a) Invent other mental training-exercises, regardless of whether the task or situation you select is easy or difficult.

b) Be careful to *avoid* feeling yourself into any task or situation, or visualizing any object which causes you to *feel* deep fear, disgust, or any other upsetting emotion or physical discomfort.

c) Should lack of self-confidence be your problem, for instance, then don't imagine yourself in a situation which makes you feel insecure. If, as a mental training-exercise, you were to project yourself into feeling insecure, you would condition this feeling in yourself more and more and, instead of bolstering your self-confidence, you would diminish it ever more. However, you can overcome this insecurity and other negative feelings by concentrating and projecting yourself into those positive feelings which are the *opposite* of your negative feelings.

But don't lie to your unconscious and suggest to yourself that you are happy, if you are *not* happy; or that you feel self-confident and secure, if you feel insecure. Returning to the example of lack of self-confidence: almost certainly your life has contained some experience where, at least, you came close to feeling self-confident and secure. Endeavor to *recreate that feeling of self-confidence!* If you don't succeed immediately, try again and again, at different times of the day and also on different days; finally you will succeed. But never try too hard and if you feel tired, break off for that particular time or day.

Furthermore, don't merely recreate descriptively the occasion on which you felt self-confident; try to *recapture the feeling!* Repeat this projection of feeling secure and self-confident every day for a couple of minutes or so and continue repeating the projection during several weeks until you notice definite progress. Then, and only then, try to detach this feeling from the particular instance or situation in which you *originally* experienced it. This separation is necessary in order to generalize the feeling of self-confidence instead of attaching it to its original cause only.

d) Follow the same procedure in order to overcome any other negative attitude you may have.

e) Once you have mastered the ability to project your feelings at will into various situations and activities, you may begin to concentrate on the contents of hypnoidal suggestions and meditate on them. To do this successfully, the following hints are valuable: for example, one paragraph of the hypnoidal suggestions deals with mental-emotional self-direction.

Try to imagine and *feel* as if you were actually in a situation in which you direct yourself satisfactorily. In short, imagine and *feel* yourself as *being* in a situation in which you put your constructive intention or intentions into action.

f) If it is difficult for you to *feel* yourself into a certain situation in which you act and react in a positive manner such as applying constructive self-direction, it will help you to recall an incident in which you actually succeeded in positive self-direction. Try to recapture the *emotional echo of gratification* you very likely felt at that time. It is immaterial whether or not the occasion was a particularly important one. Quite an ordinary incident may serve your purpose. For instance, you might have liked going to a show on some evening, but you had to write an important letter. You were reluctant to write that letter and you could have postponed it a day or two. Nevertheless, you decided to stay home and get the whole thing off your chest. In this case, probably, you had a feeling of gratification at having made and carried out a sensible decision.

Again it should be pointed out that constructive self-direction does not imply constant struggle with oneself and perpetual self-denial. Constructive self-direction only means to act in agreement with one's better insight. *The more skillful you become in handling this ability, the less inner conflict is involved.*

And should you, on rare occasions, decide to act against your better insight, well, if it is not too important an occasion—every rule has its exception!

g) Another paragraph of the hypnoidal suggestions concerns itself with *conditioned emotional reflexes.*

You should realize that you feel conditioned emotional reflexes in the same manner as you feel spontaneous emotional reflex-reactions, namely, independently of your selective thinking, or before your selective thinking has had time to set in.

Conditioned emotional reflexes as well as spontaneous emotional reactions are distinguished by the pleasant or unpleasant quality of their effect on us. It is natural, of course, that you wish to erase those unpleasant emotional reactions which have gradually been conditioned in you and, instead, endeavor to replace them by more pleasant and favorable reflex-reactions. To accomplish this, you have to be consistent in your attempts and *feel* yourself into such emotional reactions as will lead towards the reflex-reactions to which you aspire.

h) When you use hypnoidal suggestions as training-exercise for concentration and meditation, recall any other positive emotional reactions you may have had in the past and *which coincide more or less vividly* with the meaning of the hypnoidal suggestions you have chosen as training-exercise. While reading the paragraphs of the hypnoidal suggestions, try to reactivate any positive emotional response and *feel yourself into this response for several seconds up to a couple of minutes.*

(B) *Meditation*

1) Make yourself as comfortable as possible. Try to reduce to a minimum any external disturbance such as extreme noise and any physical unease such as uncomfortable clothes, uncomfortable position, and so on.

2) Detach yourself from all thoughts and feelings not connected with the goal on which you wish to meditate.

3) Meditate only on *one* goal or on those paragraphs of hypnoidal suggestions with a special interrelated meaning at the same time.

4) Don't start meditation when you are particularly irritable, fidgety, or tired.

5) Above all, be and remain calm and relaxed during your endeavor to meditate.

6) Concentrate fully in thought and feeling on the essentials of your goal or on the meaning of the hypnoidal suggestions.

7) Although it is considered preferable to meditate early in the morning before breakfast, it is far more important in the *personalized* form of meditation to choose exactly the time when you feel as close as possible to being relaxed and ready to meditate. Besides, in the method of hypnoidal self-development, it is advisable to meditate before you go to sleep in the evening or before you take a nap in day-time.

8) Meditate at approximately the same time every day.

9) In order to meditate successfully, you need not assume any particular position of body such as a certain way of crossing your legs. The oriental forms of meditation favor positions of this type and other similar ones, probably because such positions cause physical sensations which provide a background accompaniment to meditation comparable to the bass notes which underscore a musical theme.

If one and the same physical background-sensation is repeatedly linked with concentrated thinking and feeling, their interaction will intensify the effect of meditative thinking and feeling.

10) A similar effect can be created during meditation within the method of hypnoidal self-development. It suffices that you join your hands as in prayer, but with merely the tips of your fingers touching each other. To avoid fatigue, rest your elbows on some kind of support such as chair-arms or a table. First, for a minute or so, *concentrate* on nothing but the physical sensation you experience by joining your fingertips. During this act of concentration you will become aware of a sensation of an overall strength which will provide the intensifying background sensation to your subsequent meditation on some specific goal, or on hypnoidal suggestions.

It is, of course, not strictly necessary to make use of this hand-position in meditation, but it is very helpful.

11) When you have settled down to meditate, take *one* deep breath with your *mouth closed. Inhale* with your diaphragm; don't inhale by expanding your chest. *Be relaxed! Breathe gently! Never force the depth of inhalation!*

When you *exhale,* do it slowly through your *opened mouth.* This type of breathing serves to enrich the blood with oxygen and promotes a sensation of well-being. It is advisable to start and to terminate meditation with a pleasant sensation. Breathing in this manner is recommended here solely to create a feeling of well-being and *not* as a breathing-exercise per se. Breathing-exercises without competent training and supervision are not advisable because under certain circumstances they may become harmful. The method of hypnoidal self-development does not require breathing-exercises.

12) Don't confuse wishful thinking with meditation! Avoid mere wishful thinking! Reach beyond the theoretical desire to attain your goal or goals and *direct your meditative thinking and feeling as if you were actually in the process of achieving your goal.*

13) If you meditate on a specific goal you wish to attain, outline your goal *in writing,* enumerating all the positive factors which you think will make it possible for you to achieve your goal. For instance, should you wish to be more successful in your business or profession, figure out first what has hampered you in your efforts thus far. Then itemize the positive factors which will be helpful. Meditate on the positive factors, never on the negative ones.

   Apart from your personal requirements, the overall prerequisites for success are, of course, justified self-confidence, good reasoning, tenacity and inner strength which will help you to develop and carry out sound ideas and decisions.

14) Never meditate on the negative aspects of what you wish to accomplish. If you meditate on the ability to relax at will, for instance, don't concentrate and meditate on how uncomfortable it is to feel tense!

Or, for example, if you suffer from lack of self-confidence, never concentrate and meditate on your desire to get rid of this painfully negative feeling. Instead, imagine a situation in which you can feel sure of yourself.

15) Should thoughts and feelings unrelated to the subject you have chosen intrude themselves *while* you are meditating, interrupt your meditation and start out afresh.

You may find yourself obliged to repeat this procedure several times, but don't devote more than five minutes to it within one and the same session. Should you still be unable to direct your thoughts and feelings exclusively toward the subject of your meditation, then give it up for that day. It may take several weeks before you will be able to meditate properly; but don't get discouraged! Ultimately, you will succeed in directing your thoughts and feelings with an "effortless effort."

16) Meditation can be considered successful when it is sustained for a minimum of two or three consecutive minutes.

17) But you may extend successful meditation beyond two or three minutes up to ten and fifteen minutes a day.

Do not devote more than ten minutes a day to successful meditation either on your goal or on the meaning of hypnoidal suggestions. It is essential to *restrict* successful meditation to ten minutes a day at the very most, otherwise meditation may turn into *unrestricted* and futile day-dreaming.

18) Successful meditation can give you a sensation of becoming completely welded with your goal or the meaning of hypnoidal suggestions. It is a process in which "thought and being become identical."

19) While you meditate, *be relaxed, but stay alert!* The alertness of your mind is necessary to make meditation successful. Drowsiness, *while* you meditate, interferes with the effect of meditation.

20) However, *towards the end of your meditation, permit yourself to glide into drowsiness;* this leads us to step two.

41. MEDITATION IN COMBINATION WITH THE HYPNOIDAL STAGE—STEP TWO

a) When you meditate on your personal goal and feel drowsiness coming on *towards the end of your meditation, give in to it* and let yourself glide into sleep. In this manner you take the contents of your meditation through the hypnoidal stage along into sleep.

b) It is immaterial whether you sleep only for a short while or longer; but to sleep or to take a brief nap *after* successful meditation is important.

Taking the contents of your meditation through the hypnoidal stage into sleep favors beneficial mental imprints on your unconscious. For this reason it is advisable to meditate shortly *before* you intend to go to sleep in the evening or *before* you intend to take a nap during the day.

c) When you feel that you succeed in what you set out to accomplish, it will be sufficient for you to meditate twice or three times a week. But don't give meditation up completely.

42. HOW TO SELF-ADMINISTER HYPNOIDAL SUGGESTIONS

a) To obtain good results, self-administer hypnoidal suggestions at least four times a week.

b) The day on which you intend to self-administer hypnoidal suggestions while you are in the hypnoidal stage, *meditate* on the meaning of that paragraph, or those paragraphs of the suggestions which you intend to self-administer the same day while you are falling asleep.

c) *Meditation* on the paragraph(s) on the same day is essential.

d) Meditate on the general meaning contained in the paragraph(s) and also on the meaning the contents have for you personally.

e) Do not meditate on the contents of more than three paragraphs of the hypnoidal suggestions during one period of meditation and do not self-administer more than these three paragraphs while you are in the hypnoidal stage.

f) *The best time to meditate* on hypnoidal suggestions is *just before you settle down to sleep* in the evening or before you take a nap in daytime.

g) Should this schedule be inconvenient, then *meditate* at a more convenient time during the day, but preferably at about the same time each day.

h) While you are falling asleep, read the hypnoidal suggestions, but now *in the indicated hypnoidal monotony-rhythm.* Do this *quite mechanically,* because any attempt to pay attention or merely register the meaning of the suggestions interrupts the hypnoidal stage and thereby interferes with the intensified mental receptivity brought on by increasing drowsiness.

i) For this reason it is preferable that you *memorize* the paragraph(s), if you possibly can. Then, while you are in the hypnoidal stage, silently recite them in the indicated hypnoidal monotony-rhythm. In this case, you will probably want to self-administer not more than one paragraph of the hypnoidal suggestions. As already explained, recite the suggestions quite mechanically but don't permit your thoughts to wander while you are reciting the suggestions. This too would interfere with the effectiveness of the hypnoidal stage.

j) By means of hypnoidal monotony-rhythms, the suggestions are injected into the unconscious. And, while our conscious self recedes and the gateway to our innermost self is opened, the meaning of the suggestions is absorbed by the unconscious.

k) Don't pay attention whether or not you stop reading or reciting in the middle of a paragraph; in other words, don't prevent yourself from dozing off! Relax and let drowsiness envelop you more and more while you glide into actual sleep.

l) During the ensuing period of natural sleep, the meaning of the hypnoidal suggestions that has been carried deep into your unconscious by the monotony-rhythm will be consolidated and actively integrated as a constructive element within your personality make-up.

m) Self-administer regularly one to three paragraphs of the suggestions throughout three weeks. Then switch to other paragraphs of the hypnoidal suggestions and self-administer *these* paragraphs for three weeks until you have self-administered all the paragraphs you have selected as the ones from which you wish to benefit.

Now you may self-administer all of the selected paragraphs of hypnoidal suggestions alternately.

But always self-administer the same paragraph or group of paragraphs during one and the same week.

In this manner you will have very good results within about six months.

Of course, hypnoidal suggestions played back to you on records or tapes achieve the best results, because you remain unhampered by any effort and your increasing drowsiness and passivity let you benefit from the hypnoidal stage and the suggestions to the full extent.

Besides, recorded suggestions continue to instill their meaning into the unconscious through the various levels of the hypnoidal stage, whereas you would stop reading or reciting the hypnoidal suggestions as you go deeper into drowsiness and finally fall asleep.

Nevertheless, even without records or tapes, you can get excellent results with self-administered hypnoidal suggestions, if you follow the directions carefully.

43. GENERALIZED HYPNOIDAL SUGGESTIONS

From my collection of many different hypnoidal suggestions in numerous types of hypnoidal monotony-rhythms, I have selected the following eight paragraphs. They are particularly well suited for *successful self-administration* without records or tapes.

The text of hypnoidal suggestions must not be judged by literary standards. Words and sentences have been chosen solely for their suitability to convey their meaning most forcefully through the monotony-rhythms during the hypnoidal stage.

The text lines of each of the following paragraphs are marked alphabetically: (a), (b), (c), and so on. These letters serve to indicate the manner in which the hypnoidal monotony-rhythms are to be used when being self-administered. You will find a separate indicator under each paragraph.

After you have chosen the paragraph or paragraphs you wish to self-administer, write down the complete text in the specific monotony-rhythm as directed by the indicator.

The act of writing down the text yourself will help you not only to read or recite the suggestions fluently while you are in the hypnoidal stage, but will also impress their meaning and rhythm on your conscious mind.

PARAGRAPH I: TO CONDITION SOUND
MENTAL-EMOTIONAL REFLEXES

(a) I SUCCEED .... (a)
(b) IN DEVELOPING AND CONDITIONING WITHIN MYSELF (b)
(c) SOUND MENTAL-EMOTIONAL REFLEXES .... (c)
(d) AND .... (d)
(e) MY SOUND MENTAL-EMOTIONAL REFLEXES HELP ME (e)
(f) TO RESPOND WITH ALL MY FEELINGS................ (f)
(g) TO MY CONSTRUCTIVE THINKING................... (g)
(h) AND .... (h)
(i) MY SOUND AND HELPFUL MENTAL-EMOTIONAL RE-
     FLEXES .... (i)
(j) ARE AND REMAIN CO-ORDINATED .... (j)
(k) WITH MY CONSTRUCTIVE THINKING .... (k)
(l) AND .... (l)
(m) THEREFORE I SUCCEED .... (m)
(n) IN CREATING A GOOD WAY OF LIVING............. (n)
(o) ENJOYABLE TO MYSELF .... (o)
(p) AND TO THOSE AROUND ME. .... (p)

INDICATOR: Begin with line (a)
            Repeat   "   (a) and   ADD line (b)
            Repeat (a), (b)   "   ADD " (c)
            Repeat (a), (b) and (c) *twice*
            Repeat (a) to (c)   and   ADD " (d)
            Repeat (a) to (d)   "   ADD " (e)
            Repeat (e) *twice*
            Repeat (a) to (e) and   ADD " (f)
            Repeat (f) *twice*
            Repeat (a) to (f) and   ADD " (g)
            Repeat (e), (f), (g) *twice*
            Repeat (a) to (g) *twice*
            Repeat (a) to (g) and   ADD " (h)
            Repeat (a) to (h) and   ADD " (i)
            Repeat (a) to (i) and   ADD " (j)
            Repeat (a) to (j) and   ADD " (k)
            Repeat (i), (j) and (k) *twice*
            Repeat (a) to (k) and   ADD " (l)
            Repeat (a) to (l) and   ADD " (m)
            Repeat (a) to (m) and   ADD " (n)
            Repeat (a) to (n) and   ADD " (o)
            Repeat (a) to (o) and   ADD " (p)
            Repeat (m) to (p) *twice*
            Repeat (a) to (p).

PARAGRAPH II: TO STIMULATE INNER STRENGTH

(a) I FEEL INNER STRENGTH .... (a)
(b) I HAVE INNER STRENGTH.......................... (b)
(c) AND .... (c)
(d) MY INNER STRENGTH .... (d)
(e) IS AND REMAINS WELL INTEGRATED .... (e)
(f) WITHIN MY WHOLE BEING .... (f)
(g) MY INNER STRENGTH IS BENEFICIAL.............. (g)
(h) AND MY BENEFICIAL INNER STRENGTH .... (h)
(i) PERMEATES ALL MY THINKING AND FEELING....... (i)
(j) THEREFORE .... (j)
(k) I CAN AND I DO DIRECT AND APPLY............... (k)
(l) MY BENEFICIAL INNER STRENGTH .... (l)
(m) WISELY AND HELPFULLY .... (m)
(n) IN EVERYTHING .... (n)
(o) THAT I THINK, FEEL AND DO. .... (o)

INDICATOR: Begin with line (a)
              Repeat   " (a) and   ADD line (b)
              Repeat (a), (b) *twice*
              Repeat (a), (b)   "   ADD " (c)
              Repeat (a) to (c)   "   ADD " (d)
              Repeat (a) to (d)   "   ADD " (e)
              Repeat (a) to (e)   "   ADD " (f)
              Repeat (d) to (f) *twice*
              Repeat (a) to (f) and   ADD " (g)
              Repeat (a) to (g)   "   ADD " (h)
              Repeat (a) to (h)   "   ADD " (i)
              Repeat (a) to (i)   "   ADD " (j)
              Repeat (a) to (j)   "   ADD " (k)
              Repeat (a) to (k)   "   ADD " (l)
              Repeat (g) to (l) *twice*
              Repeat (a) to (l) and   ADD " (m)
              Repeat (m) *twice*
              Repeat (a) to (m) and ADD " (n)
              Repeat (a) to (n)   "   ADD " (o)
              Repeat (a) to (o).

PARAGRAPH III: TO STIMULATE GOOD REASONING AND INTUITIVE FACULTIES

(a) I SUCCEED IN THINKING AND REASONING . . . . (a)
(b) SOUNDLY, JUSTLY . . . . (b)
(c) CLEARLY AND EFFECTIVELY . . . . (c)
(d) AND I SUCCEED . . . . (d)
(e) IN KEEPING MY THOUGHTS AND FEELINGS . . . . (e)
(f) POSITIVE . . . . (f)
(g) WELL-BALANCED . . . . (g)
(h) ALERT . . . . (h)
(i) YET PLEASANTLY RELAXED . . . . (i)
(j) AND . . . . (j)
(k) I SUCCEEDED IN PERCEIVING AND SENSING SOUNDLY (k)
(l) AND DISTINCTLY . . . . (l)
(m) WITH MY INTUITIVE FACULTIES . . . . (m)
(n) AND MY POSITIVE THOUGHTS BLEND HARMONIOUSLY (n)
(o) WITH MY INTUITIVE FACULTIES . . . . (o)
(p) IN EVERYTHING . . . . (p)
(q) I AM THINKING, FEELING AND DOING . . . . (q)

```
INDICATOR: Begin with line (a)
           Repeat      " (a)   and   ADD line (b)
           Repeat (a), (b)      "    ADD  "   (c)
           Repeat (a) to (c)    "    ADD  "   (d)
           Repeat (a) to (d)    "    ADD  "   (e)
           Repeat (a) to (e)    "    ADD  "   (f)
           Repeat (a) to (f)    "    ADD  "   (g)
           Repeat (a) to (g)    "    ADD  "   (h)
           Repeat (a) to (h)    "    ADD  "   (i)
           Repeat (a) to (i)    "    ADD  "   (j)
           Repeat (a) to (j)    "    ADD  "   (k)
           Repeat (a) to (k)    "    ADD  "   (l)
           Repeat (a) to (l)    "    ADD  "   (m)
           Repeat (a) to (m)    "    ADD  "   (n)
           Repeat (a) to (n)    "    ADD  "   (o)
           Repeat (a) to (o)    "    ADD  "   (p)
           Repeat (a) to (p)    "    ADD  "   (q)
           Repeat (a) to (q).
```

PARAGRAPH IV: TO STIMULATE COORDINATION OF CONSTRUCTIVE THINKING WITH FEELING AND TO STIMULATE MENTAL-EMOTIONAL SELF-DIRECTION

(a) I SUCCEED .... (a)
(b) IN DEVELOPING AND USING MY INNATE ABILITY.... (b)
(c) TO THINK SENSIBLY AND CONSTRUCTIVELY......... (c)
(d) AND WITH MY FEELING I SUCCEED.................. (d)
(e) IN RESPONDING POSITIVELY .... (e)
(f) TO MY SENSIBLE AND CONSTRUCTIVE THINKING. ... (f)
(g) MY CONSTRUCTIVE THINKING AND FEELING........ (g)
(h) ARE AND REMAIN WELL CO-ORDINATED............. (h)
(i) AND WITH MY WELL CO-ORDINATED, ... (i)
(j) CONSTRUCTIVE THINKING AND FEELING .... (j)
(k) I SUCCEED .... (k)
(l) IN BUILDING UP AND KEEPING UP .... (l)
(m) SOUND MENTAL-EMOTIONAL SELF-DIRECTION .... (m)
(n) IN EVERYTHING I THINK, FEEL AND DO. .... (n)
(o) MY BENEFICIAL INNER STRENGTH HELPS ME .... (o)
(p) TO APPLY SOUND MENTAL-EMOTIONAL SELF-
    DIRECTION .... (p)
(q) TO MY OWN BENEFIT .... (q)
(r) AND THE BENEFIT OF OTHERS. .... (r)

INDICATOR: Begin with line (a)
            Repeat   " (a) and   ADD (b)
            Repeat (a), (b)   "   ADD (c)
            Repeat (a) to (c)   "   ADD (d)
            Repeat (a) to (d)   "   ADD (e)
            Repeat (a) to (e)   "   ADD (f)
            Repeat (a) to (f) *three times*
            Repeat (a) to (f) and   ADD (g)
            Repeat (a) to (g)   "   ADD (h)
            Repeat (g) and (h) *three times*
            Repeat (a) to (h) and   ADD (i)
            Repeat (a) to (i)   "   ADD (j)
            Repeat (a) to (j)   "   ADD (k)
            Repeat (a) to (k)   "   ADD (l)
            Repeat (a) to (l)   "   ADD (m)
            Repeat (k) to (m) *three times*
            Repeat (a) to (m) and   ADD (n)
            Repeat (a) to (n) and ADD (o), (p), (q), (r)
            Repeat (o), (p), (q), (r) *three times*
            Repeat (a) to (r).

PARAGRAPH V: TO STIMULATE GOOD INSIGHT AND SELF-EVALUATION

(a) WITH INCREASING EASE .... (a)
(b) I SUCCEED .... (b)
(c) IN EVALUATING HONESTLY .... (c)
(d) EVERYTHING .... (d)
(e) THAT IS GOOD IN ME. .... (e)
(f) AND I SUCCEED .... (f)
(g) IN DEVELOPING AND UTILIZING .... (g)
(h) EVERYTHING THAT IS GOOD IN ME. .... (h)
(i) I ALSO CAN AND DO .... (i)
(j) RECOGNIZE WITHIN MYSELF .... (j)
(k) ANY TRAITS AND HABITS .... (k)
(l) WHICH I SHOULD CORRECT .... (l)
(m) AND .... (m)
(n) IN PRACTICING SOUND SELF-EVALUATION .... (n)
(o) I REALIZE AND FEEL MY BENEFICIAL INNER
     STRENGTH .... (o)
(p) AND MY BENEFICIAL INNER STRENGTH .... (p)
(q) AND CONSTRUCTIVE SELF-DIRECTION HELP ME ..... (q)
(r) TO LIVE UP TO MY SOUND AND HONEST SELF-
     EVALUATION .... (r)
(s) FOR MY OWN BENEFIT .... (s)
(t) AND THE BENEFIT OF OTHERS. .... (t)

INDICATOR: Begin with lines (a) to (e)
           Repeat lines   (a) to (e) *three times*
           Repeat (a) to (e) and ADD lines (f), (g), (h)
           Repeat (f), (g), (h) *three times*
           Repeat (a) to (h) and ADD (i), (j), (k), (l)
           Repeat (i), (j), (k), (l) *three times*
           Repeat (a) to (l) and ADD (m)
           Repeat (a) to (m) and ADD (n), (o)
           Repeat (n), (o) *three times*
           Repeat (a) to (o) and ADD (p), (q)
           Repeat (p), (q) *three times*
           Repeat (a) to (q) and ADD (r), (s), (t)
           Repeat (p) to (t) *three times*
           Repeat (a) to (t).

PARAGRAPH VI: TO STIMULATE MENTAL AND CREATIVE FACULTIES

(a) BY SOUND MENTAL AND EMOTIONAL REFLEXES .... (a)
(b) AND FIRM BUT RELAXED SELF-DIRECTION .... (b)
(c) I SUCCEED .... (c)
(d) IN DEVELOPING AND ACTIVATING WITHIN MYSELF.. (d)
(e) THE GOOD QUALITIES OF MY MENTAL FACULTIES ... (e)
(f) AND ALSO THE GOOD QUALITIES .... (f)
(g) OF MY CREATIVE ABILITY. .... (g)
(h) THEREFORE .... (h)
(i) AND WITHIN THE SHORTEST TIME POSSIBLE .... (i)
(j) I CAN AND WILL MAKE GOOD AND FRUITFUL USE .. (j)
(k) OF ALL MY MENTAL AND CREATIVE RESOURCES .... (k)
(l) AND WITH ALL MY SOUND STRENGTH, ... (l)
(m) SOUND DETERMINATION .... (m)
(n) AND WELL-DIRECTED AMBITION .... (n)
(o) I WILL CARRY OUT IN THOUGHT AND PRACTICE .... (o)
(p) EVERYTHING THAT IS NECESSARY .... (p)
(q) TO ACHIEVE THE BEST POSSIBLE RESULTS .... (q)
(r) IN ALL MY ACTIVITIES. .... (r)

INDICATOR: Begin with lines (a), (b)
    Repeat (a), (b) *twice*
    Repeat (a), (b)   and ADD (c), (d)
    Repeat (c), (d) *twice*
    Repeat (a) to (d)   and ADD (e), (f)
    Repeat (e), (f) *twice*
    Repeat (a) to (f)   and ADD (g), (h)
    Repeat (g), (h) *twice*
    Repeat (a) to (h)   and ADD (i), (j)
    Repeat (i), (j) *twice*
    Repeat (a) to (j)   and ADD (k), (l)
    Repeat (k), (l) *twice*
    Repeat (a) to (l)   and ADD (m), (n)
    Repeat (m), (n) *twice*
    Repeat (a) to (n)   and ADD (o), (p)
    Repeat (o), (p) *twice*
    Repeat (a) to (p)   and ADD (q), (r)
    Repeat (q), (r) *twice*
    Repeat (a) to (r) *twice*.

PARAGRAPH VII: TO FURTHER SOUND RELAXATION

(a) BY EXERTING SOUND EMOTIONAL AND PHYSICAL
     REFLEXES .... (a)
(b) I SUCCEED .... (b)
(c) IN RELEASING ANY KIND OF TENSION .... (c)
(d) AUTOMATICALLY OR AT WILL .... (d)
(e) THEREFORE .... (e)
(f) I CAN AND I DO ENJOY .... (f)
(g) BENEFICIAL AND HEALTHFUL .... (g)
(h) MENTAL AND PHYSICAL RELAXATION .... (h)
(i) AND MY ABILITY TO RELAX .... (i)
(j) AUTOMATICALLY OR AT WILL .... (j)
(k) ENABLES ME TO BE, FEEL AND FUNCTION WELL .... (k)
(l) IN EVERY RESPECT. .... (l)
(m) I CAN AND I DO ALLOT .... (m)
(n) TO EVERYTHING I AM THINKING AND DOING ...... (n)
(o) THAT AMOUNT OF ENERGY AND ABILITY .... (o)
(p) WHICH IS NECESSARY TO ENABLE ME .... (p)
(q) TO BE AT MY VERY BEST .... (q)
(r) AND TO FEEL CONFIDENT AND PLEASANTLY AT EASE (r)

INDICATOR: Begin with line (a)
            Repeat   " (a) and ADD line (b)
            Repeat   " (a), (b) and ADD line (c)
            Repeat lines (a), (b), (c) *twice*
            Repeat lines (b), (c) *twice*
            Repeat (a), (b), (c) and ADD line (d)
            Repeat (a) to (d)   "   ADD   "   (e)
            Repeat (a) to (e)   "   ADD   "   (f)
            Repeat (f) *twice*
            Repeat (a) to (f)   "   ADD   "   (g)
            Repeat (a) to (g)   "   ADD   "   (h)
            Repeat (f), (g), (h) *twice*
            Repeat (a) to (h)   and ADD "   (i)
            Repeat (a) to (i)   "   ADD   "   (j)
            Repeat (a) to (j)   "   ADD   "   (k)
            Repeat (a) to (k)   "   ADD   "   (l)
            Repeat (f) to (l) *twice*
            Repeat (a) to (l)   and ADD "   (m)
            Repeat (a) to (m)   "   ADD   "   (n)
            Repeat (a) to (n)   "   ADD   "   (o)
            Repeat (a) to (o)   "   ADD   "   (p)
            Repeat (a) to (p)   "   ADD   "   (q)
            Repeat (a) to (q)   "   ADD   "   (r)
            Repeat (m) to (r) *twice*
            Repeat (a) to (r).

PARAGRAPH VIII: TO FURTHER THE INTEGRATION OF THE STIMULATED FACULTIES INTO YOUR PERSONALITY

(a) WHILE I SLEEP IN THE NIGHT .... (a)
(b) OR WHENEVER I SLEEP .... (b)
(c) MY SLEEP IS SOUND AND REFRESHING .... (c)
(d) AND .... (d)
(e) ALL MY BENEFICIAL THOUGHTS AND FEELINGS .... (e)
(f) WHICH I TAKE OVER INTO MY SLEEP .... (f)
(g) LINGER ON WHILE I SLEEP .... (g)
(h) AND BECOME ACTIVELY INTEGRATED .... (h)
(i) INTO MY WHOLE BEING .... (i)
(j) AND ALL THE PROGRESS I MAKE .... (j)
(k) IN DEVELOPING SOUND AND CONSTRUCTIVE
       ATTITUDES .... (k)
(l) BECOMES AND REMAINS AN ACTIVE PART .... (l)
(m) OF EVERYTHING .... (m)
(n) I THINK, FEEL AND DO. .... (n)

INDICATOR: Begin with line (a)
    Repeat   " (a) and   ADD line (b)
    Repeat (a), (b)   "   ADD " (c)
    Repeat (c) *twice*
    Repeat (a) to (c) and ADD " (d)
    Repeat (a) to (d) " ADD " (e)
    Repeat (a) to (e) " ADD " (f)
    Repeat (a) to (f) " ADD " (g)
    Repeat (a) to (g) " ADD " (h)
    Repeat (e) to (h) *twice*
    Repeat (a) to (h) and ADD " (i)
    Repeat (e) to (i) *twice*
    Repeat (a) to (i) and ADD " (j)
    Repeat (a) to (j) " ADD " (k)
    Repeat (a) to (k) " ADD " (l)
    Repeat (a) to (l) " ADD " (m)
    Repeat (a) to (m) " ADD " (n)
    Repeat (j) to (n) *twice*
    Repeat (a) to (n).

44. IN CONCLUSION

"Strength of mind is exercise and not rest!" said Alexander Pope in his *Essay on Man*. However, we have to realize that in Pope's time, the human mind was not so overtaxed with the complexities of living and learning as it is in our day. It is necessary, therefore, to keep a sound balance between the ability to exercise our mind and spirit and the equally important capacity to relax and enjoy periods of leisure.

The method of hypnoidal self-development helps us to develop this sound balance and to realize that we ourselves can and should infuse our life with meaning and purpose. This realization has been emphasized time and again by various cultures and philosophies. Often it is expressed in profound and sometimes rather abstruse language; then again it is reflected in quite a simple but nonetheless enlightening manner as in the legend of "The Chinese Inn."

This legend tells us that travelers, seeking the inn's hospitality, would find the tables decked with finest linen, set with dinnerware of choice porcelain and brightened with fragrant flowers; in short, everything would be supplied for a festive meal, except one item—there would be nothing to eat! The travelers themselves had to bring along their food!

And so you will have to bring along your own provision of sustaining values to contribute to the feast of a rich and useful life.

Set out to discover these values for yourself!

Hypnoidal self-development will help you to recognize them.

APPENDIX I

GUIDE TO SELF-EXAMINATION

HOW TO USE THE GUIDE
TO SELF-EXAMINATION

You will discover in the course of answering the questions that they will help you very much to evaluate your good and your "not so good" qualities. With the aid of the "Guide" you will get to know yourself better than ever before.

Bear in mind that the questionnaire is *not* designed for actually sick people; the questions are intended for those who are potentially capable of finding their own answers and means of necessary correction.

Some questions you will be able to answer in full, others only in part, and perhaps some not at all.

While you are answering the listed questions, others may arise in your mind. *This process of posing questions to yourself will be an added contribution to your progress in gaining insight.*

Be as sincere and objective with yourself as you possibly can. Only by rejecting the assumption that we know best—and by substituting for this attitude an endeavor to search for the best—can we advance in objectivity. Let's start!

a) Take sufficient writing-paper. Sit down comfortably and give yourself time. Write down your detailed answers to the questions. Answer them with complete honesty.

b) Don't force yourself to answer too many questions at a time. On the other hand, if you feel like answering a great many questions at one time, then by all means do so! It may take you a couple of weeks, or so, to go through all the questions of the "Guide to Self-Examination."

c) Should you want to relate any experiences, thoughts, or emotions which are not covered by the listed questions, write down whatever you recall and, if possible, make a note regarding what prompted you to remember.

d) In connection with some questions, or without any apparent connection, thoughts based on *free association* may occur to you. Write them down. Don't censor yourself. Elaborate freely. But make a note indicating whether you think that the associations are conjured up by certain questions of the "Guide," either directly, indirectly, or not at all.

The method of free association is most helpful in personality-development. Sigmund Freud was not the first one to discover it. The German poet Friedrich Schiller in his correspondence with Christian Gottfried Koerner pointed out that free association should be recommended to anyone who wishes to be productive. Then, in 1823, the German writer Ludwig Boerne advised: "write down, without fabrication or hypocrisy everything that comes into your head . . . you will be quite out of your senses with astonishment at the new and unheard-of thoughts you have had."

e) Immediately on completion, you may want to read your answers or whatever else you have written down. You may do so, of course, but it is preferable that you let at least a few days pass before reading what you have written.

f) While evaluating your completed answers, try to determine whether your attitudes and your emotional reactions affect you or others, favorably or unfavorably. Should you consider any of them unfavorable, try to discover whether the reason for this lies in your disposition or whether your unfavorable attitudes are due to environmental circumstances.

Regardless of whether your unfavorable attitudes and character-traits are based on your inherent disposition or whether you have acquired them, try to remember under what circumstances they appeared first and still manifest themselves.

g) Try also to discover, objectively, *your favorable* character-traits and attitudes. Find out whether you possess them by disposition or whether you have acquired them.

h) Once you have terminated this investigation, make out a kind of balance-sheet, enumerating your favorable as well as your unfavorable attitudes and character-traits; then weigh them against each other. This helps you to a better understanding of how you function psychologically and to conduct yourself in a more satisfactory manner, both mentally and emotionally.

However well we may function psychologically, it is always commendable to improve our personality-assets and to correct any personality-liabilities we may have. The method of hypnoidal self-development is a reliable aid in achieving this goal.

i) Some of the questions in the "Guide" are designed to stimulate your constructive attitudes toward the general values in life. Recognition of these values can undoubtedly help you to develop your personality.

But keep in mind that the values referred to throughout this book and also in the "Guide" are meant to be used solely as a means of directive thought stimulation. Whether or not you accept these values, from here on you will have to search for and find your own.

j) Disregard questions which you are sure don't apply to you and your problems.

k) In everything you write, be it answers to questions or be it based on free associations, objectivity and honesty with yourself are essential. This cannot be stressed often enough.

l) In your answers to questions, or anything you write in connection with them, refer to the listed numbers in the *questionnaire* for your convenience, but also for reference in case you should wish to obtain *individualized* hypnoidal suggestions.

m) Whether your aim is to develop your personality-assets or to correct whatever shortcomings you may have, proper use of the hypnoidal stage will be of inestimable help to you.

GUIDE TO SELF-EXAMINATION: QUESTIONS

Answer the questions exactly in sequence and not at random! This is essential.

1. What gives you pleasure?
2. What gives you contentment?
    In answering questions 1 and 2, write down every major or minor source of enjoyment you can think of. Elaborate on them.
3. As a child, were you closer to your father or to your mother? How good or how poor is your present relationship with them?
4. What is your *most unpleasant* early memory?
5. What other unpleasant memories do you have?
6. What other *later* unpleasant memories do you have?
7. How was (and is) your parent's relationship to each other and how did you (or do you) feel about it?
8. How is your relationship to your (a) brother(s), (b) sister(s), (c) other relatives, (d) in-laws?
    Were you or are you afraid of certain persons?
9. As a child, what kind of animals did you like or dislike?
10. As an adolescent, were there any persons, things or situations you were afraid of?
11. Do you remember any particular childhood habit(s)? If so, enumerate and describe.
12. What habits, if any, did you retain?
13. Were you ever, or are you now, afraid that anything unforeseen might happen to you or to anybody who is close to you? If so, are you or were you afraid of anything specific?
14. Do you think you are generous? If so, give reasons why you think you are generous.
15. As a child, were you or were you not generous?

16. Did you, or do you, have hostile impulses toward one person or several persons? If so, towards whom?

17. State under what circumstances you felt, or feel, hostile impulses and give the reason or reasons why you felt, or feel, that way?

18. How old were you when you fell in love for the first time?

19. At what age did you have your first sex experience?

20. What was your *emotional* reaction to your first sex experience?

21. What is your general attitude towards children?

22. Do you have children?
How many? boys? girls?

23. Do you prefer boys to girls or girls to boys? Why?

24. Does your husband (wife) prefer boys or girls? Why?

25. What do you understand by *love?* Does one of the following quotations express your feeling about love? If so, which one and what is your reason for choosing that particular one?

(a) Love has no thought of self!
Love buys not with the ruthless usurer's gold
Without a heart! Love sacrifices all things
to bless the thing it loves.

Bulwer-Lytton

(b) Love is the tyrant of the heart; it darkens reason, confounds discretion; deaf to counsel, it runs a headlong course to desperate madness.

John Ford

(c) Better to love amiss than nothing to have loved.

Crabbe

(d) It is strange that man will talk of miracles, revelations, inspiration and the like, as things past, while love remains.

Thoreau

(e) What have I done? What horrid crime committed?
To me the worst of crimes—outliv'd my liking.

Colley Cibber

(f) Love allows us to experience another's personality as a world in itself, and so extends our own world ... love is not deserved, is unmerited—it is simply grace ... But love is not only grace; it is also enchantment.

Victor Frankl

26. Have you ever hated someone or is there someone in your life whom you hate now? Give reasons.

27. Are you afraid of life?

28. Do you feel that "something is missing" in your life? If so, do you know *what* you miss or is it merely an overall, vague feeling which overcomes you from time to time? Whatever your answer is, can you remember when you first had that feeling and under what circumstances?

29. Do you feel like complaining about one or another thing? If so, write down exactly what it is and investigate whether you are completely justified in your complaints or whether you tend to exaggerate, at least in part?

30. Would you say that most of your complaints are of an emotional or of a physical nature?

31. Do you know what circumstances provoke your emotional or physical unease? If so, enumerate these circumstances. In case you are not aware of them, try to discover what they are.

32. Do you feel bad emotionally first and *then* physically, or is it the other way round?

33. Have you ever tried to do something about what bothers you? If so, with what results?

34. In case you have never done anything about what bothers you, explain why not?

35. In case you tried to ease your discomfort(s) or to make any changes in your life-situation without getting satisfactory results, did you or do you blame this on anybody or on yourself or on circumstances? Answer in detail.

36. What is your most pleasant early memory?

37. What other pleasant early memories do you have?

38. What other *later* pleasant memories do you have?

39. When you were a child, did you like to play with other children?

40. Did you feel accepted by your playmates?

41. If so, did you enjoy it?

42. Did you feel left out of things? (a) always? (b) only sometimes?

43. In case you felt, or were actually left out of things, do you think you know the reasons? If so, what were the reasons?

44. Did you have temper tantrums as a child? If so, why?
45. Did you have imaginary playmates?
46. Did you invent games which you played all by yourself? If so, what type of games?
47. *Why* did you like or dislike certain animals?
48. Did you dislike playing with other children
    (a) because they took your toys away?
    (b) for other reasons? If so, what reasons?
    (c) because you were afraid of other children in general or only of one or two of them?
    (d) because it bored you to play with other children?
49. Did you prefer to play by yourself when you were a child? If so, give particulars.
50. Did you or do you find it difficult or impossible to concentrate? If so, give reasons.
51. As a child, whom did you love most?
    "   "   "   "   "   "   admire most?
    "   "   "   "   "   "   dislike most?
    "   "   "   "   "   "   hate most?
    "   "   "   "   "   "   imitate most?
    "   "   "   "   "   "   avoid imitating?
52. As a child, were you afraid of animals, of the dark, of certain situations? Or were you afraid of other things?
53. Did your childhood fears diminish when you became an adolescent?
54. Did your fears increase or were new fears added when you reached adolescence?
55. If you succeeded in overcoming your fears, did they just disappear or do you know what helped you?
56. Did you ever tease cruelly or torture an animal?
57. If so, do you remember why you did it and under what circumstances?
58. What did you do to the animal?
59. What kind of animal did you mistreat?
60. Do you have any particular habit-pattern(s) in your daily life at the present time or did you have any particular habit-pattern(s) in the past? In the latter case, what helped you to break the habit-pattern(s)?

61. Do you prefer your present domestic circumstances to your previous ones or vice versa? In each case, give reasons.

62. Were you ever, or are you now, afraid that anything unforeseen may happen to anybody whom you dislike?

63. If so, do you, or did you, fear that anything *specific* might happen to the person whom you dislike and what *is* the specific thing you are or were afraid of?

64. Are there any tangible reasons why you are or were afraid that anything might happen to a person whom you dislike?

65. As a child, what types of games did you like to play?

66. As a child, what types of games did you dislike to play?

67. Are you satisfied in your profession (occupation)?

68. If you are dissatisfied or unhappy in your present profession (occupation), write down why this is so.

69. Did you choose your profession (or occupation) yourself or did your parents or anybody else influence your choice?

70. Do you or did you ever think that "love" and "sex" are the same?

71. Enumerate mistakes which you admit easily and mistakes which you find difficult to admit (a) to yourself (b) to others.

72. How do you feel about financial generosity?

73. How do you sleep?

74. When you wake up in the morning, are you well rested?

75. Do you dream frequently? If so, do you remember some of your dreams, or, at least, brief portions of them? If so, write them down, even if they are incoherent and/or fragmentary.

76. Have you had the same dream repeatedly? (a) at times? (b) frequently? (c) never? (d) do you remember the contents of this or these specific dreams?

77. Do you or did you ever envy anybody? If so, who is or was it and what is the reason for your envy?

78. Do you feel lonely?

79. Do you feel lonely even when you are with people? If so, why do you think you feel that way and do you know what you could do to change this feeling? Have you ever tried to change this feeling?

80. Are you afraid of illness in general?

81. Are you afraid of any specific disease?

82. Are you really afraid or do you just worry about falling ill?
83. Do you have actual reasons to be concerned about your health or are you inclined to worry about almost anything?
84. Are you particularly afraid of death?
85. Do you think there is a life hereafter?
86. Did you ever hate your friends? (a) Any particular friend? (b) One or several of your relatives? (c) If so, what are your reasons? Distinguish clearly between *hate* and *dislike*.
87. Do you consider your present sex adaptation: (a) good (b) adequate (c) unsatisfactory?
88. To what type of person do you feel attracted in regard to (a) appearance (b) aptitudes (c) education (d) temperament (outgoing temperament or reserved) (e) manners (f) background (g) disposition?
89. Do you consider yourself, or your partner sexually inadequate? If so, since when and, in your opinion, for what reason?
90. What are your and your sex-partner's attitudes toward each other:
    (a) Are you normally considerate?
       Is your partner normally considerate?
    (b) over-considerate?
    (c) affectionate?
    (d) indifferent?
    (e) demonstrative?
    (f) over-demonstrative?
    (g) unconcerned about the partner's reaction?
    (h) inconsiderate in other respects, for instance, cleanliness, etc.?
    (i) inconsiderate regarding quantity and/or quality of sexual needs?
    (j) excessive in sexual demands?
    (k) repelled by sexual demands?
91. Do you think about sex activities (a) frequently (b) seldom (c) never?
92. Did you ever or do you now feel disgust for any part of the human body? If so, give reasons.
93. Do you like or dislike aggressiveness in your sex-partner?

94. Are you aggressive or are you more passive in your sexual approach?

95. Did your parents prefer boys to girls or vice versa?

96. If your parents preferred boys to girls or girls to boys, do you remember how you found this out and what was your reaction to it?

97. Have your parents ever particularly approved, or disapproved of your viewpoints and/or actions? If so, did your parents' approval encourage, or their disapproval disturb, or even hurt you? Or were you more or less indifferent?

98. Have you felt sometimes that you didn't care for anything? If so, can you give reasons for this feeling? Besides, do you feel that way (a) often (b) or hardly ever?

99. With which of the following quotations do you sympathize:

   (a) For never can true reconcilement grow,
       Where wounds of deadly hate have pierced so deep.

   Milton

   (b) In time we hate that which we often fear.

   Shakespeare

   (c) Whom they have injured they also hate.
   (d) Hatreds are the cinders of affection.

   Sir Walter Raleigh

   (e) Better a dinner of herbs where love is, than a stalled ox and hatred therewith.

   Proverbs, 15:17

100. Did you ever or do you now have guilt-feelings? If so, about what do you feel guilty?

101. Do you worry easily?

102. What do you worry about most frequently?

103. What do you worry about most intensely?

104. Do you think the following quotation expresses truth?

   That is the bitterest of all—to wear the yoke of our own wrong-doing.

   George Eliot

105. Do you or did you ever feel an aggressive impulse to *emotionally* harm other people? Or to humiliate them? To dom-

inate them? Or hurt them in some particular manner? If so, is this impulse directed against men, women, or children?

106. Do you think or did you ever think that no one really cares for you? If so, give particulars.

107. How do you feel about emotional generosity?

108. Do you desire prestige?

109. Do you feel anxiety over responsibilities? If so, what are these responsibilities and in what way do they cause you to feel anxiety?

110. Do you like to assume responsibilities in general? If so, what are these responsibilities?

111. Do you succeed in directing your thoughts away from your worries into more constructive channels or do you feel compelled to continue worrying? Elaborate on your answer in detail.

112. Do you know the difference between *worrying* about a situation or *facing* a complicated or unpleasant situation by *thinking through it methodically?*

113. What in particular makes you feel lonely?

114. Do you or did you ever think that no one really knew and understood you? If so, give particulars?

115. Do you or did you ever feel an aggressive impulse to harm people *physically?* If so, is this impulse directed against men, women, or children? Under what circumstances is this impulse particularly strong?

116. Do you feel at a disadvantage or awkward with the opposite sex? If so, can you explain why you feel that way?

117. Do you feel unbearably lonely (a) sometimes (b) often (c) all the time (d) only under certain circumstances?

118. What in particular makes you feel lonely?

119. Do you feel an aggressive impulse only against a particular person and, if so, do you know why?

120. Are you ambitious (a) to get into the limelight (b) to excel in whatever you do (c) to gain wealth (d) to gain power?

121. Do you find fault with others easily?

122. What fault do you object to particularly in others?

123. Do you feel that *you* have many faults?

124. Do you or did you ever strive to correct your faults and shortcomings?
125. Are you the only one to recognize your faults and shortcomings?
126. Do you or did you ever discuss your faults and shortcomings with other people? If so, with whom?
127. Did or do others recognize your faults and shortcomings? If this is the case, do these people help you or do they tease or scold you? Or are they indifferent?
128. How do you evaluate yourself: (a) physically, (b) intellectually (c) emotionally (d) morally (e) socially, (f) constructive faculties (g) creative potentialities (h) relationship with others?
129. If you take the initiative to discuss your shortcomings with other people, do you feel resentful afterwards?
130. In your opinion, what are your shortcomings?
131. Have you attempted to correct or succeeded in correcting most of your shortcomings or only a few of them? Or none at all?
132. If anybody tries to help you, do you resent this or are you cooperative?
133. Do you feel that kindness is a desirable character-trait?
134. On what occasion have you been particularly kind to a person? Or to an animal?
135. On what occasion has anybody been particularly kind to you? Give details.
136. If you have been kind to another person, do you expect appreciation?
137. Are you normally concerned or overly concerned about your relationship to other people?
138. Does kindness in itself give you gratification regardless of whether or not your kindness is appreciated?
139. Are you arrogant?
140. Are you helpful to others? If so, describe what you mean by being helpful.
141. Do you like being helpful to others or do you consider it an unpleasant duty? Always or only occasionally?

142. Do you feel that extra-marital relationships are permissible or objectionable?

143. Do you have certain viewpoints on how people should conduct themselves morally?

144. Have you ever felt complete hopelessness in your life? If so, give reasons why.

145. Were you successful in conquering this feeling of utter hopelessness and, if you were, how did it happen?

146. Are you concerned about your own moral conduct and/or the morals of others? If so, what is your main concern?

147. What is your viewpoint on morality in general?

148. Are you superstitious?

149. Do you feel that you exert good self-control? If so, give an example or examples.

150. As a rule, do you think a great deal about yourself? If so, what is the main subject of your thoughts about yourself?

151. Are you inquisitive (a) in general (b) only concerning certain things? Give details.

152. Do you like to watch people when they are unaware of your presence?

153. Do you indulge in wishful thinking often? Or only occasionally?

154. Do you have a tendency to self-effacement in your relationship with others? If so, give examples.

155. Do you or did you ever have fantasies of success? If so, what forms did these fantasies take?

156. If you indulge in wishful thinking, what is (are) the subject(s) of your wishful thinking?

157. Is it easy for you to confide in other people?

158. Did you ever have an intimate friend?

159. Do you like to live alone or do you prefer to be married?

160. Do you feel that certain actions or omission of certain actions bring good luck or bad luck? Give particulars.

161. If there are only one or two people in whom you feel that you can confide, who are they (a) relatives (b) friends (c) husband (wife)?

162. Do you believe in revenge? Or punishment?

163. Which of the two following quotations do you endorse?

(a) God save me from my friends, I can protect myself from my enemies.

> Attributed to Marshal de Villars
> on taking leave of Louis XIV

(b) It is sublime to feel and say of another, I need never meet, or speak, or write him; we need not reinforce ourselves or send tokens of remembrance; I rely on him as on myself; if he did thus and thus, I know it was right.

> Emerson

164. Have you ever felt genuine friendship for somebody and have you ever *proved* your friendship towards anybody? If so, in what way?

165. What do you understand by friendship?

166. Do you differentiate strongly in regarding someone as a friend? a companion? or an acquaintance?

167. Are you inclined to trust: (a) people in general (b) only your friend or friends (c) nobody?

168. Have you ever been severely disappointed by a friend?

169. Do you feel it is correct to say?

> Friendship is love without wings.
> Byron

170. Do you collect things? If so, what do you collect? Are you proud of the things you collect?

171. Do you feel that you need somebody and that only by living with somebody could your life be worth living and bring contentment? If so, do you feel that way in general or in connection with a specific person?

172. Do you suffer from (a) shyness (b) indecision (c) inability to get ahead in life (d) any other difficulties? If so, do you blame anybody for your difficulty(ies), and why?

173. Do you like to be surrounded by many people or do you prefer the company of only one or two? If the latter is the case, what type of companion(s) do you prefer?

174. Do you feel that people want to impose their opinions or attitudes on you? If so, (a) who does, or did so? (b) of what

do these opinions and attitudes consist? (c) do they try to impose their opinions on you only occasionally? (d) always? (e) if only occasionally, on what occasions?

175. Do you think that pre-marital sexual relationship is morally permissible or objectionable: (a) in general (b) with the man (woman) you want to marry?

176. Whenever you are reproached for your shortcomings, do you consider these reproaches justified, at least on some occasions?

177. Do you resent these reproaches even if they are justified?

178. Whenever you feel that reproaches are justified, do you accept them in an appreciative spirit?

179. When you feel that reproaches are *not* justified, do you feel (a) indifferent (b) hurt (c) show your reaction to the person who actually or allegedly misjudged you? If you show your reaction, in what manner do you show it?

180. Whatever your answers are to the preceding questions (179), have you ever changed in your reactions? If so, why do you think you changed?

181. Do you think courtesy is old-fashioned and unnecessary? If "yes," give reasons.

182. What are your main interests?

183. Do you have any problem regarding alcohol or drugs?

184. Do you suffer from (a) general tension (b) muscular tension (c) emotional tension (d) in the morning (e) during the day (f) in the evening (g) regularly (h) seldom (i) not at all? Do you realize what makes you tense?

185. If you have any problem regarding alcohol or drugs, what emotional, physical, or environmental circumstances are the cause, in *your* opinion?

Does anybody else have an opinion about this problem? If so, does this opinion concur with yours? If not, what is the difference?

186. Which of the two following quotations do you endorse?
   (a) "Too much courtesy is discourtesy."
   (b) "No one blames you for being polite."
   Give reasons for your choice.

187. Would you choose success at the expense of some other person?

188. Which of your character-traits do you (a) approve of (b) admire (c) disapprove of?

189. Which of the following quotations do you prefer:

    (a) Eye for eye, tooth for tooth, hand for hand, foot for foot . . .

    (b) The object of punishment is prevention from evil; it never can be made impulsive to good.

        Horace Mann, Lectures on Education

190. Do you always observe strictly certain "rules," set either by yourself or acquired by hearsay or tradition?

191. Are you inclined to procrastinate (a) in your work? (b) in other things?

192. If you had to choose between success in money-matters and (a) love, (b) friendship, (c) honor, which one would you choose?

193. Are you forgetful about things you have to do? If so, give examples.

194. After you have gone to bed and have turned off the light, do you fall asleep immediately or do all kinds of thoughts come to your mind? If the latter is the case, give a brief survey of the nature of these thoughts.

195. While you work, do you feel pressed for time, even if there is no necessity: (a) often? (b) always? (c) hardly ever?

196. Do you believe you can plan well ahead (a) in general? (b) only in certain instances? Give examples of your ability or inability to plan well ahead.

197. What hobby or hobbies do you have, if any?

198. What is your favorite recreational activity?

199. Which of the following quotations do you endorse?

    (a) And so all growth that is
        Not towards God
        Is growing to decay.

        George MacDonald

    (b) I can no more understand a man praying than I can understand him carrying a rabbit's foot to bring him luck.

        H. L. Mencken

(c) The world is, of course, 'incurably religious.' Why? Because everyone who reflects at all must have conceptions about the world which go beyond the field of science; that is, beyond the present range of intellectual knowledge . . . Religion will be with us so long as a man hopes and aspires and reflects upon the meaning of existence and the responsibilities it entails.

Robert A. Millikan

(d) When I am low in spirits and full of misery, I never feel any impulse to seek help, or even mere consolation, from supernatural powers.

H. L. Mencken

(e) It is a strange thing that most of the feeling that we call religion, most of the mystical outcrying which is one of the most prized and used and desired reactions of our species, is really the understanding and the attempt to say that man is related to the whole thing, related inextricably to all reality, known and unknowable.

John Steinbeck

200. Do you feel that you have the right to be happy?
201. Do you feel there is a difference between having a good sense of humor and being a practical joker?
202. Do you feel that emotional likes and dislikes interfere with your logical thinking? If so, does it happen often or only on rare occasions? Describe these occasions.
203. The following excerpt from a case history may show you how emotions can interfere with recognition of facts. Miss X. was interested in a man who wanted to marry her, but she couldn't make up her mind to accept his proposal. She had several reasons for her hesitation, most of them justified. Nevertheless, she saw the man almost every day, but after many months of waiting for her final answer, he started to show interest in another woman. When he spoke about marrying this other woman—and he married her—Miss X. felt jilted and rejected. Miss X., an intelligent and otherwise logically thinking person, ignored emotionally that it was she who had rejected the man in the first place and that his interest in another woman was only the consequence of her

own attitude towards him. This may seem quite obvious to you, but try to check your own attitude(s) and try to recall circumstances under which you have reacted similarly, namely, completely on your emotional level. (The circumstances, of course, may have been quite different in your case.)

204. Do you feel wishful thinking is mainly focused on personal advantage?

205. Do you feel there is a difference between *daydreaming* and *wishful thinking?* If you do, can you explain the difference?

206. Do you feel that daydreaming—provided it is not morbid daydreaming—may result in activating our creative fantasy?

207. What recreational occupation do you dislike? (For instance, the husband likes to go fishing, but his wife dislikes it, or the wife likes to go to the movies, but the husband is bored by them, and so on.)

208. When you are confronted with certain circumstances in which you are involved emotionally, do you *always* try to judge the situation objectively or only in certain cases? Try to find out *when* and *why* you can be objective and *when* and *why* this is not possible for you.

209. The following anecdote reveals how conclusions can lead to most unfortunate and even dangerous consequences. According to the anecdote, the owner of a jumping flea was very proud because this intelligent flea would jump on command. So he made the flea perform whenever he had an audience. But one day the owner of the flea had the notion to make an experiment. He tore out the hind legs of the flea and then commanded him to jump. The flea, of course, could no longer jump, whereupon the owner turned around and said apologetically to the audience: "Since I tore out his hind legs, he doesn't hear well any more!"

Have you ever met a similar type of false reasoning (a) in others? (b) in yourself? Try to remember examples.

210. Do you think that a good sense of humor enhances one's life? If so, think of an example.

211. If you dislike some recreational activity, do you always try to avoid it?

212. Once I heard a minister say over the radio that if one wants

to *destroy* one's enemy, one shouldn't hate but love him! What is your reaction to it?

213. Do you realize that "destruction of the enemy" excludes love? In question 214, the minister's use of the word "destroy" doesn't make hate or love a point of discussion; he merely recommends a different *weapon* for destruction and calls that weapon "love." But the weapon which is used for destruction is immaterial. It is "destruction" from which we should turn away. We should go a step farther and understand that even without having destruction or hate in mind, we may at times *destroy by wrongly applied love.* And it is not always our enemy whom we destroy!

   Have you encountered a situation of this kind or experienced it personally?

214. Do you daydream (a) often? (b) seldom? (c) never? And if you daydream, what are your daydreams about?

215. Do you think you have artistic faculties? If so, give particulars.

216. The following anecdote illustrates the interference of personal inclinations with clear thinking:

   A man is accused of drunk driving. The judge sentences him to three days in jail. Whereupon the man, feeling ill-treated, says: "That's what drives a man to drink!"

   Can you think of similar fallacious reasoning by which you were affected or which affected others?

217. Do you feel you are successful . . . or unsuccessful in life? In either case, give reasons why you feel that way.

218. Do you hesitate to make a decision if you cannot consult somebody about it? If so, give an example of the type of decision you would not make on your own and what is your present reaction to it?

219. Do you like to tease others?

220. Did anybody ever help you to be or prevent you from being successful?

221. Do you always make up your mind without listening to other people's opinions? If so, why do you have this attitude?

222. Do you consider happiness as a privilege and do you agree with the following statement by Aristotle:

"Happiness is a kind of energy; and an energy is evidently produced and not like a property merely possessed"? If you feel different about "happiness," give reasons why.

223. Do you agree with the following viewpoint: "A man does have feelings, and you throw away your best chance of understanding him if you deliberately forget that these feelings may be very similar to yours. If you make a man angry, you know what he feels, because you had the experience of being angry yourself." (Anthony Standen)

224. Do you often think and say: "I know exactly how you feel, I had the same experience!"

225. Do you generally accept news-items that you read or hear as unbiased and acceptable statements of facts, provided that they agree with your own views?

226. Do you agree or disagree that when one is teasing or joking, it is most important to sense and avoid what would make others feel uncomfortable? If you don't agree, give your reasons.

227. Returning to the questions 225 and 226: if you answered question 226 affirmatively and agree with the viewpoint expressed in 225, do you realize that you might be making a mistake, because one and the same experience may cause different mental-emotional reactions in different people? Anger, for instance, although stemming from the same cause, may differ in quality and intensity in different individuals.

228. Are the "little things in life" sufficient to make you feel good or happy?

229. Do you agree with Hawthorne's viewpoint: "A man's bewilderment is the measure of his wisdom"? Have you ever experienced that kind of bewilderment?

230. A similar viewpoint (229) has been expressed more recently by Carl Jaspers: "He who has ceased to be astonished has ceased to question. He who acknowledges no mystery is no longer a seeker. Because he humbly acknowledges the limits of possible knowledge, the philosopher remains open to the unknowable that is revealed at these limits. Here cognition ceases, but not thought . . . another and deeper kind of thought. It is not detached from being and oriented toward

an object, but it is a process of my innermost self, in which thought and being become identical."

231. Do accomplishments, even minor ones, make you feel content?

232. Do you feel that to be "wise" amounts to being practically infallible?

233. Do you recognize the dangerous fallacy of attitudes such as: "I like cucumber salad, consequently *you* should like cucumber salad too . . . or what's good for me, is good for you" . . . and so on.

234. Do you agree with the idea expressed in the following words by Carl Sandburg: "Time is a sandpile we run our fingers in. It is high enough to last a lifetime, though, and big enough to build many castles. If we spend too much of it fretting over day-by-day tactics . . . we probably won't get half as much done, half as much fun out of it as we will if we concentrate on the grand strategy in disposing of our share of eternity."

If you agree, do you conduct your life according to the meaning expressed in these words? Or in accordance with the meaning expressed in other viewpoints you encountered in this questionnaire?

You have probably noticed that the sequence of the questions does not always coincide with their contents. You will have found questions related to a particular subject scattered among questions dealing with other matters. This has been done deliberately.

Once you have answered the questions in the sequence presented in the questionnaire, it is advisable to sort them out and *group the related* subjects together as best you can.

In doing so, you may well discover that you have given contradictory answers on one or the other subject. To check up on this will enable you to gain a good deal of additional insight into your attitudes and ways of thinking.

Should you have no safe place in which to keep the notes resulting from your "appointments with yourself," destroy them after they have served their purpose.

APPENDIX II

RECOMMENDED BOOKS

BARTLETT, FREDERIC. Thinking, An Experimental and Social Study. New York: 1958

COHEN, MORRIS RAPHAEL. A Preface to Logic. New York: 1956

DUDENEY, H. E. Amusements in Mathematics. New York: 1958

DUDENEY, H. E. Canterbury Puzzles. New York: 1958

FLESCH, RUDOLF. The Art of Clear Thinking. New York: 1951

FREUD, SIGMUND. The Interpretation of Dreams. New York

GARDNER, MARTIN. Mathematics, Magic & Mystery. New York: 1956

GARDNER, MARTIN. The Scientific American Book of Mathematical Puzzles & Diversions. New York: 1959

GUTHEIL, EMIL A. The Handbook of Dream Analysis. New York: 1951

HADFIELD, J. A. Dreams and Nightmares. London: 1954

HALL, CALVIN S. The Meaning of Dreams. New York: 1953

KAUFMAN, GERALD L. New Word Puzzles. New York: 1957

LUCEY, R. M. A Problem a Day. London: 1937

MADER, A. E. Logic for the Millions. New York: 1947

MEYER, JEROME. Book of Puzzle Quiz and Stunt Fun. New York: 1956

STEBBING, SUSAN L. Thinking to Some Purpose. London: 1952

TITCHMARSH, E. C. Mathematics for the General Reader. New York: 1959

Generalized hypnoidal suggestions on records may be obtained by writing to Dr. Margaret Steger, P.O. Box 791, Sherman Oaks, California.

INDEX

Index   255

24, 25, 146, 158; collective, 183, 184; easier access to the, 174, 181; function(s) of, 186; guilt-feelings, suppressed into the, 103; imposing a deception on, 164

Undercurrents, emotional, 33; harmful, unconscious, 155

Understanding of oneself and others, 55

Values, emotional and spiritual, 63; essential to relationship between men and women, 63; spiritual, 59

Vinci da, Leonardo, 158

Wagner, Richard, 158

Wakefulness, 126, 155, 156, 166, 168, 169

Waking condition, 118, 119, 135

Warning-signals, 66

Walter, Grey W., 162, 166, 185

Well-being, psychological, 12

Whitman, Walt, 76

Willpower, wrongly applied, 51

Will to power, 65

Wisdom, 27, 43, 44; certain degree of, 82; intuitive kind of, 82; nature of, 82

Wish, fulfillment of the, 195

Word(s), 170; absorption, 173; abstract, 171; concrete, 171; intensification of the meaning of, 186, 188; meaning of, 191; spoken, 12; suggestive, 132

Work, conscious, preliminary, 24, 25; preparatory, 12, 14, 15, 24-27, 29, 164, 188, 195; stimulates activities of the unconscious, the right kind of, 25; the wrong kind of, 25

Working-skill, lack of, 194

Worry to, profitably, 52

Years, formative, 48